Passages in the Life of a Radical, and Early Days

BAMFORD'S PASSAGES IN THE LIFE OF
A RADICAL

THE REFORMER'S BOOKSHELF.

Large Crown 8vo, cloth, **3s. 6d.** *each.*

The Labour Movement. By L. T. HOBHOUSE, M.A Preface by
R B HALDANE, M P

Sixty Years of an Agitator's Life. G J HOLYOAKES Autobiography
2 vols

Bamford's Passages in the Life of a Radical. Edited and with an
Introduction by HENRY DUNCKLEY 2 vols

The Economic Interpretation of History. By Prof. THOROLD
ROGERS 2 vols

The Industrial and Commercial History of England. By Prof.
THOROLD ROGERS 2 vols

Charles Bradlaugh: A Record of His Life and Work By His Daughter,
HYPATIA BRADLAUGH BONNER 2 vols

The Inner Life of the House of Commons. Selected from the
Writings of WILLIAM WHITE 2 vols.

The Gladstone Colony. By JAMES FRANCIS HOGAN, M P

Life of Richard Cobden. By JOHN MORLEY. 2 vols

The Political Writings of Richard Cobden. A New Edition. With
Preface by Lord WELBY, and Introductions by Sir LOUIS MALLET
and WILLIAM CULLEN BRYANT, and a Bibliography With Frontis-
pieces 2 vols

British Industries under Free Trade. Edited by HAROLD COX

Labour and Protection. Edited by H W MASSINGHAM

Labour Legislation, Labour Movements, Labour Leaders. By
GEORGE HOWELL 2 vols

BAMFORD'S PASSAGES

IN THE

LIFE OF A RADICAL

AND

EARLY DAYS

IN TWO VOLUMES

EDITED, WITH AN INTRODUCTION,

BY

HENRY DUNCKLEY

("VERAX")

SECOND IMPRESSION

VOL. II

London

T. FISHER UNWIN

PATERNOSTER SQUARE

MCMV

CONTENTS OF "PASSAGES IN THE LIFE OF A RADICAL."

PASSAGES IN THE LIFE OF A RADICAL

PASSAGES IN THE LIFE OF A RADICAL.

CHAPTER I.

RIOTS OF 1815 AND 1816—WILLIAM COBBETT—HAMPDEN CLUBS—
DELEGATE MEETINGS—LEADERS OF REFORM—THE FIRST
TRAITOR.

IT is matter of history that whilst the laurels were yet cool
on the brows of our victorious soldiers on their second occupation of Paris, the elements of convulsion were at work
amongst the masses of our labouring population; and that a
series of disturbances commenced with the introduction of
the Corn Bill in 1815, and continued, with short intervals, until
the close of the year 1816. In London and Westminster riots
ensued, and were continued for several days whilst the bill
was discussed; at Bridport, there were riots on account of the
high price of bread; at Bideford there were similar disturbances to prevent the exportation of grain; at Bury, by the
unemployed, to destroy machinery; at Ely, not suppressed
without bloodshed; at Newcastle-on-Tyne, by colliers and
others; at Glasgow, where blood was shed; at Preston, by
unemployed weavers; at Nottingham, by Luddites, who destroyed thirty frames; at Merthyr Tydvil, on a reduction of
wages; at Birmingham, by the unemployed; and at Dundee,
where, owing to the high price of meal, upwards of one
hundred shops were plundered. At this time the writings
of William Cobbett suddenly became of great authority; they

were read on nearly every cottage hearth in the manufacturing districts of South Lancashire, in those of Leicester, Derby, and Nottingham ; also in many of the Scottish manufacturing towns. Their influence was speedily visible. He directed his readers to the true cause of their sufferings—misgovernment; and to its proper corrective—parliamentary reform. Riots soon become scarce, and from that time they have never obtained their ancient vogue with the labourers of this country.

Let us not descend to be unjust. Let us not withhold the homage which, with all the faults of William Cobbett, is still due to his great name. Instead of riots and destruction of property, Hampden clubs were now established in many of our large towns, and the villages and districts around them. Cobbett's books were printed in a cheap form ; the labourers read them, and thenceforward became deliberate and systematic in their proceedings. Nor were there wanting men of their own class, to encourage and direct the new converts. The Sunday Schools of the preceding thirty years had produced many working men of sufficient talent to become readers, writers, and speakers in the village meetings for parliamentary reform. Some also were found to possess a rude poetic talent, which rendered their effusions popular, and bestowed an additional charm on their assemblages ; and by such various means, anxious listeners at first, and then zealous proselytes, were drawn from the cottages of quiet nooks and dingles, to the weekly readings and discussions of the Hampden clubs.

One of these clubs was established in 1816, at the small town of Middleton, near Manchester; and I, having been instrumental in its formation, a tolerable reader also, and a rather expert writer, was chosen secretary. The club prospered, the number of men increased, the funds raised by contributions of a penny a week became more than sufficient for all out-goings, and, taking a bold step, we soon rented a chapel which had been given up by a society of Kilhamite Methodists. This place we threw open for the religious worship of all sects and parties, and there we held our meetings on the evenings of Monday and Saturday in each week. The proceedings of our society; its place of meeting—singular as being the first place of worship occupied by reformers (for so in those days we were termed), together with the services of religion connected with us—drew a considerable share of public attention to our transactions, and obtained for the leaders some notoriety. They, like the young aspirants of the present, and all the other days, whose heads are as warm as their hearts, could sing with old John Bunyan—

> " Then fancies fly away,
> We fear not what men say."

Several meetings of delegates from the surrounding districts were held at our chapel, on which occasions the leading reformers of Lancashire were generally seen together. One of our delegate meetings deserves particular notice. It was held on Sunday, the 16th December, 1816, when it was determined to send out missionaries to other towns and villages, particularly to Yorkshire. The experiment was considered somewhat hazardous, for at that time the great towns of Yorkshire, Halifax, Bradford, and Leeds, to which they were bound, had shown but small sympathy with the cause of reform. They went, however, and, I believe, made an impression which awakened the cause in that county. At this meeting a man of the name of William Wilson appeared as the delegate from Moston; he was known to several present, and, being considered a good reformer, was chosen secretary for the occasion. He thus took copies of all the resolutions and proceedings. Soon afterwards it was discovered that he was in communication with the police of Manchester. He then left the district, abandoning his wife and a young family of children, and was next heard of as a police officer in London, to which place his wife and children followed him. Can this have been our first traitor?

On the 1st of January, 1817, a meeting of delegates from twenty-one petitioning bodies was held in our chapel, when resolutions were passed declaratory of the right of every male to vote, who paid taxes; that males of eighteen should be eligible to vote; that parliaments should be elected annually;

that no placeman or pensioner should sit in parliament; that every twenty thousand inhabitants should send a member to the House of Commons; and that talent and virtue were the only qualifications necessary. Such were the moderate views and wishes of the reformers in those days, as compared with the present. The ballot was not insisted upon as a part of reform.* Concentrating our whole energy for the obtainment of annual parliaments and universal suffrage, we neither interfered with the House of Lords, nor the bench of bishops, nor the working of factories, nor the corn laws, nor the payment of members, nor tithes, nor church rates, nor a score of other matters which in these days have been pressed forward with the effect of distracting the attention and weakening the exertions of reformers; any one or all of which matters would be far more likely to succeed with a House of Commons elected on the suffrage we claimed than with one returned as at present.† Quoting scripture, we did, in fact say, first obtain annual parliaments, and universal suffrage, and, "all these things shall be added unto you."

Some of the nostrum-mongers of the present day would have been made short work of by the reformers of that time; they would not have been tolerated for more than one speech, but handed over to the civil power. It was not until we became infested by spies, incendiaries, and their dupes—distracting, misleading, and betraying—that physical force was mentioned amongst us. After that our moral power waned, and what we gained by the accession of demagogues, we lost by their criminal violence, and the estrangement of real friends

* 1812 It is interesting to compare with these demands the "six points" of the "Charter"—universal suffrage, vote by ballot, equal electoral districts, annual parliaments, abolition of property qualification of members, and the payment of members.   † Under the Reform Act of 1832.

CHAPTER II.

IT may not be amiss to state that the opinions contained in this work, whether of persons or transactions, are those of the writer at the period they refer to. Time, the ameliorator of all things, has not passed him without leaving some experience; and the lessons of that severe handmaid, making him better acquainted with mankind and himself, have somewhat matured his judgment and increased his charity; changing also, he hopes for the better, some of his views both of men and things. Hence, though elsewhere he will speak of the conduct of Henry, now Lord Brougham, strongly, as he felt at the time; he would, in his present frame of mind, make large allowances. Our educators are, after all, the best reformers, and are doing the best for their country, whether they intend so or not. In this respect, Lord Brougham is the greatest man we have. He led popular education from the dark and narrow crib where he found it, like a young colt, saddled and cruelly bitted by ignorance, for superstition to ride. He cut the straps from its sides and the bridle from its jaws, and sent it forth strong, beautiful, and free.*

Still, we want something more than mere intellectuality;

* Mr. Spencer Walpole observes that Brougham was "the first politician who made the subject [of popular education] his own" The earliest education returns (1818) were due to him. His Bill for the Establishment of an Education Board in London (1837) led to the formation of the Committee of the Privy Council two years later. He was the chairman of the Society for the Promotion of Useful Knowledge, the offspring of an enthusiasm now perhaps somewhat disparaged, but at that time a very quickening force.

that is already vigorous in produce, whilst souls lie comparatively waste. The Persians of old first taught their children
to speak the truth, and that was a wise beginning; but, like
the embalming of the Egyptians, lost to the present day.
The young mothers of England, and the anxious fathers,
should do more—they should give life to the souls of their offspring, and encourage and strengthen as well as comfort their
young hearts. Their constant lesson should be, "With thy
whole soul, love and support whatsoever is right. With thy
whole soul, hate and oppose whatsoever is wrong. Fear not
anything, save the contamination of sin." The schoolmaster
might then finish the intellect; and the spirit of Him who
said, "Father, forgive them," should be invoked to shed its
dove-like mercy over all. Education so grounded and built
upon, would bring us hearts, and brave ones too, brimful of
nobleness and truth, and heads to work anything requisite
for their country. Intellect neglected may be repaired; but
a soul once in ruin, nothing human can restore.

Nor would the writer at the present day be found praying
for annual parliaments, though he would endeavour to attain
the same end by better means. Annual general elections
would, he is convinced, be a great political evil to the country;
and reviewing all that he has seen of elections, he does say,
they are generally conducted in a manner which is disgraceful
to civilised society. The infamy they generate is equalled by
the bungling knavery of their management. He needs not go
into their history, but he would ask a rational man to note the
proceedings of one of these " good old English " events ; and
then say whether it were not more like " hell broke loose "
than anything human. Who could wish for annual recurrence
of these things throughout the nation? Frequent enough
their visitation when they can no longer be avoided. General
elections annually would be annual curses ; and single borough
or county elections are best let alone until there be good cause.
As, in his petition to the House of Commons, in 1837, the
writer would pray that we might have the benefit without the
disturbing force. He would say, let the House of Commons
be, like that of the Lords, indissoluble ; members to render an

account of their conduct annually ; individual members liable to be displaced by their constituents at any time, and elected, displaced, or retained, as private servants are, viz., as they do well their duty, or otherwise. The sense of the electors to be taken annually—by ballot in districts; all elections to be by ballot. No hustings, no nomination farce, no mob gatherings, no ruffianism, no demagogueism, no canting and deception of the multitudes, nor opportunity for the display of insolence and ignorance to win a passing clap or huzza. Many evils would be done away with, excitement would be moderated, sober-mindedness would take the place of extravagance, Court intrigue or ascendency of faction would not have the power of dispersing the people's servants, nor of throwing the country into a ferment of brute passion, to take advantage of it. Such a plan would the writer substitute for that of annual parliaments, and so far his opinions have changed on that point.

CHAPTER III.

MEETINGS AT THE CROWN AND ANCHOR TAVERN, LONDON—
HENRY HUNT—THOMAS CLEARY—WILLIAM COBBETT—MAJOR
CARTWRIGHT—LORD COCHRANE.

THE Hampden Club of London, of which Sir Francis Burdett
was the chairman, having issued circulars for a meeting of
delegates at the "Crown and Anchor," for the purpose of discussing a Bill to be presented to the House of Commons,
embracing the reform we sought, I was chosen to represent the
Middleton Club on that occasion. I shall not notice the abuse
which this small honour brought upon my shoulders, further
than to say, that it gave me an unexpected insight into the
weakness of some whom I had considered as the best of
friends to myself and the cause. I thus early got a dose of
disgust which would have banished me from amongst them,
had I not considered that by retiring I should abandon my
duty and gratify my new enemies. I therefore took up my
cross, forgave them, and attended my appointment in London.

I had scarcely alighted from the coach at the "Elephant and
Castle," ere I was accosted by Benbow,* who took me to his
own lodgings near Buckingham Gate, where I became comfortably settled for the present. He had been in London
some time, agitating the labouring classes at their trades
meetings and club-houses. That night he conducted me to
the Crown and Anchor Tavern; and whilst I stood gazing
around a large hall, which seemed wonderfully grand and
silent for a tavern, a gentleman came out of a room and

* William Benbow, shoemaker, of Birch, near Middleton.

18

accosted my companion, who increased my curiosity and awe by pronouncing the name of Mr. Hunt.* He invited us within; and we there found a small party of delegates, recently arrived, in friendly conversation with Mr. Cleary, the secretary of the London Club. This was an event in my life. Of Mr. Hunt I had imbibed a high opinion, and his first appearance did not diminish my expectations. He was gentlemanly in his manner and attire, six feet and better in height, and extremely well formed. He was dressed in a blue lapelled coat, light waistcoat and kerseys, and topped boots; his leg and foot were about the firmest and neatest I ever saw. He wore his own hair; it was in moderate quantity and a little grey. His features were regular, and there was a kind of youthful blandness about them which, in amicable discussion, gave his face a most agreeable expression. His lips were delicately thin and receding; but there was a dumb utterance about them which in all the portraits I have seen of him was never truly copied. His eyes were blue or light grey—not very clear nor quick, but rather heavy; except as I afterwards had opportunities for observing, when he was excited in speaking; at which times they seemed to distend and protrude; and if he worked himself furious, as he sometimes would, they became blood-streaked, and almost started from their sockets. Then it was that the expression of his lip was to be observed—the kind smile was exchanged for the curl of scorn, or the curse of indignation. His voice was bellowing; his face swollen and flushed; his griped hand beat as if it were to pulverise; and his whole manner gave token of a painful energy, struggling for utterance.

Such was the appearance of Mr. Hunt as I saw him that night, and on subsequent occasions. His every-day manners, exhibiting the quality and operations of his mind, will, of necessity, occupy some portion of the future pages of this work. He was constantly, perhaps through good but misapplied intentions, placing himself in most arduous situations. No repose, no tranquillity for him. He was always beating against a tempest of his own or of others' creating. He

* Henry Hunt, known as " Orator Hunt." He died in 1835.

had thus more to sustain than any other man of this day and station, and should be judged accordingly.

Thomas Cleary, the secretary of the Hampden Club, was also in the room; he was perhaps twenty-five or twenty-six years of age, about middle stature, slightly formed, and had a warmth and alacrity in his manner which created at once respect and confidence. He was, and I have no doubt is yet, if he be living, worthy of and enjoying the esteem of all who know him. Hunt ferociously traduced his character at a subsequent election for Westminster, but the shame recoiled on the calumniator. Afterwards he attempted to fix upon Cleary the stigma of being a Government spy, and intimated that he tried about this time to involve some of the delegates in illegal transactions—a charge as absurd as it was false.

The day of meeting arrived; Sir Francis Burdett was in the country, and the worthy old Major Cartwright * took the chair. With a picture of that venerable patriot in my recollection, let me pause, and render the tribute due to integrity and benevolence. He was far in years—I should suppose about seventy; rather above the common stature, straight for his age; thin, pale, and with an expression of countenance in which firmness and benignity were most predominant. I see him, as it were, in his long brown surtout and plain brown wig, walking up the room, and seating himself placidly in the head seat. A mild smile played on his features, as a simultaneous cheer burst from the meeting. Cobbett stood near his right hand. I had not seen him before. Had I met him anywhere save in that room and on that occasion, I should have taken him for a gentleman farming his own broad estate. He seemed to have that kind of self-possession and ease about him, together with a certain bantering jollity, which are so natural to fast-handed and well-housed lords of the soil. He was, I should suppose, not less than six feet in height; portly, with a fresh, clear, and round cheek, and a small grey eye, twinkling with good-humoured archness. He was dressed in a blue coat, yellow swansdown waistcoat, drab kersey small-

---

* Thomas Cartwright, a major in the militia, a Reformer from 1780— hence styled the "Father of Reform."

clothes, and top boots. His hair was grey, and his cravat and linen were fine, and very white. In short, he was the perfect representation of what he always wished to be—an English gentleman-farmer.

The proceedings of the meeting it is not requisite that I should go into; they have long been matters of record. The absence of the baronet was the subject of much observation by the delegates; and yet, in deference to his wishes, as was understood, a resolution was introduced and supported by Cobbett, limiting the suffrage to householders. This was opposed by many, and especially by the delegates from the manufacturing district; some of whom were surprised that so important a concession should be made to the opinion of any individual. Hunt treated the idea with little respect, and I thought he felt no discomfort at obtaining a sarcastic fling or two at the baronet. Cobbett advocated the restricted measure, scarcely in earnest, and weakly, and alleging the impracticability of universal suffrage. The discussion proceeded for some time and no one grappled the objection; until, fearing the resolution would be adopted, I in a few words explained how universal suffrage might be carried into effect, by taking the voters from the Militia list, or others made on the same plan. Hunt took up the idea, in a way which I thought rather annoyed Cobbett, who at length arose, and expressed his conviction of its practicability, giving me all the merit of his conversion. Resolutions in favour of universal suffrage and annual parliaments were thereupon carried, and soon afterwards the meeting was adjourned to the day following. Several of our country delegates were now presented to Cobbett by Benbow, who appeared to act almost as master of the ceremonies. I was not however introduced to the great man, and soon after he left the room.

On the day when Parliament was opened, a number of the delegates met Hunt at the Golden Cross, Charing Cross, and from thence went with him in procession to the residence of Lord Cochrane,* in Palace Yard, where a large petition from Bristol, and most of those from the north of England,

* Afterwards Lord Dundonald.

were placed in his lordship's hands. There had been some
tumult in the morning; the Prince Regent had been insulted
on his way to the house, and this part of the town was still in
a degree of excitement. We were crowded around, and accompanied by a great multitude, which at intervals rent the
air with shouts. Now it was that I beheld Hunt in his
element. He unrolled the petition, which was many yards
in length, and it was carried on the heads of the crowd
perfectly unharmed. He seemed to know almost every man
of them, and his confidence in, and entire mastery over them,
made him quite at ease. A louder huzza than common was
music to him; and when the questions were asked eagerly,
"Who is he?" "What are they about?" and the reply was,
"Hunt! Hunt! huzza!" his gratification was expressed by
a stern smile. He might be likened to the genius of commo-
tion, calling forth its elements, and controlling them at will.
On arriving at Palace Yard, we were shown into a room
below stairs, and whilst Lord Cochrane and Hunt conversed
above, a slight and elegant young lady, dressed in white, and
very interesting, served us with wine. She is, if I am not
misinformed, now Lady Dundonald. At length his lordship
came to us. He was a tall young man; cordial and un-
affected in his manner. He stooped a little, and had somewhat of a sailor's gait in walking; his face was rather oval;
fair naturally, but now tanned and sun-freckled. His hair
was sandy, his whiskers rather small, and of a deeper colour;
and the expression of his countenance was calm and self-
possessed. He took charge of our petitions, and being seated
in an armchair, we lifted him up and bore him on our
shoulders across Palace Yard, to the door of Westminster
Hall, the old rafters of which rung with the shouts of the
vast multitude outside.

CHAPTER IV.

ABOUT this time I was formally introduced to Mr. Cobbett, by
Benbow. He received me in a manner which was highly
gratifying to my feelings. This was at his office, or rooms, in
Newcastle Street, Strand. A number of other delegates were
present, but I thought Cobbett gave the preference above all,
to our friend Fitton of Royton, whose sarcastic vein had
particularly pleased him. Fitton had, in a speech at a public
meeting, designated a certain class in Manchester, " The Pig-
tail Gentry; " a ludicrous idea certainly, and one which made
Cobbett laugh till his sides shook. No man could enjoy a bit
of sarcasm better than he.

A number of us went one morning to visit Sir Francis
Burdett at his house in Park Place. The outside was but
of ordinary appearance; and the inside was not much better,
so far as we were admitted. To me it seemed like a cold,
gloomy, barely furnished house; which I accounted for by
supposing that it was perhaps the style of all great mansions.
We were shown into a large room, the only remarkable thing
in which was a bust of John Horne Tooke. Sir Francis came
to us in a loose grey vest coat, which reached far towards his
ankles. He had not a cravat on his neck; his feet were in
slippers; and a pair of white cotton stockings hung in
wrinkles on his long spare legs, which he kept alternately
throwing across his knees, and rubbing down with his hands,
as if he suffered, or recently had, some pain in those limbs.

He was a fine-looking man on the whole, of lofty stature, with a proud but not forbidding carriage of the head. His manner was dignified and civilly familiar; submitting to rather than seeking conversation with men of our class. He, however, discussed with us some points of the intended Bill for Reform candidly and freely, and concluded with promising to support universal suffrage, though he was not sanguine of much co-operation in the house. Under these circumstances we left Sir Francis; approving much that we found in and about him, and excusing much of what we could not approve. He was one of our idols, and we were loath to give him up.

Still I could not help my thoughts from reverting to the simple and homely welcome we received at Lord Cochrane's and contrasting it with the kind of dreary stateliness of this great mansion and its rich owner. At the former place we had a brief refection, bestowed with a grace which captivated our respect, and no health was ever drunk with more sincere goodwill than was Lord Cochrane's; the little dark-haired and bright-eyed lady seemed to know it, and to be delighted that it was so. But here scarcely a servant appeared, and nothing in the shape of refreshment was seen.

On the afternoon of a Sunday, Mitchell went with me to endeavour to find a former playfellow of mine, who was now a soldier in the Foot Guards. He had fought the campaigns of Portugal, Spain, and France; and we now found him a colour-serjeant at Knightsbridge barracks. The brave fellow received us with every demonstration of friendship. I told him what business had brought us to London, and that my fellow visitor was here on the same errand. Our business made no difference with him; he brought forth his ration, and we took a hearty lunch, after which we went with him to the non-commissioned officers' room at the canteen. About half-a-dozen serjeants were there, to whom my friend introduced us, making known, without the least reserve, or show of it, the business we were come upon to the metropolis. That seemed not to weigh with them, and we were soon in a free conversation on the subject of parliamentary reform. When objections were stated, they listened candidly to our replies, and a good-humoured discussion, half serious, half joking, was promoted on both sides. I and Mitchell had with us, and it was entirely accidental, a few of *Cobbett's Registers*, and Hone's political pamphlets, to which we sometimes appealed, and read extracts from. The soldiers were delighted; they burst into fits of laughter; and on the copies we had being given them, one of them read the Political Litany through, to the further great amusement of himself and the company. Thus we passed a most agreeable evening, and parted only at the last hour. Mitchell and I returned to the city; neither of us, I firmly believe, having any further thought of the circumstance than to regret that evenings so rationally and so peaceably spent came so seldom.

Very soon after this a law was passed, making it death to attempt to seduce a soldier from his duty. Could it possibly be that the occurrences of this evening led to the enactment of that law?

Several times I attended meetings of trades' clubs, and other public assemblages of the working men. They would generally be found in a large room, an elevated seat being placed for the chairman. On first opening the door, the place seemed dimmed by a suffocating vapour of tobacco, curling from the cups of long pipes, and issuing from the mouths of the smokers, in clouds of abominable odour, like nothing in the world more than one of the unclean fogs of their streets, though the latter were certainly less offensive and probably less hurtful. Every man would have his half-pint of porter before him; many would be speaking at once, and the hum and confusion would be such as gave an idea of there being more talkers than thinkers, more speakers than listeners. Presently, "order" would be called, and comparative silence would ensue; a speaker, stranger or citizen, would be announced with much courtesy and compliment. "Hear, hear, hear," would follow, with clapping of hands and knocking of knuckles on the tables till the half-pints danced; then a speech, with compliments to some brother orator or popular statesman; next a resolution in favour of parliamentary reform, and a speech to second it; an amendment on some

minor point would follow; a seconding of that; a breach of
order by some individual of warm temperament; half a dozen
would rise to set him right, a dozen to put them down, and
the vociferation and gesticulation would become loud and con-
founding.   The door opens, and two persons of middle stature
enter; the uproar is changed to applause, and a round of
huzzas welcome the new-comers.   A stranger like myself
inquiring—Who is he, the foremost and better dressed one?—
would be answered, "That gentleman is Mr. Watson the elder,
who was lately charged with high treason, and is now under
bail to answer an indictment for a misdemeanour in consequence of his connection with the late meeting at Spa Fields."
The person spoken of would be supposed to be about fifty
years of age, with somewhat of a polish in his gait and
manner, and a degree of respectability and neatness in his
dress.   He was educated for a genteel profession, that of a
surgeon; had practised it, and had in consequence moved in
a sphere higher than his present one.   He had probably a
better heart than head; the latter had failed to bear him up
in his station, and the ardour of the former had just before
hurried him into transactions, from the consequences of which
he had not yet escaped.   His son at this time was concealed
in London, a large reward having been offered for his apprehension.   The other man was Preston, a co-operator with
Watson, Hooper, and others, in late riots.   He was about
middle age, of ordinary appearance, dressed as an operative,
and walked with the help of a stick.   I could not but entertain a slightful opinion of the intellect and trustworthiness of
these two men, when, on a morning or two afterwards, at
breakfast with me and Mitchell, they narrated with seeming
pride and satisfaction their several parts during the riots.
Preston had mounted a wall of the Tower, and summoned the
guard to surrender.   The men gazed at him—laughed; no one
fired a shot—and soon after he fell down, or was pulled off by
his companions, who thought (no doubt) he had acted fool
long enough.

Such were two of the most influential leaders of the London
operative reformers.   I repeat that I thought meanly of their

qualifications for such a post. But how blind is human perception, how slow should we be to condemn! I myself was at the same moment going hand and heart with some who were as little to be depended upon as the above, and yet I could not perceive my situation. The blind were then leading the blind.

During the debate on the report of the Green Bag* Committee, I obtained an order for admission to the gallery of the House of Commons. I well recollect, though I cannot describe, all the conflicting emotions which arose within me as I approached that assembly, with the certainty of now seeing and hearing those whom I considered to be the authors of my country's wrongs. Curiosity certainly held its share of my feelings; but a strong dislike to the " boroughmonger crew " and their measures held a far larger share. After a tough struggle at elbowing and pushing along a passage, up a narrow staircase, and across a room, I found myself in a small gallery, from whence I looked on a dimly lighted place below. At the head of the room, or rather den, for such it appeared to me, sat a person in a full loose robe of, I think, scarlet and white. Above his head were the royal arms, richly gilded; at his feet several men in robes and wigs were writing at a large table, on which lamps were burning, which cast a softened light on a rich ornament like a ponderous sceptre of silver and gold, or what appeared to be so. Those persons I knew must be the Speaker and the clerks of the House; and that rich ornament could be nothing else than the " mace "—the same thing, or one in its place, to which Cromwell pointed and said, " Take away that bauble; for shame—give way to honester men." On each side of this pit-looking place, leaving an open space in the centre of the floor, were some three or four hundreds of the most ordinary-looking men I had ever beheld at one view. Some were striking exceptions; several young fellows in military dresses gave relief to the sombre drapery of the others. Canning, with his smooth, bare, and capacious forehead, sat there, a spirit beaming in his looks like that of the

* The " Green Bag " contained papers on the state of the country intended to justify the suspension of the Habeas Corpus Act.

leopard waiting to spring upon its prey. Castlereagh, with his handsome but immovable features; Burdett, with his head carried back, and held high as in defiance; and Brougham, with his Arab soul ready to rush forth and challenge war to all comers. The question was to me solemnly interesting, whilst the spectacle wrought strangely on my feelings. Our accusers were many and powerful, with words at will, and applauding listeners. Our friends were few and far between, with no applauders save their good conscience, and the blessings of the poor. What a scene was this to be enacted by the "collective wisdom of the nation." Some of the members stood leaning against pillars, with their hats cocked awry; some were whispering by half-dozens; others were lolling upon their seats; some, with arms a-kimbo, were eye-glassing across the house; some were stiffened immovably by starch, or pride, or both; one was speaking, or appeared to be so, by the motion of his arms, which he shook in token of defiance, when his voice was drowned by a howl as wild and remorseless as that from a kennel of hounds at feeding time. Now he points, menacing, to the ministerial benches —now he appeals to some members on this side—then to the Speaker; all in vain. At times he is heard in the pauses of that wild hubbub, but again he is borne down by the yell which awakes on all sides around him. Some talked aloud; some whinnied in mock laughter, coming, like that of the damned, from bitter hearts. Some called "order, order," some "question, question;" some beat time with the heel of their boots; some snorted into their napkins; and one old gentleman in the side gallery actually coughed himself from a mock cough into a real one, and could not stop until he was almost black in the face.

And are these, thought I, the beings whose laws we must obey? This the "most illustrious assembly of freemen in the world?" Perish freedom then, and her children too. O! for the stamp of stern old Oliver on this floor; and the clank of his scabbard, and the rush of his iron-armed band, and his voice to arise above this babel howl—"Take away that bauble"—"Begone; give place to honester men."

Such was my first view of the House of Commons; and such the impressions strongly forced on my feelings at the time. The speaker alluded to was Henry Brougham. I heard at first very little of what he said, but I understood from occasional words, and the remarks of some whom I took for reporters, that he was violently attacking the ministers and their whole home policy. That he was so doing might have been inferred from the great exertions of the ministerial party to render him inaudible, and to subdue his spirit by a bewildering and contemptuous disapprobation. But they had before them a wrong one for being silenced, either by confusion or menace. Like a brave stag, he held them at bay, and even hurled back their defiance with "retorted scorn." In some time his words became more audible; presently there was comparative silence, and I soon understood that he had let go the ministry, and now, unaccountable as it seemed to me, had made a dead set at the reformers. Oh! how he did scowl towards us—contemn and disparage our best actions and wound our dearest feelings! Now stealing near our hearts with words of wonderful power, flashing with bright wit and happy thought; anon like a reckless wizard changing pleasant sunbeams into clouds, "rough with black winds and storms," and vivid with the cruellest shafts. Then was he listened to as if not a pulse moved; then was he applauded to the very welkin. And he stood in the pride of his power, his foes before him subdued, but spared; his friends derided and disclaimed, and his former principles sacrificed to "low ambition," and the vanity of such a display as this.

I would have here essayed somewhat with respect to Canning, and the character and effects of his eloquence; but little appertaining to him remained on my mind. Every feeling was absorbed by the contemplation of that man whom I now considered to be the most perfidious of his race. I turned from the spectacle with disgust, and sought my lodgings in a kind of stupor, almost believing that I had escaped from a monstrous dream.

Such was my first view of Henry Brougham; and such the impressions I imbibed and long entertained of that extraordinary man. He sinned then, and has often done so since, against the best interests of his country; bowing to his own image, and sacrificing reason and principle to caprice or offended self-love. But has he not done much for mercy, and for the enlightenment of his kind? See the African dancing above his chains! Behold the mild but irresistible light which education is diffusing over the land! These are indeed blessings beyond all price—rays of unfading glory. They are Lord Brougham's; and will illumine his tomb when his errors and imperfections are forgotten.

CHAPTER V.

SOON afterwards I left the great Babylon, heartily tired of it,
and returned to Middleton, where events rapidly pressed on
my attention.

On the morning of Sunday, the 8th of March, Benbow
called on me at Middleton. I had lost sight of him since my
return from London; the Habeas Corpus Act was already
suspended, and I supposed from some remarks of his that he
had thought it best not to be so much in public at Manchester
as he previously had been. He had, however, taken a great
share in getting up and arranging the Blanket Meeting; and
now, after commending the intended proceeding, and dwelling
on the good effects it would produce, he asked me to join in
the meeting and expedition, and to bring as many of my
neighbours as I could. I flatly refused; and stated my
reasons, which will shortly appear. He enlarged his com-
mendations, calculating with certainty that the Blanketeers
would march to London, thousands in number; and that their
petitions would be graciously, if not with some awe, received
by the Prince Regent in person. I maintained my opinions—
he answered with reproaches; I treated the plan as a chimera,
and held lightly the judgment of its proposers and concoctors.
Benbow went away in a huff, and I remained with a lowered
opinion of my former comrade.

On the night of Sunday, the 9th of March, I was requested

to attend a meeting in the house of one of my neighbours,
where a number of friends wished to hear my opinion with
reference to the Blanket Meeting. I went to them and spoke
freely in condemnation of the measure. I endeavoured to
show them that the authorities of Manchester were not likely
to permit their leaving the town in a body, with blankets and
petitions, as they proposed ; that they could not subsist on
the road ; that the cold and wet would kill numbers of them,
who were already enfeebled by hunger and other deprivations;
that soldiers always marched in divisions for the easier pro-
curement of food and lodgings ; and that an irregular multitude like themselves, could not, on an emergency, be pro-
visioned, and quartered. That they need not expect to be
welcome wherever they went, especially in such of the rotten
boroughs as fell in their way, against the franchise of which
they were petitioning ; that the inhabitants would bolt their
doors against them ; and that if they took possession by force
there was the law to punish them. That many persons might
join their ranks who were not reformers but enemies to reform,
hired perhaps to bring them and their cause into disgrace; that
if these persons began to plunder on the road, the punishment
and disgrace would be visited on the whole body ; that they
would be denounced as robbers and rebels, and the military
would be brought to cut them down or take them prisoners.
In conclusion, I earnestly cautioned them against having anything to do with the proposed meeting, and intimated that the
parties who had got it up were not to be depended upon ; that
their blind zeal overran every reasonable consideration ; and
that if they, my neighbours, took part in the meeting, they
would probably repent when it was too late. Whether it was
in consequence of what I said I cannot tell ; but I was afterwards gratified on hearing that no person from Middleton went
as a Blanketeer.

But of this meeting, which was our first great absurdity, I
must write more particularly.

It was one of the bad schemes which accompanied us from
London, and was the result of the intercourse of some of the
deputies with the leaders of the London operatives—the

Watsons, Prestons, and Hoopers. Mitchell and Benbow had cultivated a rather close acquaintance with these men, little suspecting, I have no doubt, that their new friends had already fallen under the influence of instigators who betrayed all their transactions to the Government. But the London leaders, or at least such of them as I conversed with, were, as I have shown, men of frank character and bearing, and apparently of sincere intention; and their manner, flattering by the confidence it bestowed, naturally led to a reciprocal feeling, and to the formation of connections, the effects of which now began to appear.

Our maxim had hitherto in all our proceedings been— "Hold fast by the laws." It was the maxim of Major Cartwright, our venerable political father, and had been adhered to with a religious observance. But doctrines varying from this now began to be broached, and measures hinted, which, if not in direct contravention of the law, were but ill-disguised subterfuges for evading its intentions.

The meeting took place according to appointment; but I not being there, my brief description must be taken as the account of others. The assemblage consisted almost entirely of operatives, four or five thousand in number; and was held on that piece of ground (St. Peter's Field) which afterwards obtained so melancholy a celebrity. Many of the individuals were observed to have blankets, rugs, or large coats, rolled up and tied, knapsack like, on their backs; some carried bundles under their arms; some had papers, supposed to be petitions rolled up; and some had stout walking sticks. The magistrates came upon the field and read the Riot Act; the meeting was afterwards dispersed by the military and special constables, and twenty-nine persons were apprehended, amongst whom were two young men, named Bagguley and Drummond, who had recently come into notice as speakers, and who being in favour of extreme measures, were much listened to and applauded. But my warm friend, Benbow, took care not to make his appearance on that occasion.

On the Riot Act being read, about three hundred persons left the meeting to commence their march to London. Some

of them formed a straggling line in Mosley Street, and marched
along Piccadilly, being continually joined by others, until the
whole body was collected, near Ardwick Green. The appearance of these misdirected people was calculated to excite in
considerate minds pity rather than resentment. Some appeared to have strength in their limbs and pleasure in their
features, others already with doubt in their looks and hesitation in their steps. A few were decently clothed and well
appointed for the journey; many were covered only by rags
which admitted the cold wind, and were already damped by a
gentle but chilling rain. Some appeared young, with health
on their cheeks, every care behind and hope alone before;
the thoughts of others were probably reverting to their homes
on the hill-sides, or in the sombre alleys of the town, where
wives and children had resigned them for a time, in hopes of
their return with plenty, and never more to part. Here a youth
was waving his hand to a damsel pale and tremulous with
alarm; yonder an attenuated being, giving back, after kissing
it, a poorly child to the arms of its mother—he hastens towards his comrades with willing but feeble steps, looking back
on those, so poor, but oh! how dear—the child is hushed
with a caress, the mother turning it gently to her cold and
nurtureless bosom, nurtureless of everything save deep and
tender love. Her looks are still directed the way he goes; he
has disappeared: and whilst her tears flow the poor but
cleanly mantle is drawn over the little one, and in a conflict
of grief, hope, and fear, she thoughtfully wends to her obscure
and cheerless abode. A body of yeomanry soon afterwards
followed those simple-minded men, and took possession of the
bridge at Stockport. Many then turned back to their homes;
a body of them crossed the river below, and entered Cheshire;
several received sabre wounds, and one man was shot dead on
Lancashire hill. Of those who persisted in their march it is
only necessary to say that they arrived at nine o'clock at night
in the market place at Macclesfield, being about one hundred
and eighty in number. Some of them lay out all night, and
took the earliest dawn to find their way home. Some were
well lodged and hospitably entertained by friends; some paid

for quarters, and some were quartered in prison. Few were those who marched the following morning. About a score arrived at Leek, and six only were known to pass Ashborne bridge. And so ended the Blanket Expedition! "What would you really have done," I said to one of them, "supposing you had got to London?" "Done?" he replied, in surprise at the question; "why iv wee'd nobbo gett'n to Lunnun, we shud ha' tan th' nation, an' sattl't o'th dett." Such, and about as rational, were some of the incoherent dreams which at this time began to find favour in the eyes of the gross multitude.

But another cause was assigned for the dispersion of the Blanketeers. It was said that a purse containing from thirty to fifty pounds having been made up, was given to one of the principal leaders, with instructions to proceed on the London road a day or two in advance, to procure food and lodgings for money, where they could not be had for friendship or a more urgent motive. That "the good man," by some mistake, got out of the right way, and wandering far into Yorkshire, he never found himself till the money was all spent; and the Blanketeers, thus losing their commissary and paymaster, were broken by the same means which had dispersed more numerous armies, viz., want of necessaries; and thus "the nation" was saved for that time. However true or otherwise this account may be, it is certain that the man suddenly disappeared (but others did the same) and was out of the way a month or two, after which he paid a visit to Middleton on his return, as he said, from Yorkshire to Manchester. He was always somewhat doubted afterwards; and his last appearance in this quarter was in the character of an adroit crimp to a fortune-promising attorney.

It was about this time, though I have not the exact date, that the first out-of-door meeting was held at Rochdale. Fitton, Knight, myself, and several other public characters were invited to attend, and I did so. The day was cold and very wet; the hustings were fixed on the bare moor of Cronkeyshaw. None of the speakers save myself kept their appointment; nothing in the form of resolution or petition had been prepared, and I had to select and arrange these from an old "Statesman" newspaper which I found at the rendezvous, the "Rose," in Yorkshire Street. The town wore an appearance of alarm, and a company or two of soldiers were under arms in the main street. The meeting was, however, well attended, and the hearts of the people seemed to warm in proportion to the merciless cold of the wind and rain, which latter teemed upon us during the whole of the proceedings. On our return, the poor redcoats were still carrying arms, though, as one of the woollen weavers remarked, it would be to little purpose should they be wanted, "as the water was already running over at the muzzles of their guns, they might squirt us," he said, "but could not shoot us." On this occasion I received pay for my attendance. On our return to the "Rose," besides refreshments, the Committee presented me with four shillings, and I accepted the money because I thought I was entitled to it, having lost work to that value at home. But I never, except on this occasion, took money or any other remuneration for attending reform meetings. I considered it a mean thing, though the practice was coming much into use, and several of my friends, without any scruple, continued to do so until "their occupation" was gone. It was a bad practice, however, and gave rise to a set of orators who made a trade of speechifying, and the race has not become extinct. These persons began to seek engagements of the kind ; some would even thrust themselves upon the committee for remuneration, and generally received it. He who produced the greatest excitement, the loudest cheering, and the most violent clappings, was the best orator, and was sure to be engaged and well paid, and in order to produce those manifestations, the wildest and most extravagant rhodomontade would too often suffice. Such speakers quickly got a name ; the calls on them were frequent ; and they left their work or their business for a more profitable and flattering employment ; tramping from place to place hawking their new fangles, and guzzling, fattening, and replenishing themselves at the expense of the simple and credulous multitude. Steadiness of conduct and consistency of principle were soon placed as it were at a distance from us. Our unity of action was relaxed ; new speakers sprung like mushrooms about our feet ; plans were broached, quite different from any that had been recognised by the Hampden Clubs ; and the people, at a loss to distinguish friends from enemies, were soon prepared for the operations of informers, who, in the natural career of their business, became also promoters of secret plots and criminal measures of various descriptions. The good and fatherly maxim of the worthy old major, "Hold fast by the laws," was by many lost sight of.

How far the moral of these facts is applicable to the present day will be judged by an observant public, and may perhaps not be deemed ill-timed by some of the more intelligent of those who have been found amongst the persons styled Chartists. If from the records of past errors good can be extracted for present emergencies, it will be well, and let us endeavour to do so. History is a faithful monitor, requiring only to be consulted in a truth-seeking spirit, when she will vouchsafe to become a friendly counsellor, saying to her inquirer, "Come blind one and see ; come lost one, and behold thy way." Nations may read their fate in the histories of nations ; and individuals may be advised by a memoir so humble as mine.

At dusk on the evening of Tuesday, the 11th of March, the day after the Blanket meeting, a man dressed much like a dyer was brought to my residence by Joseph Healey, who had found him inquiring for me in the lower part of the town. The stranger said he had something of a private and important nature to communicate, in consequence of which I and the stranger and Healey went to the sign of the " Trumpeter," where we were accommodated with a private room. The man now told us that he was deputed by some persons at Manchester to propose that in consequence of the treatment which the Blanketeers had received at the meeting and afterwards, " a Moscow of Manchester " should take place that very night. The man paused and looked at us severally. I intimated that I knew what he meant, and desired him to go on. He said it would entirely depend on the co-operation or otherwise of the

country people ; that other messengers had been sent to every
reform society within twenty miles of the town; that if the
answers were favourable to the project, the light of the
conflagration was to be the signal for the country people to
come in—and, in such case, the Middleton people were
requested to take their station on St. George's Field.   He said
the plan had been arranged by a meeting held at Manchester ;
that the whole force would be divided into parties, one of
which was to engage the attention of the military and draw
them from their barracks ; another was to take possession
of the barracks and secure the arms and magazine ; another
was to plunder and then set fire to the houses of individuals
who were marked out; and a fourth was to storm the New
Bailey and liberate the prisoners, particularly the Blanketeers
confined there.   I said it was a serious thing to undertake,
and that an answer could not be returned from Middleton
until some friends had been consulted.   On my rising to go
out, the man appeared alarmed, and begged I would not betray
him.   I assured him he had nothing to fear, and desired him
to stay with Healey until my return, which would be very
soon, on which he seemed reconciled to my going.   I speedily
went to five of my acquaintance, chiefly members of the
committee, and desired them to repair immediately to Healey's
house, where business of importance would be laid before
them.   I then brought up the stranger and the doctor, and
telling the man he might confide in us, he repeated nearly
word for word what he had said at the " Trumpeter."   I then
said I would have nothing to do with the scheme ; that it was
unlawful, inhuman, and cowardly.   I told him he appeared to
be a simple young fellow, and was probably the dupe of some
designing villain.   My friends agreed with my opinion, both as
to the proposal and the instrument who broached it : we bade
him, however, not to mistrust us ; gave him refreshment, and
sent him away, more in sorrow for his peril (being persuaded
he was in the hands of villains) than of resentment for the
decoy he had attempted.   We bade him good night, and he
went his way.

The young man said his name was Samuel Priestley; I

observed that he had lost a finger from his left hand ; he said
he lived at Bank Top, Manchester. I afterwards made inquiries respecting him on the spot, but never could hear of
such a person in the place or neighbourhood. This statement,
however, cannot now injure him.

After he was gone we consulted about this strange message
and unknown messenger. We had not heard of the plot
before, and though we doubted not that it had been sanctioned,
as the man stated, by the Manchester committee, that circumstance did not increase our confidence. We had no reliance
on their sagacity or their integrity as a body ; men who could
get up and countenance the Blanket Expedition had no weight
with us. They were moreover reported to be under the
influence of spies from the police; a suspicion which many
circumstances tended to strengthen. The plot itself did the
same ; the unknown messenger, the precipitation, " to be done
that very night," the population for twenty miles around an
immense town to be brought upon it by midnight, and then to
be divided, apportioned, and set to work by men of whom they
knew nothing ! The proposal was too absurd, as well as
iniquitous, to excite anything save wonder and disgust, even
with simple and inexperienced ones like ourselves. Besides,
would Major Cartwright have sanctioned such a measure ?
Certainly not. And then we almost regretted that we had
suffered the emissary to depart

It was deemed prudent that Healey and I should on that
night sleep from home, and at some place where our stay
could be proved, should anything arise to render such a step
necessary ; and none could tell what might be necessary, as in
those days of alarm and uncertainty no one knew what was
impending. An old female reformer accordingly gave us her
house and bed, and turning the key, locked us in, whilst we,
in our simplicity, were quite satisfied with having taken so
wise a precaution against any false evidence which might by
possibility be brought to connect us with the plot of which we
had been apprised. We retired to rest and lay talking this
strange matter over until sleep overtook us. I was first to
awake, and seeing a brightness behind the curtain, I stepped

to the window, and sure enough beheld in the southern sky a
stream of light which I thought must be that of a distant fire.
It was a fine crisped morning, and as I looked, a piece of a
moon came wandering to the west from behind some masses
of cloud. Now she would be entirely obscured ; then streaks
of her pale beams would be seen breaking on the edges of the
vapours ; then a broader gleam would come ; then again it
would be pale and receding ; but the clouds were so connected
that the fair traveller had seldom a space for showing her un-
veiled horn. I saw how it was; my conflagration had dwindled
to a moonbeam, and as I stood with the frost tingling at my
toes " an unlucky thought" (as we say, when excusing our
own sins we impute them to a much abused sable personage)
came into my head to have a small joke at the doctor's
expense ; and as it was a mode of amusement to which I
must confess I was rather prone, I immediately began to carry
it into effect. I gave a loud cough or two ; the doctor thereupon grunted and turned over in bed ; when, in the very
break of his sleep, I said aloud, as I crept beneath the bed-
clothes, "there's a fine leet i'th' welkin, as th' witch o' Brand-
wood sed when the devil wur ridin' o'er Rossenda." " Leet,"
said the doctor ; " a fine leet, weer ? weer ? " " Why go to th'
windo' an' look." That instant my sanguine friend was out of
bed and at the window, his head stuck behind the curtain.
" There's a great leet," he said, " to'rd Manchester." " There
is indeed," I replied, "it's mitch but weary wark is gooin' on
omung yon foke." " It's awful," said the doctor ; " thei'r
agate as sure as we're heer." " I think there's summut up,"
I said. I was now snugly rolled in the clothes, and perceived
at the same time that the doctor was getting into a kind of
dancing shiver, and my object being to keep him in his shirt
till he was cooled and undeceived, and consequently a little
sprung in temper, I asked, " Dun yo really think then ot th'
teawn's o' foyer ? " " Foyer," he replied ; "there's no deawt
on't." " Con yo see th' flames, doctor ? " " Nowe, I conno'
see th' flames, but I con see th' leet ut coms fro' em." " That's
awful," I ejaculated. " Aye, it's awful," he said ; "come an'
see for yo'rsel'." " Nowe, I'd reyther not," I answered ; " I

dunno' like sich scets; it's lucky ut we're heer—they conno' say ut we'n had owt to do wi' it, at ony rate, con they, doctor?" "Nowe," he said, "they conno'. It keeps changin'," he said. "Con yo' yer owt?" I asked. "Nowe, I conno' yer nowt," he said. I, however, heard his teeth hacking in his head, and stuffed the sheet into my mouth to prevent my laughter from being noticed. "Ar' yo' sure, doctor?" I asked. No reply. "Is it blazin' up?" I said. "Blazin' be hanged!" was the answer. "Wot dun yo' myen, doctor—is it gwon eawt then?" "Gullook!" he said, "it's nobbut th' moon, an' yo' knewn it oth' while." A loud burst of laughter followed, which I enjoyed till the bed shook; my companion muttering imprecations and sundry devil's prayers against all "moon doggs an' welkin lookers," by which terms I knew he meant myself for one.

CHAPTER VI.

CONSEQUENCES OF THE SUSPENSION OF THE HABEAS CORPUS—
STATE OF THE COUNTRY—STOPPAGE OF PUBLIC MEETINGS
—SECRET ONES COMMENCED.

PERSONAL liberty not being now secure from one hour to
another, many of the leading reformers were induced to quit
their homes, and seek concealment where they could obtain it.
Those who could muster a few pounds, or who had friends to
give them a frugal welcome, or who had trades with which
they could travel, disappeared like swallows at the close of
summer, no one knew whither. The single men stayed away
altogether; the married ones would occasionally steal back at
night to their wan-cheeked families, perhaps to divide with
them some trifle they had saved during their absence, perhaps
to obtain a change of linen or other garment for future concealment, but most of all, as would naturally be the case, to
console, and be consoled by their wives and little ones. Perhaps one had found an asylum amongst kind friends, and had
brought home a little hoard, the fruits of his own industry and
carefulness, or of their generosity. Perhaps he had been
wandering in want, not daring to make himself known, until
his beard disguised him, his shoes and stockings were trampled
from his feet, and his linen was in rags; when at length, worn
out and reckless, he would venture home, like the wearied
bird which found no place to rest. Perhaps he had been discovered to be a reform leader, and had been threatened, mayhap pursued, and, like a hunted hare, now returned to the
·place of former repose. Then he would come home stealthily
under cover of darkness; his wife would rush into his arms,

his little ones would be about his knees, looking silent pleasure —for they, poor things, like nestling birds, had learned to be mute in danger.

But with all precautions, it did sometimes happen that in such moments of mournful joy the father would be seized, chained, and torn from his family before he had time to bless them or to receive their blessings and tears. Such scenes were of frequent occurrence, and have thrown a melancholy retrospection over those days. Private revenge or political differences were gratified by secret and often false information handed to the police. The country was distracted by rumours of treasonable discoveries, and apprehensions of the traitors, whose fate was generally predicted to be death or perpetual imprisonment. Bagguley, Johnson, Drummond, and Benbow were already in prison at London; and it was frequently intimated to me, through some very kind relations-in-law, that I and some of my acquaintances would soon be arrested. This sort of information was always brought to Middleton by parties who, being in the manufacturing line, visited Manchester twice or thrice a week for the purpose of disposing of their goods. They appeared to be well acquainted with the movements of the police; they could tell when king's messengers arrived or departed; how many State warrants had been issued; who would be next apprehended; and such like useful and pleasant things, which they always took care to make known in such quarters as made it sure to reach those they wished to render unhappy by anticipation of troubles they could not now avoid. And, strange to say, many of their predictions were verified. King's messengers did arrive: Government warrants were issued; and the persons they mentioned were taken to prison. A cloud of gloom and mistrust hung over the whole country. The suspension of the Habeas Corpus Act was a measure the result of which we young reformers could not judge, save by report, and that was of a nature to cause anxiety in the most indifferent of us. The proscriptions, imprisonments, trials, and banishments of 1792 were brought to our recollections by the similarity of our situation to those of the sufferers of that period. It seemed as if the sun of freedom were gone down, and a rayless expanse of oppression had finally closed over us   Cobbett, in terror of imprisonment, had fled to America; Sir Francis Burdett had enough to do in keeping his own arms free; Lord Cochrane was threatened, but quailed not; Hunt was still somewhat turbulent, but he was powerless, for he had lost the genius of his influence when he lost Cobbett,* and was now almost like Sampson, shorn and blind.   The worthy old Major remained at his post, brave as a lion, serene as an unconscious child; and also, in the rush and tumult of that time, almost as little noticed.   Then, of our country reformers, John Knight had disappeared; Pilkington was out of the way somewhere; Bradbury had not yet been heard of; Mitchell moved in a sphere of his own, the extent of which no man knew save himself; and Kay and Fitton were seldom visible beyond the circle of their own village; whilst, to complete our misfortunes, our chapel-keeper, in the very tremor of fear, turned the key upon us, and declared we should no longer meet in the place.

Our society, thus hopeless, became divided and dismayed; hundreds slunk home to their looms, nor dared to come out, save like owls at nightfall, when they would perhaps steal through by-paths or behind hedges, or down some clough, to hear the news at the next cottage.   Some might be seen chatting with and making themselves agreeable to our declared enemies; but these were few, and always of the worst character.   Open meetings thus being suspended, secret ones ensued; they were originated at Manchester, and assembled under various pretexts.   Sometimes they were termed "benefit societies," sometimes "botanical meetings," "meetings for the relief of the families of imprisoned reformers," or "of those who had fled the country"; but their real purpose, divulged only to the initiated, was to carry into effect the night attack on Manchester, the attempt at which had before failed for want of arrangement and co-operation.

* In March, 1817, on the suspension of the Habeas Corpus Act, Cobbett went to America, where he remained two years.

CHAPTER VII.

SEARCH FOR A TEMPORARY HOME—DOCTOR HEALEY'S PATERNITY
—SOME ACCOUNT OF HIMSELF—A GLANCE AT THE AUTHOR'S
ANCESTRY — HEALEY'S UNCLE RICHARD, HIS HOUSE AND
FAMILY—VIEW FROM KNOWE HILL.

WEARIED at length with the continued alarms of my intended
arrest and committal to prison, I consented to leave home for
a day or two to find some place where, unknown, I might
earn a subsistence until the cloud was blown over, and I could
return in safety.   Healey, who also had expectations of being
wanted shortly, determined to accompany me with a like view;
and so, in the thick, grey morning, with light purses and somewhat heavy hearts, we left our humble but dear homes, and
struck into the open country—

> "Down a quiet green lane where two rindles flow;
> Unto lands where the night-hunters stealthily go;
> Cross'd Roche's dark stream; o'er a barren heath hied;
> And up to the moorlands wild and wide."

Healey wished to see his uncle Richard, who was a farmer
and publican on the moors to the north-west of Middleton;
and soon, as the sun broke out and the mist cleared, we found
ourselves traversing Hopwood Ley in that direction.   How
delicious was the air, wafting breezy and free over the budding
woods!   Now sweeping up the hollows, now coming through
the dew pearls and shaking the hazel bloom, now bearing
towards us the bold note of the throstle, anon receding to
nestle softly in the dingles with the melody of the blackbird!
How happy were those simple children of nature—happy in

45

their loves, in their rude nests ; in their offspring, and in their
unconsciousness of danger. The lapwing's plaintive cry as it
wheeled above was in unison with our feelings ; the bird also
seemed, like ourselves, to have no resting-place ; whilst the
cony, frisking before us, and disappearing, showed us he had a
home. But the bracing air, the warm, life-giving sun, the
glorious beings of nature around and above us, whilst they
excited our attention, gradually dispelled the gloom of our
feelings, and we also began to be cheerful if not happy, remembering that there is no hill without its vale, no storm
without its calm, no shadow without its sun. So we went on
—now climbing a hedge, now leaping a rindle, now starting a
hare, or springing a woodcock, now treading a bit of swamp,
now up a knoll through the gorses, then by the skirt of a
meadow, and round to the hill-foot, by the music of a stream,
where—

> "Spring moves on as glad we gaze,
> Calling the flowers wherever she strays.
> Come from the earth, ye dwellers there,
> To the blessed light, and the living air:
> For the snowdrop hath warned the drift away;
> And the crocus awaiteth your company ;
> And the bud of the thorn is beginning to swell;
> And the waters have broken their bonds in the dell.
> And are not the hazel and slender bine
> Blending their boughs where the sun doth shine ?
> And the willow is bringing its downy palm,
> Garland for days that are bright and calm ;
> And the lady-flower waves on its slender stem ;
> And the primrose peeps like a starry gem."

Thus tramping o'er Spinthreeds and the Wilderness, we
approached Captain Fold, the sight of which led Healey into
some remarks on his father, his family, and his own early days.

He said he was born at Captain Fold, where his father
lived and was a famous cow-leech, being fetched by the
farmers to all parts of the country when their cattle were
sick ; that he also dabbled a little in medicines for the human
frame, and was successful in most of the cases which he
undertook ; and they were such as had baffled common

applications. That his father was a devout man of the Methodist persuasion, and a firm believer in witches and witchcraft, which persuasion he also inherited. That in those days there were many sudden and uncommon disorders, which few persons understood, and fewer still could cope with. Such were often treated by his father on the " supernatural plan," and he was generally successful. He was almost sure to be sent for when cattle were supposed to be amiss from the influence of infernal spells, which he counteracted sometimes by other spells, drugs and herbs prepared at particular seasons, and under certain forms and ceremonials. He had also great faith in the power of faith, and the efficacy of private prayer. He died, however, leaving my companion unprovided for, and he was put apprentice to a cotton weaver at Bolton, where he learned the business, but under such oppressions and cruelties from his master and dame, as instilled into him a thorough abhorrence of tyranny. At the expiration of the term of his bondage he came to Chadderton, where he had a married sister living; and after introducing a new method of twisting-in-warps, by which he saved a little money, and clothed himself respectably, he paid his addresses to his present wife and was accepted, and came to Middleton to reside with his wife and her parents. He accounted for his getting into the surgical profession by supposing that he derived a taste for it from his father. He first began by selling simple drugs; after which he got some books, and ventured to compound and prescribe medicines. Next he succeeded in "breathing a vein"; and lastly became a tooth-drawer, and general practitioner of the surgical art; and now " he was thankful, he needed not turn his back on any of his neighbours in the same line." There was only one point he said, and that was the art obstetric, in which he was deficient; and he hoped to attain that yet. Such were my companion's past trials and present attainments. In sketching his father, however, he omitted one remarkable circumstance, and if he knew it, honour be to his filial regard for the omission; it accords, however, very closely with the son's outline of the remarkable old man. It was said that so firm was his belief in the human application of divine faith, and such his assurance of being perfected in it, that he ascended the ridge of his barn, in the presence of his assembled neighbours, and after praying for, and exhorting them, he, in the full expectation of being buoyed up, flung himself off, and fell souse on a dung-heap below. Such a misdirection was, of course, a great handle to the ungodly; but in the old man's opinion it was no disproof of the power of faith, but an intimation only of his own weakness and imperfections in that divine attainment.

Doctor Healey, or, "the doctor," as we must now call him, was about five feet six in height; thirty-two or three years of age, with rather good features, small light grey eyes, darker whiskers and hair, with a curl on his forehead, of which he was remarkably proud. He was well-set in body, but light of limb; his knees had an uncommonly supple motion, which gave them an appearance of weakness. He had an assured look, and in walking, especially when with a little "too much wind in the sheet," he turned his toes inward, and carried an air of bravado which was richly grotesque. In disposition he was, until afterwards corrupted, generous and confiding; credulous, proud of his person and acquirements. A book-buyer, but little of a reader, less of a thinker, and no recollector of literary matters. Hence, with an imperturbable self-complacency, he was supremely oblivious of the world, its history, manners, and concerns; except such as directly interfered with the good or evil of his own existence. At this time his attire was scarcely more decent than my own; both were somewhat too seedy, but that was a circumstance on which a learned doctor and a self-devoting patriot could look with indifference.

His hat was somewhat napless, with sundry dinges on the crown, and up-settings and down-flappings of the brim, which showed it to have tupped against harder substances than itself, as well as to have seen much "winter and rough weather." He wore a long drab top-coat, which, from its present appearance, might never have gone through the process of perching. His under-coat was of dark uncut fustian, which, by his almost incessant occupation in the "laboratory," preparing ointments, salves, and lotions, had become smooth and shining as a duck's wing, and almost as impervious to wet; his hamsters were similar in material and condition to his coat, whilst his legs were encased in top-boots, no worse for wear, except perhaps a leaky seam or two, and a cracked upper leather. Such was one who will have frequently to make his appearance in this work. He had within him at this time, no doubt, the germs of many faults which might not have appeared at all, had he not been thrown into connections which perverted his naturally simple, inoffensive, and even amiable nature.

But, the reader may say, we have only one of the travellers here; why does not the author furnish a portrait of the other? Behold him then. A young man, twenty-nine years of age; five feet ten inches in height; with long, well-formed limbs, short body, very upright carriage, free motion, and active and lithe, rather than strong. His hair is of a deep dun colour, coarse, straight, and flaky; his complexion a swarthy pale; his eyes, grey, lively, and observant; his features strongly defined and irregular, like a mass of rough and smooth matters which, having been thrown into a heap, had found their own sub-sidence, and presented, as it were by accident, a profile of rude good nature, with some intelligence. His mouth is small; his lips a little prominent; his teeth white and well set; his nose rather snubby; his cheeks somewhat high; and his forehead deep and rather heavy about the eyes. His hat is not quite so broken, but quite as well worn as the doctor's; his coat of brown cloth, as yet unpatched, but wanting soon to be; his waistcoat of lighter colour, bare and decent; his hamsters of dark kerseymere, grey at the knees; and his stockings of lamb's-wool, with some neat darning above the quarters of his strong nailed shoes. Such, reader, was the personal appearance of him who now endeavours to amuse thee; of the qualities of his mind and disposition an opinion may be formed from this work.

Having crossed the River Roach, we came to the foot of Crimble, where I told Healey the story of Christian and Faithful, at the hill Difficulty, and said I would be his

Faithful, and would help him up this Difficulty. I remarked that he must have many sins to answer for, through his selling of drugs at extortionate prices, quacking a little in his practice, and sometimes drawing sound teeth when he could not find faded ones. He turned on me when we got to the level, and he breathed more freely. He bade me look towards those fields and that venerable hall which one of my ancestors lost by rebellion against a king; and he narrated a story which I had heard before, how, in the Civil Wars, the eldest of two brothers held this estate of Bamford, and fought against the king, who was dethroned, and at the restoration the elder brother fled into exile and died there, leaving his children heirs only to poverty and obscurity; meantime his younger brother, who had fought on the royal side, was put into possession of the hall and estates, and thus they descended from him to the last of the name who held the property. Healey remarked that I indeed had not an estate to lose, but was taking a fair course for losing my head, and was already an outcast wanderer on lands belonging to my ancestors.

On coming to Bakslate Moor, Healey said the neighbourhood was formerly infested by witches. His father had often been called upon to counteract their infernal schemes. He firmly believed all this, and I did not combat his opinion: on the contrary, I said I was sure it had been a place of witches. He asked why I believed so. I bid him notice it; did it not look like a barren and withered land, full of slate pits, rushy knobs, and dry wiry grass, from which even asses turned away? Besides, I had been witched myself by one of them. Healey looked serious, and inquiringly. I assured him I had. I was so bewitched that on a midsummer morning one of them withdrew me to a place where I gave myself to her for life; and the charm remained so strong that I had never yet attempted to break it, nor even wished to do so. He smiled on perceiving my meaning, and said he was not alluding to the witchcraft of love.

We now began to ascend the road leading to the moors, and a climb of about two miles brought us upon the level of the hill at Ashworth Moor; soon after which we came in sight of Learock Hoyle, in modern English, "Lark's Hole," a substantial hostel and farmhouse, which Healey informed me was his uncle Richard's, or Dick's, as he sometimes called him. The old man was at work in a stone quarry near the roadside; he was about sixty years of age, strong and active for his time of life, and hearty too, for he came out of the quarry, and gave us a blunt and frank welcome, and took us into the house. His wife was a remarkably clever and good-looking woman, much younger than her husband, and the very personification of a managing, self-confident, and civil landlady. Two fine thriving lasses, taking after their mother, and a son more like his father, were their stock of children. And here this family had lived many years, contented with a sufficiency of plain comforts, at a lone house on the borders of a moor. I could not but reflect on the advantages they must derive from thus enjoying life freely in a world of their own, and with a moderation which gave promise of a long continuance. They seemed but little affected by what was going on, politically, in the districts below and around them; they were clear of the anxieties and tumults of business, which were heart-rending, and distracting the inhabitants of the great towns situated within their view, and, in fact, within their hearing (for we could distinguish the noise of the lumbering roll of the carriages, like the eternal moan of a distant sea); and contrasting the quietness of this nest, this "Hole of the Lark," with the errors and terrors of scenes I had quitted, I could not but detect my yearnings for a shelter with those I loved in some quiet nook little known and seldom visited.

Having rested and taken refreshment, we went strolling upon the moor, and ascended Knowe, or Knowl Hill, from whence we had an extensive prospect. In the distance on our left were the moors towards Todmorden and Walsden; following the horizon, we next saw the ridge of Blackstone Edge, streaked with sun gleams and dark shadows; then the moors of Saddleworth, particularly Oaphin with his white drifts still lingering, and Odermon with his venerable relics of Druidism, his "Pots an' Pans." The mountains of Derbyshire and

Cheshire rose like a region of congealed waves, whilst Vale
Royal, to the south, lay reposing in a glorious sun, and the
country towards Liverpool was bounded by a bright streak,
probably the Irish Sea. A dim white vapour indicated the
site of Preston or Blackburn ; Bolton seemed near at hand,
and Bury close on our right below. Manchester, Stockport,
Ashton, Oldham, and Rochdale were distinctly visible, and
neither last nor least regarded, was one small speck—it was
the white end of a house at Heabers, which directed our looks
to the misty vapour of Middleton, rising beside dark woods
from the vale in which the town is situated. That was the
smoke of our own hearths, heaped by those who were thinking
of us. We could almost see them : whisht ! could we not hear
the voices of our children ? of their mothers calling them
home ? And in the fond imagination we shouted their names,
but there was no reply ; and then, feeling we were cut off and
outcast, we more sadly understood the human desolateness of
Him who said, "The foxes have holes, and the birds of the air
have nests, but the Son of man hath not where to lay His head."

But even in this wild region were objects to call us back to
reality, and teach us that in every situation there is something to be thankful for ; that—

"There is mercy in every place,"

and that a bounteous Creator is nowhere unmindful of those
He has called into life. A beautiful spring of water, pure as a
cup from heaven's banquet, was gently brimming over a basin
of white sand and pebbles, into which it arose. A sward of
sweet green grass lined the margin of a silvery band that lay
glimmering and trickling on the sunny side of the hill, whilst
here and there were tufts of rushes glistering with liquid
pearls. We took the water in our hands and drank "to our
families and friends "; "to our suffering brethren everywhere"; "to the downfall of tyranny and soon"; and "to
liberty," with three huzzas. An old black-faced tup lifted
his horns from the heather, looked gravely at us, and giving a
significant bleat, scampered off, followed by such of his
acquaintance as were browsing near.

CHAPTER VIII.

THE VALLEY OF HOLCOMBE—HEALEY IN FULL PRACTICE—THE WOMAN OF MUSBURY.

ON the morning following we bid our worthy host and his family good-bye, and after taking the way towards Edenfield a short distance, we struck into a deep stony road on our left, and descended to the valley of Holcombe. We had counted our stock of money after turning out, and found it to be greatly diminished; for as Uncle Richard refused pay for our board and lodging, we had spent in liquor more freely than we otherwise should have done, and our finances were now exceedingly light. Our intention was to enter Bolton that night, where Healey had a brother possessed of property, who he thought would either assist him with a little money, or find him a retreat for a short time, whilst I could easily get a loom in some of the neighbouring villages. But this plan was afterwards abandoned, as will shortly be seen.

After traversing this beautiful valley for some distance we entered a publichouse and took seats in the kitchen. A stumpy, rosy-cheeked lass, with cherry-ripe lips, and arms as red as apples, served us with ale; after which a decent elderly dame came in and told her to " goo an' get some moor o' that stuff, for Mary's tooth wur no betther." I nudged the doctor, who immediately took the hint, and informed the dame, with his best grace, that if any of the family were ill of the tooth-ache he could either cure it or take out the tooth. She said her daughter had got it very bad, and was in another room. Healey said he was a surgeon, and would extract it if she liked. " Well, really," said she, with surprise, looking at his unctuous clothes, "yo may be a dochtur, but you look'n more like a kawve-lad." Healey seemed offended, and I assured the dame that he was "as regular a bred surgeon as ever wur born ov a woman"—and in confirmation Healey pulled out a case of lancets and his tooth-drawing instrument. At this moment a young woman entered the room with her face rolled in flannel, and one cheek puffed and swollen. Her mother told her what Healey said, and being in extreme anguish, she suffered him to examine her mouth, after which he assured her it would be a mere flea-bite, and he could have the tooth out in "no time," and at last she consented to have it drawn. I never liked to hear the crash of bones pulled out of living flesh, and so I walked into the yard, but had not been there a minute ere a piercing scream called me in again, and I beheld the young woman on the floor sputtering blood, and the doctor also on the floor near the fire, and literally swamped in a pool of cream, the mug of which lay in fragments beside him. I saw there was no murder in the case, and if my life had been at stake I could not have refrained from loud and hearty laughter. I assisted the young woman to rise, but my mirth was abated when, on spitting out, two teeth instead of one dropped into her lap. The doctor, meantime, had got up and began to wipe the fluid from his face and clothes; he was quite silent and looked very rueful. The old woman now came into the place, and with her two men, one of whom we soon understood to be a constable, and the other an overseer. "These ar um," she said, "yo seen what havock theyn made, an iv ye hadno comn they met ha' kilt us for owt I kno.' That little devil pretended to be a docthur, an' put a pair o' pincers into th' wench's meawth, an' has very nee poo'd her yed off; an' th' tother's no better nor him. Beside, theyn brokken my mug an' shed my kryem." "An' look at theese," said the patient, casting an enraged glance at the doctor, "hee's poo'd two teeth eawt istid o' one." The doctor begged to be heard; the constable said he "had bin sworn at Howkham Kwort, an' munt do his duty; an' iv thur wur a charge he munt take us afore a magistrate." The over-seer said, "that wur reet, ackwordin' to Burn's justice." I did not relish the idea of going before a magistrate just at that time, lest something might escape as to who we were and what had brought us into that part, so I said I and my friend were quite ready to go with the gentlemen anywhere to have this misfortune explained; but as they appeared to be men of good understanding and respectable manners, and seemed to know something of law, I thought the matter might as well be talked over a little, and if a glass of something to drink were added it would not, at any rate, make matters worse than they were. This was declared to be very reasonable by all parties, and accordingly we adjourned with the officers to another room, and were soon afterwards joined by two persons, apparently farmers; and a jug of warm ale with some grated ginger in, and I think also a dash of the first syllabled liquid, being placed on the table, with tobacco and pipes, we drew round the fire. Healey now requested that the young woman might be called, and she making her appearance, he very submissively requested to see the teeth; they were produced, and he then wished to examine her mouth without his instruments, which was also conceded after some persuasion, when he cleverly slipped one of the teeth, a sound one, into the orifice from which it had been taken, gently compressed the gum to make it close up, and ordering a squib of rum, with directions to keep it in her mouth a minute, and then put it out, he declared she was as well as ever. The patient did as she was bid, only instead of putting out the rum she swallowed it, and then said she thought she was better. This made Healey proud as chanticleer, and taking a hearty draught of the ale, he said he would not stand in second place to any doctor they could produce in the whole country. The overseer was next instituted chairman, and the dame of the house was called; asked what was her charge, she said as her daughter was better, she would only charge five shillin' for "th' mug breakin' an' kryem sheedin', an' if that wur sattl't o' wud be reet." The doctor said he thought the case was a very hard one, for he had done his patient a great service at the risk of his limbs almost. The young woman, he said, was in a most favourable position for the operation, the extractors were fixed, and he was bringing out the tooth very nicely, when she screamed, threw up her foot, with which she took him in the ribs, and sent him to the other end of the room, where he alighted slap against the wall, and falling on the mug, broke it, and was at the same time seriously bruised himself. The young woman was asked if that was true. She replied, she believed it was; and the company then agreed that, as there was no charge except for damage, the patient had best pay half-a-crown for tooth-drawing, and the doctor three shillings for the mug and cream. The doctor heard the decision with a kind of inward groan, for nothing hurt his feelings more than paying money when he should be receiving it. He, however, threw down one of the few sixpences which he had left, and the old woman took it in settlement of the damage. This matter being adjusted, we were partaking another pot, when a man came in from Bolton, and in conversing said the Radicals were in great alarm there, it being reported that King's officers had arrived in London for the purpose of arresting some of the leaders, and that the police were very sharp on the look-out for them. This information was not lost by us, and we exchanged significant glances without being observed.

We were talking on various matters when the door was opened, and a personally fine-looking woman, with an infant at the breast, advanced timidly and said she wished to speak to the overseer. Her outer garments were of very homely material, being seemingly cotton fents dyed blue, but neatly fitting her person, and very clean. She had a pair of light clogs on her feet, and her stockings were, I could perceive, well darned above the buckles. Her petticoat and bedgown were of the same blue cotton, and the latter was open at the bosom, where a fine boy lay smiling at his pap. Her apron was striped calico, and her headgear consisted of a striped napkin, apparently also a fent, over a mob cap, very white, from beneath which a lock of black hair had escaped, and hung as if in contrast with a bosom of as pure white as ever appertained to human nature. Her features also were handsome; her cheeks were faintly tinged on a very pale ground; her mouth was somewhat wan; she seemed rather

exhausted, and as she stood the tears came into her dark
and modest eyes. "Weer dusto com fro'," asked the overseer, "an' wat dusto want? theawrt a new un at ony
rate," he continued. She said she came from Musbury,
and wanted relief for her husband, herself, and two children, besides the infant. "An' wot dun yo do for a livin'?"
interrogated the overseer. They wove calico, she said, when
they could get work and were able; but the children at home
were ill of the measles; the shopkeeper had refused them any
more credit, and her husban' had "wurched for 'em till he
fell off his looms, and wur beginnin' o'th' feyver, th' docthur
said so." "Hang thoose docthurs," said the overseer, "why
conno' they let foke dee when thur time comes." "I hope
he'll no' dee yet," said the poor woman, tears streaming in
plenty. "I think he'd com' reawnd iv yo'd nobbut let us have
a trifle o' summut to carry on wi'; an' iv yo' win" (intreat-
ingly) "I'll hie me whom, an' I'll put th' chylt i'th' keyther
an' set at yon wark, an' I'll finish it mysel'; an' we'en not
trouble yo' ogen unless we'en sum new misfortin'." The overseer asked the farmers, who, it appeared, were ratepayers,
what they thought of the case; and the result was that he
gave her two shillings, and promised to call and see the family.
But she must tell her husband he must not begin of the fever.
"Its o' idelty, idelty; an' iv th' paupers o'th' teawn yerd 'at he
geet owt wi' bein' ill o'th' feyver, they'd o' begin." "Nowe,
nowe, theyd'n ha' no feyvers i' their teawnship." She took
the money, curtseyed, and thanked the overseer and ratepayers. One of them said she had been "a decent wench";
he knew her father in better days, and offered her a glass of
the warm ale, which she put to her lips and swallowed a
small quantity. Her cheeks turned deadly pale; she put out
her hand as if her sight was gone, her grasp relaxed, the
child dropped on Healey's knee, and I caught the fainting
woman in my arms. "Hoo's clem'd to dyeth," said one of
the ratepayers. "Hoo's as dyed as a dur nail," said the
other. "I didno' deny her relief," said the overseer. The
doctor handed the child to the landlady, and called for some
brandy, which was brought, together with a sharp smelling-

bottle, which was applied, but there was not any perceptible breathing, and she shrunk down seated upon the floor, I kneeling and still keeping her in a leaning posture.

And shall I be ashamed to say that, whilst I thus held her, tears escaped, and chased down a furrow already made by care on that cold and pale brow? Oh, no! could I have withheld my deepest sympathy from that beauteous mother, my sister in humanity, perishing thus for want of food, my heart must have turned to stone. Healey chafed her temples with the liquor, sprinkled her face with water, opened her hands, and tried to get a drop of liquid into her mouth, but her teeth were set. "Poor thing," said the doctor, "she must have been very ill." "Hoo's dun for i' this ward," said one of the men. "I relieft hur," said the overseer, "for I seed hoo'r none o' eawr reggilur paupers." "We shan ha' to have an inquest," said the constable. "Moor expense, an' moor," said the overseer; "but they conno' say 'at I neglected 'em, con they?" Whilst these observations and many others were passing, the features of the sufferer became less rigid, the jaw relaxed; a drop of brandy and water was administered; a slight tinge of pink appeared on her cheeks; the chafings and smellings were continued; a sigh after some time escaped, and in a minute or two those dark-fringed eyes unclosed; she looked inquiringly around, and soon appeared to comprehend her situation. In a short time she was restored; her child was again pressed to her bosom, the two shillings were made up to five, she took a cup of warm tea with the family, and in another hour she was slowly wending up the hill towards Musbury.

CHAPTER IX.

IT was dark when we entered the neat country town of Bury; for, after what we heard of the state of things at Bolton, we deemed it best to avoid that neighbourhood; probably, also, we were influenced by a natural leaning towards home; and, in consequence, though scarcely determined, we were travelling thitherward ere we had agreed so to end our journey. After the departure of the woman, we consented to another libation with our new acquaintance, and our stay was prolonged at some risk, as questions were asked, and suppositions expressed, which required more caution than it was agreeable to maintain. My little comrade also was, in his own estimation, become a very big man, and a most important personage. The liquor was getting into his head, and he showed his wonted inclination for "sprozing," the best exemplification of which is that of a turkey-cock spreading his feathers. It was at the sacrifice of a considerable share of vanity that he was restrained from telling the constable and overseer who and what he was, his great abilities—which he would have proved by singing and recitations (in both of which he murdered everything he uttered)—and his great practice, and the cures he had effected. I therefore got him away decently; and our next halting-place was "The Grey Mare," a public-house opposite the church in the aforementioned market town. We were both hungry, not having tasted food since morning; we bought a steak, which we wished to have cooked at this house, but were informed it could not be done; "they had something else to do than to cook steaks on Saturday nights."

59

The place indeed was full of customers, apparently country people, come to the town to make their markets, so we went on to the next house, where our meat was cooked, and we washed it down with a jug of pretty good ale. There was here also much company; and we learned from their conversation that several persons had been arrested the day before for high treason at Manchester, and that two of them were named Ogden and Johnson. This was no very encouraging news to us; nor were our feelings tranquillised when, soon after, a respectable-looking, rather elderly man came into the room, and, surveying the company round, went away without saying a word. We soon learned that he was the deputy-constable of the town, and this incident hastened our departure.

The night was cloudy and overcast, but the glare of the shops threw a good light into the street, which was well filled with market people. We were anxious to get out of the way, and resolved to take the field road, as being most calculated to favour escape if we should be pursued, as well as to prevent pursuit. We accordingly inquired the way to " Gig Bridge," and, following our directions, we found ourselves, after a short walk, on the bank of an apparently deep stream, which we knew must be the Roach; and following its course we were soon on a narrow wooden bridge, which we passed without any of that unpleasant motion which had obtained for it the reputation of a dangerous passage. The clouds now, instead of blowing off, as we had thought they would, became more thick, and the night darker. We knew little of the way; Healey not a foot of it, and I had only a slight notion of its general direction. At the worst, however, we could take the hunter's road till we came to a house. The path led us between a high bank on our right, and what, in the darkness, seemed to be a deep and tangled wood on our left. Proceeding cautiously, for the road was crooked and uneven, we came to the verge of the wood, where two roads lay before us; and we were considering which to take, when the light of a lanthorn flashed close upon us, and we asked the person who bore it (a woman) where the two roads led to. She was low in stature, with an old red cloak thrown over her shoulders, and a handkerchief,

tied hoodlike, around her head and face. She held the light
up to Healey as he stood next to her, and looked at him
steadfastly, and I had an opportunity for observing that she
was considerably aged. Some thin locks of grey hair were
streaming in the wind and flapping across her face; her eyebrows were expansive and grey; and her two quick, dark eyes,
set in wrinkles, seemed peculiarly brilliant for her age. Her
face was furrowed and brown; her features had been regular,
perhaps handsome, but now appeared careworn and anxious;
and her teeth were still even and white. She evidently had
not been a-marketing, as she had not either bundle or basket,
but held a stick, on which she leaned, in one hand, and the
lanthorn in the other. "Good mother," said Healey, "weer
dun theese two roads lyed to?" "To mony places i' this
ward," she replied, "an' mayhap some i'th' tother. This,"
pointing to the left, "lyeds to th' Frogg Hole, an' Yep-fowd,
an' Yeddy Hill, on th' Top o' Yep; an' that," pointing to the
one before us, "lyeds to th' Hollins, an' th' Cat Hole, an' th'
Castle, an' Thurston-fowd. But weer dun yo' want to goo
to," she asked, "o'er sitch a 'wilderin' counthry, an' sitch
o' neet as this?" We said we were strangers, but if we could
find Whittle or Bowlee we should be right. "Follow me,
then," she said, and immediately stepped out at a pace which
we little expected. Healey followed close after the lanthorn,
now making an observation more free than wise; now asking
questions, some of which must have sounded mysteriously to
our guide. "Yo're no' meety good uns, I daresay," she mut-
tered. "Yo're as like excisemen as owt 'at I ever see'd."
Healey seemed wishful to humour the supposition, and asked
if there were any hush shops in that part of the country.
She turned round, thrust the light's full glare close to his face,
and, with a furious voice and gesture, said, "Hush, foo; keep
the secret; iv I dunno' tell the' theaw winno' know." That
moment lanthorn and lanthorn-bearer disappeared, and the
next there was a crash and a plash. Healey had fallen
through a hedge, down a steep bank, and into the channel of
a brook. I should have followed him, but saved myself from
going over by clasping a young tree, by which I held; whilst,

stooping down, I got hold of my companion, and he was again safely landed.

After some puffing and gasping, and sundry emphatic wishes bestowed on "the owd hag," as Healey called our late guide, I reminded him that he had brought it upon himself by pretending to be an exciseman, and pressing unpleasant questions about the neighbourhood. "Where was the owd limb?" he asked. Had she sunk into th' earth, or flown into th' air? "Hoo went in a flash as quick as gun-shot—lanthorn, leet, an' o'—an' nobody should make him believe 'at hoo wur owt elze but an arrant witch." I said it was a strange occurrence, and not to be exactly accounted for at that time; but it was no use standing there—we must move in some direction, or we should not get home before daylight. So we groped about, and at last perceived a tree which lay across the gully, over which we stepped, holding by the branches, and soon had footing on a rising ground and an open field, over which we were directing our course, when our attention was excited by a laugh of almost unearthly tone, which came like a jeering yell upon the wind; and, looking towards our right, we perceived below us, at some distance, a light, dancing, as it were, and moving at a rapid pace through the profound darkness. "There gwos yon beldame, an' crone, an' hoo devil, on' bowt an' sowd infernal as hoo is," said Healey. The laugh was renewed, but sounded fainter, and almost like a scream of pain; and the next moment the light began to descend, and suddenly disappeared as if sunk into the earth. An exclamation of horror and surprise escaped my companion; and we continued over an uneven country—now by the roar of waters and weirs, now across dingles, levels, and swamps—until at length espying a glimmer which was stationary, we concluded it must come from a house, and, hastening forwards, we soon heard noises of song, laughter, and revelry; and, finding they proceeded from a human habitation which we thought must be a tavern, we opened the door and entered without ceremony.

CHAPTER X.

THE building was thatched, and consisted of several rooms on the ground floor, two of which were occupied by company. The room into which we entered was a square one, with a good fire of turf and wood burning opposite the door. On the centre of the floor stood a kind of low table, formed of an inner door which had been lifted from its hinges, and placed on bricks and logs of wood to serve as a table, and on it two candles in clay sockets were burning. About a dozen pots, of nearly all sorts and shapes, were upon the table; each pot containing ale, or what appeared to be so. The room was dimmed by tobacco smoke; but we could discern not fewer than some eight or ten men seated in various parts of it, some on stools, some on piled bricks, some on logs of wood; whilst others occupied empty firkins, mugs capsized, or any other article affording a seat. The company was not less dissimilar in appearance, though all seemed of the labouring class. Some were farm servants, some factory workers, and some were weavers; there were also one or two, who we found were poor men, but not workers at any branch, being known sots, bullies, and occasionally thieves. The other room was occupied by customers much the same as these; but the blows on their table, and the tremendous cursings, told us they were at high words about a game at cards. On our entering, all eyes were directed towards us, and the hum of their voices was hushed to silence. "Well, what dun yo' want," said a brawny dark-bearded fellow, turning towards us with a most unwelcoming look. I informed him we had lost our way, and merely called to inquire about it; but, as we were in the house, we would taste his ale if he had no particular objection. " Wot are yo', an' weer dun yo' come fro'," was demanded sternly; several of the company rising and repeating the questions. I said that if it was of consequence to the master or mistress of the place, they should know before we went away. If we drank their ale, we would satisfy them for it, and whether we had any or not, there would not be any harm done, we supposed.

" Mother! come heer; " shouted the dark man from the stair's foot; when, who should make her appearance but the same old woman who about an hour before had vanished so unaccountably. "Excisemen!" "Informers!" she screamed, at the top of a thrilling voice; and at that moment each man of the company was on his feet; hands were clutching at our throats, and a prospect of certain manglement or murder stared from those ferocious countenances. A crash in the next room, and a smashing of pots was heard; and whilst we were vainly, as it seemed, endeavouring to evade our fate, a stout, low-built man, rather decently clad, and with a weaver's green apron twisted around his middle, rushed into the room, said he knew us both well, that we were neither excisemen nor informers, and that he would pledge his life for us. The company then fell back; candles were brought, a circle was formed around us, gazing in curiosity and doubt, and at last we were permitted to sit down and partake of the ale. The old woman, however, persisted that we were excisemen, or sent by the Excise, and narrated what Healey had asked, and how she slipped the light under her cloak at a sudden turn of the road, leaving Healey to walk into a ditch, and his comrade after him. This caused a loud laugh at our expense; and it was repeated when we admitted that it was true except in one particular. Our friend the poacher, for such he was, meantime had taken the dark-bearded youth, the son, aside, and explained our names and condition to him, he whispered to his mother, and a.word was passed round, which caused an entire change of manner to us by the whole company. I felt

a curiosity to observe human nature in such a place, and
being now readily supplied with ale, I took my pipe, and
listened with some interest to the conversation ; whilst Healey
made himself agreeable by singing, in his best manner,

> " The deil cam fiddlin' thro' the toon,
> An' danc'd awa wi' th' exciseman."

We had not, however, been at peace long, ere the carders
in the next room again quarrelled, and proceeded to that
length, that a battle was determined upon. Lights—of candles
and pitch-rope, and bog-pine—were procured, and the combatants stripped, and accompanied by every man, went into a
small plot of ground behind the house. The combatants were
our friend the poacher, and another man, younger and heavier,
who chiefly earned his living by dog breaking, and under-
strapping to gamekeepers and their masters. Betwixt the
men there had been an unfriendly feeling for some time, and
now, over this potent ale, for it was good, though new, their
hostility was again excited, and probably decided. The ring
was formed with as much silence as possible. The men
stripped to their waists, and then kneeled down and tied their
shoes fast on their feet. They then dogged for the first grip,
much as game cocks do for the first fly ; and after about a
minute so spent, they rushed together and grappled, and in a
moment the dog-man gave the poacher a heavy kick on the
knee, and was at the same time thrown violently on the
ground, on his back, his antagonist alighting on him like " a
bag of bones." It was now a ground fight for some time, and
exhibited all the feats of a Lancashire battle, which I take to
have been derived from a very remote date, long before the
" Art of Self-defence," or indeed, almost any other art, was
known in these islands. There was not, however, any of that
gouging of the eyes, or biting the flesh, or tearing, or lacerating
other parts, which are so often imputed to Lancashire fighters
by cockney sportsmen and others, who know little about them.
It was all fair play, though certainly of a rough sort, and as
thorough a thing of the kind as I had ever seen. Doggy, after
gaining breath, tried to turn on his belly, which Poacher aimed

to prevent, pressing the wind out of him by his weight upon
the chest as he lay across him, and at times throttling him
until his eyes stared as if they were looking into another
world.   In one of those suffocating agonies, Doggy flung
round one leg, and locked it in one of his opponent's, and in
a moment they were twisted together like the knot of a boa-
constrictor ; and the next, Doggy turned on his belly, and got
upon his knees.   There was a loud shout, and much cursing
and swearing ; and several bets were offered and taken as to
the issues of the contest.   Poacher now laid all the weight he
could on Doggy's head and neck, to prevent him from getting
upright.   He grasped him below the arms, and kept clutching
his throat ; and the latter, for want of breath to carry on
with, kept tearing his hands from their grip : both snorted
like porpoises, and it began to appear that our friend
Poacher was the worst for wind.   Some heavy kicking now
ensued, until the white bones were seen grinning through the
gashes in their legs, and their stockings were soaked in blood.
Poacher was evidently a brave man, though now coming
second ; in one of his struggles, Doggy freed himself and
rushed on Poacher with a kick that made the crew set their
teeth and look for splintered bones : and Poacher stood it
though he felt it.   There was another clutch, and a sudden
fling, in which Poacher was uppermost, and Doggy, falling
with his neck doubled under, rolled over and lay without
breath or motion, black in the face, and with blood oozing
from his ears and nostrils.   All said he was killed, and that
opinion probably softened the shout of triumph which was set
up by those who had won their bets.   The doctor, who had
been trodden out of the ring during the battle, was now loudly
called for ; and at length, with that air of important gravity so
habitual to the " profession," he approached along an avenue
made through these wildlings, and, kneeling by the man on
one side, Poacher being on the other, holding a pitch torch in
great concernment, he felt for a pulse, declared there was
none, and, binding the arm, he pulled out a lancet, and
opened a vein cleverly, the blood, as if still in battle, dashing
hot and red in Poacher's face—a circumstance which made

some laugh and others look grave, it being taken by them as a
dying accusation of murder. The man bled freely, the blood
trickling into a dark red sud on the trodden grass. Poacher
presented a picture of horror and misery. After the accident
he stepped aside, and putting on his shirt, returned to the
ring, where he took his station as before described, looking
with intense anxiety on the livid features of his prostrate foe.
He had wiped the blood from his own eyes with his knuckles,
and the ghastly white of those cavities, contrasting with the
gore on his cheek and beard, now parched and glittering in
the torch-light, gave him an appearance of more than mortal
horror and despair. The arm being bound up, Doggy was
conveyed into the house and laid on the table, a turf or two
being placed under his head, by way of pillow. He had, to
the great joy of Poacher, begun to breathe during the bleeding,
and now appeared in a sound sleep, and the doctor assured
the Poacher he would come round in a short time; he had
only been a little "stunished," which had "brought on a
fainting fit," and he would soon be better. Poacher was most
grateful for the information; he declared he would never fight
again, and swore the doctor was the finest man in all England,
and that if one hare only was living on Lord Suffield's grounds,
he should have it for his stew-pot next Sunday. The doctor
enjoyed his triumph; he drank to the company all round, not
omitting the wounded man, who remained motionless and
prostrate. Some of them said his neck was awry, and the
doctor, examining him more minutely, bathed his head in cold
water; after which, adjusting the neck, he got two staves of a
butter tub, and placing one on each side, resting on the
shoulders, and jutting above the head, he tied them firmly but
gently with a couple of red cotton hanks, and the man soon
after opening his eyes, though scarcely sensible, he was conveyed home on the shoulders of his party. The doctor then
dressed Poacher's wounds; we soon after left the place, guided
into the road by Poacher, who was going that way, and arrived
at Middleton without further adventure.

 And, shall we part here, friend reader? On my very threshold shall we part? Nay, come in from the frozen rain, and

from the night wind, which is blowing the clouds into sheets like torn sails before a gale. Now down a step or two.* 'Tis better to keep low in the world than to climb only to fall. It is dark, save when the clouds break into white scud above, and silent, except the snort of the wind, and the rattling of hail, and the eaves of dropping rain. Come in! A glimmer shows that the place is inhabited, that the nest has not been rifled whilst the old bird was away. Now shalt thou see what a miser a poor man can be in his heart's treasury. A second door opens, and a flash of light shows we are in a weaving room, clean and flagged, and in which are two looms with silken work of green and gold. A young woman, of short stature, fair, round, and fresh as Hebe; with light brown hair escaping in ringlets from the sides of her clean cap, and with a thoughtful and meditative look, sits darning beside a good fire, which sheds warmth upon the clean swept hearth and gives light throughout the room, or rather cell. A fine little girl, seven years of age, with a sensible and affectionate expression of countenance, is reading in a low tone to her mother:

"And He opened His mouth and taught them, saying, Blessed are the poor in spirit; for theirs is the kingdom of heaven. Blessed are they that mourn; for they shall be comforted. Blessed are the meek; for they shall inherit the earth. Blessed are they which do hunger and thirst after righteousness; for they shall be filled. Blessed are the merciful; for they shall obtain mercy. Blessed are the pure in heart; for they shall see God. Blessed are the peacemakers; for they shall be called the children of God. Blessed are they which are persecuted for righteousness' sake; for theirs is the kingdom of heaven. Blessed are ye when men shall revile you, and persecute you, and shall say all manner of evil against you falsely for My sake."

Observe the room and its furniture. A humble but cleanly bed, screened by a dark old-fashioned curtain, stands on our left. At the foot of the bed is a window, closed from the

* The cottage is still to be seen. It is at the end of a row, and recent changes in the front street have almost turned it into a cellar dwelling.

looks of all street passers. Next are some chairs, and a round table of mahogany; then another chair, and next it a long table, scoured very white. Above that is a looking-glass with a picture on each side, of the Resurrection and Ascension, on glass, "copied from Rubens." A well-stocked shelf of crockery ware is the next object, and in a nook near it are a black oak carved chair or two, with a curious desk, or box to match; and lastly, above the fireplace, are hung a rusty basket-hilted sword, an old fusee, and a leathern cap. Such are the appearance and furniture of that humble abode. But my wife?

> " She look'd ; she redden'd like the rose ;
> Syne, pale as ony lily."

Ah! did they hear the throb of my heart, when they sprung to embrace me—my little love child to my knees, and my wife to my bosom?

Such were the treasures I had hoarded in that lowly cell —treasures that, with contentment, would have made into a palace

> " the lowest shed
> That ever rose in England's plain."

They had been at prayers, and were reading the Testament before retiring to rest. And now, as they a hundred times caressed me, they found that indeed, "Blessed are they that mourn, for they shall be comforted."

CHAPTER XI.

A MIDNIGHT VISITANT—A SECRET MEETING—A PLOT—OLIVER
THE SPY—HIS FIRST ESSAY IN THE WAY OF BUSINESS.

ABOUT the middle of the night, on the night after my return
home, we were awoke by a gentle knocking at our outer door.
I arose and asked who was there. A voice replied, "A
friend;" and I opened the door, and a man walked in,
muffled up to the eyes. I asked him who he was; when, half
laughing, in his natural voice he said, "Don't you know me?"
and I then recognised him as my most intimate acquaintance
and co-delegate at London. He said he had particular
reasons for coming disguised, and at that unseasonable hour,
and that he wished to see me and some half-dozen of our
most trusty reformers in the morning, at the house of a friend
whom he named, residing at Stannicliffe, a short distance
from Middleton. I promised to attend him as desired, and
he departed. At the time appointed, myself and several
others went to the house, and being shown into a private room
with our visitant, he commenced by entering into details of his
private business transactions, from which it appeared that he
was greatly embarrassed, and knew not how to extricate
himself. He had been at various places; at home he durst
not remain, and had last come from London, where he
had been in communication with some of the best friends to
reform, who, with himself, had come to a determination to
strike a decisive blow at once. He then detailed a plan which,
if acted upon with energy, would, he said, effect all that was
required. Some ten or a dozen of our best men were to

70

provide themselves with arms, and march to London, where they would be joined by others, and, at a time agreed upon, the united body were to rush upon the ministers at a cabinet council, or a dinner, and assassinate the whole of them. All London would then rise; the population would subdue all before it; the country would be our own, and a new Government would be established. Our arms were to consist of a stout walking staff, with a socket at one end for the reception of a dagger, which, he said, "may be easily made from the blade of a common knife, such as this," (taking one from the table). Pistols might also be carried by those who could procure them. When asked how the money for the journey was to be raised, he pulled a gold watch from his pocket, and said, if no other means were left, he would dispose of that to raise money. This would not do: it was rather too bare a trap. Besides, it was far wide of our code of reform, and we declined having anything to do with it. We also endeavoured to dissuade him from lending himself to such projects; and we left him without making any impression upon him.

The fact was, this unfortunate person, in the confidence of an unsuspecting mind, as I believe, had, during one of his visits to London, formed a connection with Oliver the spy, which connection, during several succeeding months, gave a new impulse to secret meetings and plots in various parts of Lancashire, Yorkshire, and Derbyshire, and ended in the tragedy of Brandreth, Ludlam, and Turner, at Derby. This was probably Oliver's first demonstration on his "professional tour:" it failed—but from that very week, private meetings, for highly criminal purposes, again commenced. Agents came from Manchester, and glided through the country, depositing their poison wherever they could. Meetings were held at Blackley; two or three at Middleton; one or two at Chadderton; the same at Failsworth; and again at Manchester, where some fools and their deluders having been collected, a partial explosion took place, of which further notice will occur shortly.

Let us not, however, in recounting these transactions, lay blame where it ought not to be. Let us not confound the

blind instrument with the intelligent agent who directed it.
If the individual before alluded to, our mysterious visitant,
erred greatly in these matters, he suffered for his error.   A
leading provincial journalist, with much apparent truth, afterwards stigmatised him as "a spy;" the sore obloquy stuck
to him long, and whether it has yet been entirely removed
admits of doubt.   But, had he been a spy, he would not have
been left to struggle with poverty and disgrace in England,
but would have been removed and provided for, as Oliver was.
Had he been a spy he would have betrayed those who never
were betrayed.   We may allow that he was credulous and
inconsiderate, and consequently unfit to be a leader in those
or any other times ; but this is far short of an admission that
he was a co-villain with Oliver.   He was an egregious dupe,
no doubt, but he was not a spy.

If it be asked, why did not you, as consistent and honest
reformers, denounce this plot to the government at once as, in
obedience to the laws, you ought to have done?   My reply is,
because we were persuaded the government knew of it already ;
that, consequently, if attempted. it would fail ; and lastly,
because we had accepted the man's confidence, and he had
placed his safety in our hands.   This last dilemma may serve
to caution others how they accept responsibilities which may
lead to criminality or dishonour.

CHAPTER XII.

TREASONABLE MEETING AT ARDWICK BRIDGE—APPREHENSION
OF THE DELEGATES—ARREST OF THE AUTHOR—OCCUR-
RENCES AT ROYTON, OLDHAM, AND MANCHESTER.

I HAD reprehended the doctor freely for attending one or two
of the private meetings before alluded to, and he had avoided
my company during nearly a fortnight, when, on the morning
of Saturday, the 29th of March, he suddenly made his
appearance at my residence, and with a woeful look asked if
I had heard of the arrest of the delegates at a private meeting,
at Ardwick Bridge, the night previous. I said I had heard of
the transaction; it was only what I had been expecting, and
I had offended him by speaking my opinion. He said he
wished I would go to his house for a short consultation; I
went, and found there one William Elson, who had been
connected with one or two of these meetings. They wished
for my advice as to what was best to be done under the
circumstances.

Amongst the persons arrested was John Lancashire, a
Middleton man, who had been delegated from a meeting at
which both of my friends, as I understood, had attended. I
blamed them for having anything to do with private meetings,
and advised them, they having committed themselves, to leave
home for a time, as I had not a doubt the police were in
possession of their names and would be after them. Elson
I said might go anywhere, as he was not much known:
Healey I advised to go to his brother at Bolton, and get some
money, and keep out of sight entirely, until something further
was known. His best way would be to avoid Manchester,

and go over Kersal moor and Agecroft bridge; and as I had
a relation in that quarter who wished to see me, I would keep
him company as far as Agecroft. My advice was adopted;
Elson went to prepare for his flight, and Healey commenced
doing the same. I was now informed that Lancashire had a
pike concealed in his house, and I went thither and got that
destroyed. On my return, instead of finding Healey ready he
was busy combing his hair, and adjusting his neckcloth. I
urged him to get away if he valued his life; and after some
further delay I saw him fairly on the road, and then went to
prepare myself, and in a few minutes I set out after him.
We had appointed to meet at Rhodes, Healey taking a
circuitous road over Bowlee, whilst I went a nearer but
still indirect way through Alkrington wood.

I was walking towards the churchyard at my usual
leisurely, but rather swift pace, quite satisfied that Healey
was out of all danger of being captured, and without the
remotest idea of any peril to myself, when a voice hallooed,
and looking back I beheld Joseph Scott, the deputy-constable
of Middleton, hastening towards me. I concluded instantly
that he wanted me; and disdaining the thought of flying, I
returned and met him, and he took hold of me, saying I was
the King's prisoner. I asked hin what for? and he said I
should see presently; and we had not gone many yards on
our return when we we were met by Mr. Nadin,* the deputy-
constable of Manchester, and about six or eight police officers,
all well armed with staves, pistols, and blunderbusses: two of
these took hold of me, and the whole party marched back to
the doctor's house.

Here they handcuffed me; and whilst they searched for the
doctor my wife, in great distress, rushed into the room, and
desired to know what I had done amiss that I should be
treated in that manner. One of the men had threatened to
shoot her at the door, but she rushed past him, and now,
whilst she clung to me distracted and terrified, another would
have rudely forced her away, but was rebuked by his superior,

* A famous local character of sombre repute of whom many stories are
still told.

which saved him from punishment and the party probably from the unpleasantness of a street battle with my neighbours. A crowd had collected in front of the house, and when we came out, and were proceeding down the street, there was a shout, and a piece of brick passed near the head of Mr. Nadin, who, probably apprehensive, and not without reason, of a volley, snatched a blunderbuss from one of the men, and, facing about, swore dreadfully that he would fire amongst the crowd if another stone was thrown. I turned round, and begged they would not commit any violence, for I was willing to suffer for the cause I had espoused. Either from the threat, or my wish, or both, my neighbours paused, and I was conducted to the Assheton Arms publichouse, at the lower end of the town. We stopped here some time, and I had an opportunity for observing the person of my principal captor, Mr. Nadin. He was, I should suppose, about 6 feet 1 inch in height, with an uncommon breadth and solidity of frame. He was also as well as he was strongly built; upright in gait and active in motion. His head was full sized, his complexion sallow, his hair dark and slightly grey; his features were broad and non-intellectual, his voice loud, his language coarse and illiterate, and his manner rude and overbearing to equals or inferiors. He was represented as being exceedingly crafty in his business, and somewhat unfeeling withal; but I never heard, and certainly never knew, that he maltreated his prisoners. At times he would indulge in a little raillery with them, possibly from a reason of his own, but I never was led to suppose that he threw away a word of condolement on those occasions. He was certainly a somewhat remarkable person in uncommon times, and acting in an arduous situation. He showed, however, that he had the homely tact to take care of his own interests. He housed a good harvest whilst his sun was up, and retired to spend his evening in ease and plenty on a farm of his own within the borders of Cheshire. I shall have to recur to him frequently in the course of this work. At present such was he who, with firm step but uneasy bearing, paced the floor of the parlour at the Assheton Arms inn. His men were all about the house, and some of them would frequently step in and communicate something to him, and orders and observations passed, which were unintelligible to me. I was seated at the further end of the room, near a table. On another table near to which he passed and repassed were a couple of blunderbusses and some pistols, and also a jug of ale and some glasses, one of which he filled and gave to me. "Yor a set o' roof devils," he said, "i' this Middleton, but we mun ha' sum moor on yo' afore lung." "We are pretty fair for that," I replied, "but," looking through the window, and seeing the people collecting, "I wudno' advise yo'," I said, "to walk me eawt oth' teawn, as yo' did'n hitherto; iv yo' dun, there will be some yeds brokken." "Dunno' consarn thesel' obeawt that," he replied with a knowing look; "theaw'l see heaw ween orthert that, afore long," and whilst we talked a coach, escorted by a party of dragoons drove up to the door; I was handed in, with Mr. Nadin and one of his men, and we drove at a rapid pace towards Chadderton, I chanting to myself—

> "Farewell! ye honey-winged gales;
> Farewell! ye sloping hills and dales;
> Ye waving woods that sweep the sky;
> Ye daisy'd meadows that lowly lie.
> No more to pluck your sweets I rove,
> My fond arm locked round my love;
> I now must bid a long adieu,
> To Midia's lonely bowers and you."

On arriving at the "Red Rose" at Chadderton the coach stopped, and some of the men having entered the house, returned and informed Mr. Nadin that "he was not at home, but his wife expected him soon, as he was only gone to Manchester." This was one of the houses at which private meetings had been held, and the person alluded to was Mr. Edward O'Connor, who, for having unwittingly permitted such a meeting, was involved in this affair, as will shortly appear. On the road towards Chadderton Hall I advised my conductor to draw up and return to Manchester, assuring him he would not capture any more of my batch that day,

and in confirmation I pointed to Chadderton Heights and
the neighbouring country, over which scores of people were
running like hunters, as if to meet the coach near Royton.
All the country was up, I said, and every one whom he might
want would be apprised of his coming. He growled a deep
oath, saying he had never seen anything like that before; the
officer commanding the dragoons, who rode by the coach door,
observed that he had seen something like it in Ireland, but
never anywhere else.

Passing Street-bridge and Rowley, we entered the village of
Royton, the streets of which were deserted, and the doors
shut. We soon returned to Rowley, and the constables made
a dash into a house in search of a man named Mellor, but he
was not there. A crowd was collected near the carriage, and
as I was expecting to move on, the door was suddenly opened,
and a long, thin, barrel of a human body was thrust into the
coach, head first—a couple of stilt-like legs being doubled up
after it. "Lock 'em together," said Mr. Nadin, and it was
no sooner said than done. This person had met some of the
runners in a back court or alley, and threatened to beat in
their brains with a walling hammer which he had in his hand.

George Howarth, for that was the name of my new companion, was a decent, labouring, married man of Royton,
and was about 6 feet 4 inches in height. He said he thought
it a very hard case—"he cudno' tell wot he'd dun amiss."
Mr. Nadin said he'd know "wot he'd done amiss" before he
was much older.

"Why, bless your life Mesthur Nadin," said George, "yore
a graidly felley for owt 'at I kno' to th' contrary, an' I never
sed nowt ogen yo' i' my lyve."

"Aye, an' I'll make thee into a graidly felley too afore I
ha' dun wi' the. Theaw'rt a moderate length to be begin wi',
but theaw'll be lunger afore theaw comes back to Reighton;
ween ha' thee hang'd," said our keeper.

"Nay, Mesthur Nadin," said George, "dunno' say so;
they axt wot I had i' mi' hont, an' I shode 'em; it wur nobbut
a bit ov a walling hommer 'at I'd bin a-borroin'."

"Aye," said Mr. Nadin, "an' theaw sed theawd knock

their brains eawt wi' it. But ween larn thee, an' o' yo'
Jacobins, heaw yo' threaten to kill th' King's officers; theaw'll
be hang'd as sure as theaw sits theer." George seemed
thoughtful upon this. He looked at the shackles and at me,
and soon after we drew up at the Spread Eagle publichouse,
in Manchester Street, Oldham.

The soldiers were here regaled with bread, cheese, and ale.
The street was filled with a great concourse of people, and
some of the military kept guard whilst the others refreshed.
George and I were seated on a form at the back of the room,
the policemen took other seats, and Mr. Nadin and the officer
placed themselves at a table, on which were set forth some
nice ham, and bread and cheese, and a flagon or two of ale.
They had all cut and drank, and helped themselves without
ceremony; and, observing George give a most wolfish look
towards the victuals, I asked him if he would like some? Had
he not breakfasted? He said he had not; he was just going
to breakfast when he happened to call for that unlucky walling
hammer.

"Captain," I said, addressing the officer of dragoons, "are
your prisoners to remain without food?"

"Oh, certainly not," he replied; "come up and take what
you choose." George and I then advanced, and each got a
decent wedge of cheese with bread to it, and a quart of ale was
also set before us.

It would have created an appetite in a satiated alderman
had he seen, as I did, the heathful gusto with which my companion disposed of huge and sundry uncut lumps of bread and
cheese; his nether jaw paused not, except when he sucked
down a stream of ale, after which it churned again as vigor-
ously as that of a wild boar. I too paid no small compliment
to the savoury viands, but was a small epicure beside my
companion, who never ceased until both our rations were
devoured, after which he finished with the last draught of ale,
and soon after the whole party set off towards Manchester.

The coach stopped at Hollinwood, whilst search was made
for a man named Wilson, who, however, was not captured.
George and I were left in the coach alone, but guarded, and

I took the opportunity to dispel any concern he might entertain on the subject of hanging, telling him, if there was any
preference in that line, I should obtain the favour before him.

A stream of people followed the coach and dragoons through
the streets of Manchester, and on approaching the Exchange,
down Market Street, the " Merchant Princes " crowded the
steps, and welcomed the poor captain with loud huzzas!

CHAPTER XIII.

THE BRIDGE OF TEARS—THE TRIBULATORY—A GROUP—A
DUNGEON—AN OLD ACQUAINTANCE—NEW COMRADES.

READER! Hath it ever been thy fortune, or misfortune, to
pass from Bridge Street, in Manchester, to New Bailey Street,
in Salford? Hath business, or pleasure, or curiosity, or charity
towards an afflicted prisoner, or mercy, or a yearning love for
some of thine own in trouble, or interest, or duty, ever led thee
that way? If so, thou hast passed a very plain bridge, with
high parapets of a dull red stone, and spanning, with two
arches, a rather broad stream, which here flows turbid, black,
and deep betwixt the said towns. That, reader, is "The
Bridge of Tears." Venice hath her "Bridge of Sighs,"
Manchester its "Bridge of Tears," and this is it.

How many hundreds of human beings have crossed this
bridge, conscious they were never to return? What strings
of victims have been dragged over it?—some in the serenity
of innocence, some in the consciousness of habitual guilt, and
others in a bowed and contrite spirit, but each followed by
weeping friends, who still loved, when all the world besides
was hostile or indifferent to their fate! Aye, times have been
when life was paltered to petty law, and the gallows was
rigged for a fraud on a bank, or a theft from a warehouse, or
a potato scramble, when children were perishing at home for
want of food.

And now a sad spectacle occurs to my recollection. It was
a fine sunny forenoon, and the church bells were tolling fune-
really, and Bridge Street was so crowded that you might have
walked on human heads. All eyes were turned towards this
Bridge of Tears, and what came there? Ah! men on horse-
back, with scarlet liveries and white wands, and trumpeters

richly invested, who sent forth a note of wail that might have
won pity from a heart of stone. Next came halberdiers and
javelin men, and then a horseman of lofty but gentle bearing,
who, as he rode, turned and cast a kind look towards one who
followed, sitting high in a chair of shame placed in a cart.
And who is he? that youth so heart-broken and hopeless, that
draws tears from all eyes, at whose approach all heads are
bared, all expressions are hushed, save sobs and prayers? For
though he was but "a poor Irish lad," they said "he was very
comely," and "it was a great pity," and "hard that he could
not be spared," and then, "might God support and comfort
him!" High he sat, with his back to the horses, his whole
person exposed, his feet and well-formed limbs being incased
in white trousers, stockings, and pumps, as if he were going to
a bridal. His vest also was light coloured, and a short jacket
displayed his square and elegant bust; his shirt was open at
the collar, and his brown hair was parted gracefully on his
forehead, and hung upon his shoulders. Despair and grief
beyond utterance were stamped on his countenance. He
seemed faint at times, and his colour changed, and he tasted
an orange, listening anon to the consolations of religion.
Tears would gush down his cheeks, and as he stooped to wipe
them with his handkerchief he was somewhat withheld by the
cords which bound him to that seat of shame. A coffin, a
ladder, and a rope were in the cart below him, whilst by its
side walked a dogged-looking fellow, whose eyes were perhaps
the only ones unmoistened that day. This was indeed a passage
of tears, and a day of sadness, and of contemplation on the
mysteries of life and death, with the consolement at last that
now "his troubles were ended," and "all tears were wiped
from his eyes."

Such was the spectacle of that "poor Irish lad," George
Russel, who was hanged on Newton Heath, for—stealing a
piece of fustian, or, as the old ballad had it—

> "To rob the croft
> I did intend,
> Of Master Sharrock's,
> At Mill-gate end."

Far be it from my wish, friend reader, to palliate wrong of
any degree; but let us hope, and, if necessary, entreat that
all waste of life like this may have now passed for ever from
England; that all useless inflictions may be ameliorated; and
that henceforth Justice may be enthroned with Equity and
Mercy, for without these she is but a sanguinary executioner.

Now, reader, what do we next approach? A building of
sombre appearance, with flanking towers and shot-holes, and
iron spikes jutting above high walls, and ponderous black
fetters hung above the barred window and grated portal.
That, reader, is the Golgotha, the living sepulchre of those
victims I have described. It is commonly called "The New
Bailey," * but that being a term of obsolete meaning, I shall
take the freedom to coin an expressive one, and call it "The
Tribulatory."

The coach drove up to these cage-looking gates; the people
by hundreds were trodden back by the dragoons; the gates
flew open, as if saying, "Come! Come!" to victims for a
feast, and I and George entered, and were immediately conducted into an interior courtyard, where a number of gentlemen
and several military officers stood to receive us, and my
fellow-prisoner being taken away, I was left in the midst of a
circle formed by these new observers. The late Rev. W. R.
Hay and the late Mr. Norris, both magistrates, were there.
The late Colonel Teasdale, of the First Dragoon Guards, then
a major, I believe, scanned me from top to toe; and, perhaps,
piqued at my cool reserve, a young officer of the same regiment, very laddish, and with limbs long enough for windmill
arms, stepped a foot, and said, "You look very fierce this
morning," to which I quietly replied, "'Tis well *you* cannot."
A person, whom I took to be the Boroughreeve of Manchester
for the time, uttered a small impertinence, which I answered
by a look; and Messrs. Hay and Norris coming up, the former,
after a civil recognition, told me that I was arrested on suspi-

---

* The gaol no longer exists. The latest incident in its history was the
execution of the "Manchester Martyrs" in 1867 for the murder of Constable Brett.

cion of high treason, and would be immediately sent to London for examination by the Secretary of State, under whose warrant I was a prisoner. I thanked the magistrates for their information, and said I was willing to be examined anywhere, but not having a change of linen, could I not write to my wife for some? Mr. Hay said I might, and they would take care it was sent, but I must leave the letter unsealed, as it must be examined before it was forwarded, and when the things arrived there they would give instructions to have them transmitted to London. With this arrangement I was satisfied, and thanked the magistrates for their kindness. I bowed to them, and was conducted into the governor's office, where I wrote home to the above effect, and also encouraged my wife and child to be of good cheer, for I was unconscious of any crime, and hoped soon to be with them again. A turnkey then led me up a winding stone stair, very clean, and sanded with white sand; at the top was a long arched gallery, also well limed and clean, and here, opening a strong nailed door, he motioned me to step inside, which I did, when, swinging the door to with a bang that sounded through the corridor, he turned the key, and I was left alone.

My cell was the first on the second floor, on the left side of the governor's office, and I thought they had shut me in there to have a quick eye and ear upon me. The dungeon was as compact as if cut from solid rock, and the floors and wall, like all that I had seen, were unexceptionable with regard to cleanliness. It was of an oblong form, probably about nine feet in length, by five in width; the door was at one end, and a window of a half circle in form was at the other; it was unglazed, but by a careful forethought against any accidental tumbling out, by sleep walkers or others, it was provided with a cross net work of massy iron bars. There were also a couple of wooden shutters inside, which the occupant might close when he had no wish for the free winds to come with their visits of mock condolement, or to catch a glimpse of the moon and her glorious children, to remind him of some one at home and her clustering brood around her. On each side of the cell, close to the wall, stood a narrow bed on cross legs, and beneath the

window was a stone ledge, which might serve for a seat, or a
step to get up to the window shutters.

I had been in this place some time, and was pacing backwards and forwards to preserve warmth, when a noise in the
yard excited my curiosity, and getting up to the iron bars of
the window, I was astonished and concerned on beholding
there my neighbour, the doctor, stalking, or rather staggering
along the flags below, with all the dignity he could assume.
With his hands resting upon his hips, his legs extended to a
straddle, and an air of authority, he shouted to some persons
who were laughing at him—" Bring me that bundle, I say ; I
am a reformer, and such will I live and die. My name is
Dr. Healey, and I will never flinch, so help me God! I say,
bring hither that bundle." I could not contain any longer ;
flinging myself on one of the beds I gave way to a hearty
burst of laughter, and soon afterwards heard them conduct
his majesty into one of the lock-ups.

I now expected every moment being called out for my
journey, and began to wish it, as I had become very cold.
Four o'clock arrived, and I heard the turnkeys locking the
prisoners in their cells for the night ; and, soon after, four
young lads were put into the cell in which I was. They
asked me what I was there for ; and having satisfied them,
they showed not any reservations in letting me know they
had each been convicted of felony. They were good-tempered
lads, and appeared to be naturally well disposed ; one of them
gave up his share of bed to me, for which I divided amongst
them my supper of bread and cheese ; and after having sung
a number of flash songs, and exchanged inquiries with their
acquaintance in other cells, they betook themselves to repose,
and I did the same as well as my situation and excited mind
permitted.

CHAPTER XIV.

COMPANIONS FOR A JOURNEY—COMFORTABLE EQUIPMENTS—
HOW THE DOCTOR HAD BEEN OVERTAKEN AND CAPTURED
—STOCKPORT—DISLEY—DERBY—LEICESTER.

AT five o'clock on Sunday morning I heard the welcome
rattling of keys, and soon after I was taken into the yard,
where to my surprise I found, besides Healey, John Lancashire, a weaver, from Middleton; Joseph Sellers, a cutler
and grinder, from Manchester; Nathan Hulton, a bleacher,
I think, from New Mills, in Derbyshire; John Roberts, a
cooper, from Manchester; Robert Ridings, a weaver, from
Failsworth; and Edward O'Connor, publican, of the "Red
Rose," at Chadderton. I had expected being conducted to
London alone, and certainly was not prepared for a mix-up
with these men, who I knew were part of those taken at the
plot meeting at Ardwick. Being here, however, and without
the power to extricate myself, I resolved to make the best
of my situation, and soon recalled my wonted cheerfulness.
Healey was as grim as a sweep: he had been tumbling in
a dirty, smoky lock-up all night, and was now ready to
perform "The Moor of Venice." I shook my head, and, in
order to rouse him, said he was a fine fellow to bring himself
into that place. He turned quickly, as I expected, and said,
What did I think of myself? Was not I in as great a
hobble as he was?—which retort turned the laugh against
me as I intended, and put us all in good humour; and the
doctor then went to a water-tap and washed his face.

Having been arranged in two parties, of four and four,
we were heavily ironed by the legs. Mr. Nadin, who super-

intended the operation, ordered out body and neck collars, and
armlets, with chains; but Mr. George Williams and Mr.
Stephen Dykes, King's messengers, into whose company we
were transferred, objected to the use of those irons, and they
were put in the boot of the coach, which awaited us at the
gates. Besides the messengers we were accompanied by
Joseph Mills and James Platt, both officers of the Manchester
police. The messengers then formally took us into custody in
the King's name, and gave us to understand that if we conducted ourselves with propriety on the road, every indulgence
would be extended to us. We assured them we would try
to deserve their kindness; and, congratulating each other
on our removal from a place to which, above all others, we
had a dislike, we mounted the coach, and left The Tribulatory
at six o'clock on the morning of Sunday, the 30th of March,
1817.

And now, whilst we traverse the dull streets, void of
inhabitants, save watchmen retiring from their beats, drowsy
topers staggering home, with bleared eyes, torn clothes, and
empty pockets, and here and there a sprightly maid on hands
and knees, cleaning steps and door-plates, let us recur to the
doctor, and give an account of his apprehension, as I had
learned it from him whilst we were being ironed.

On leaving home, he took with him, besides his top-coat, a
bundle of clothes, his tooth-drawing and bleeding instruments,
and a Barclay's dictionary in quarto; intending to raise
money on the latter, if no other means presented itself. The
Middleton constables, after seeing me safely lodged at the
Assheton's Arms, got a hint about the doctor, and set out after
him at full speed, but without cry. The little man had stepped
into a shop in Simister Lane, in hopes of selling his dictionary,
which, after some time lost in conversation, was declined;
and he was returning down the lane, when a woman called
him into a house to draw a tooth. He gladly accepted the invitation, performed the operation cleverly, pocketed his fee, and
was coming away to join me, but was too late. The constables got a view of him, and, encumbered as he was, with
top-coat, bundle, and dictionary, it would have been useless

attempting to run, so he resigned himself to his fate, and was taken in great triumph to the Royal Oak publichouse, at top of Bowlee. There were about half a dozen constables and helpers; and now, having made good their capture, they sat down, determined to enjoy themselves after their morning's exertions. A plentiful ale posset was first despatched, after which there came hot and cold ale, and, lastly, some potent glasses, many of which were paid for by farmers and others, who, knowing the doctor, came to see him, and bid him good-bye. Of all these things the doctor partook to his wish, which was not a small one according to his size; one of the farmers also bought his dictionary, and the little man was, in a short time, as happy as a king, and for anything he seemed to know to the contrary, as potent. An hour or two were passed in jocular entertainment, the doctor spouted and sung for them as was his wont, and a verse of a fine old song, on a genial subject, made his captors almost as jovial as himself.

> "I love no roast but a nut-brown toast,
>   Or a crab laid on the fire;
> But little bread will do my stead—
>   Much bread I nought desire.
> No frost, no snow, no wine I trow,
>   Could hurt me if it would;
> I am so wrapp't, and thoroughly lapp't,
>   Of this jolly good ale, and old.
> Back and side, go bare, go bare;
>   Both foot and hand go cold;
> But belly, God send thee good ale enough,
>   Whether it be new or old."

From this last place they adjourned to the "Black Boy" in Old Millgate, where the party dined, and the doctor again went through his performances, to the great amusement of a room full of country and townspeople, who were glad to obtain admission by feeing the waiters. He was next taken to the Police Office; his presence at which place was said to have given the chief of the police great satisfaction; and shortly after he made his appearance at The Tribulatory, as before described.

And now let us proceed on our journey. Our appearance at Stockport, where the horses were changed, seemed to excite much interest and attention, and we learned from the observations of several of the townspeople that we were known as "The Manchester Rebels." At Disley we breakfasted; and the doctor so much enjoyed it that he said if that was being a State prisoner, he wished he had been one five years before— an expression which, coupled with the hearty compliment we all paid to the viands, probably impressed our conductors with the belief that we had been most cruelly famished ere we became prisoners. At Derby we had just got seated comfortably at dinner when our Jehu came in, whip in hand, saying, as usual, "Coach, gentlemen; coach, coach." Mr. Williams told him to go back, and when we were ready we would let him know; he seemed not to comprehend this, and showed an air, until he was bid peremptorily to walk out; the coach, he was informed, was ours, and must wait for us, and not we for it. The vehicle had been specially hired for the journey.

We had by this time so won the good opinion of the King's messengers that they did me the honour to say privately the irons should be taken off, and we should travel the remainder of the journey as common passengers, if I would give my word for the sure conveyance of the party. I said I could not do that: three of the men only were personally known to me; a fourth I knew only by name, and the others I had never seen before that morning. Besides, their conduct towards us had been so kind that I should be extremely sorry if they incurred any blame by endeavouring to render us comfortable: we could do as we were, the conveyance which carried us carried our chains also. On emerging from the courtyard into the street we found that a considerable crowd had collected, many being persons of respectable appearance. They gazed with a strong curiosity; several lent us a hand to mount; the coach dashed forward, and as we waved a farewell we received their cheers in return.

Nothing requiring notice occurred until we arrived at Leicester, where we stopped at the head inn. The landlord, supposing probably that we were transported felons, showed us into a taproom, ejecting a number of coach cads, stable helpers, and others to make way for us. He refused to find a better room, and was impertinent and rude towards the King's messengers, until they exhibited their badges of office, informed him who and what they were, and demanded, at his peril for refusing, the best accommodation the house afforded. The master then became a most obsequious servant, showed us into a large and elegantly furnished room, and in a very short time set before us a good warm supper. The windows here looked into the street, and they were presently darkened by curious gazers, who climbed up the shutters to get a peep at us, and hung to one another like bees swarming about a hive. Before we left this house we were each presented with a nightcap; and on remounting the coach several gentlemen, whom we understood to be magistrates, handed us a glass of wine each, with which we drank their good healths and drove off.

CHAPTER XV.

A NIGHT JOURNEY: ITS OBJECTS AND REMINISCENCES—MUSIC AND POETRY — REDBURN — CHATTERTON — LONDON — BOW STREET.

THE night was gleamy and starlight; and as the coach dashed forward we soon entered upon what seemed a pretty rural country. Now we passed a large substantial-looking farm house, with its homestead; now a loving couple were overtaken walking arm in arm by some deep and bowered lane; next the mirth of home-wending youths would be heard; or mayhap the strains of a devout hymn from some chapel-comers. Anon a white cottage would lend us a blink from its cheerful hearth. Ah! what a paradise seems the lowliest shed when viewed from the vista of a prison door, how enviable appear the humblest mortals that walk abroad of their own free will, and what a dove-nest is that where a fair hand is seen closing the white chamber curtains for the night! Yes, it is at such moments, and under impressions produced by such objects, that we can best appreciate the blessings of the poorest hearth, of the humblest home, in which, as I have before intimated, if there be contentment, happiness will surely abide. Wise indeed is he, and wealthy beyond all riches, who enjoys with a thankful heart the blessings, few though they be, which he finds bestowed on his humble estate; remembering gratefully that "better is a dinner of herbs where love is than a stalled ox and hatred therewith." But we seldom find out these things until it be too late: we count not our jewels perhaps until the dearest are lost.

Our party of four was now inside the coach, and we began to sing. Ridings, who understood music, gave one or two pieces with a pathos and solemnity which I never heard expressed before.

" Glory to thee, my God, this night,"

brought the singing parties of our own homes to our recollection; and we all participated in the emotions of our amiable and talented musician. O'Connor sometimes laughed, sometimes cried like a child; at last he broke out into that mournful lament—

" Where is my cabin-door fast by the wild wood?
   Sisters and sire, did ye weep for its fall?
Where is the mother that look'd on my childhood?
   And where is my bosom-friend, dearer than all?
Oh! my sad soul, long abandon'd by pleasure,
   Why didst thou dote on a fast-fading treasure?
Tears, like the rain-drop, may fall without measure,
   But rapture and beauty they cannot recall."

To which we all responded as chorus—

"Where is my cabin-door, fast by the wild wood? "

Morning at length broke, and as we approached the dark woods and green meadows of Woburn, I gave my

SERENADE.

The grey dawn of morning is spreading on high;
And Venus is glowing so bright in the sky;
The cattle are lowing, the tender lambs bleat;
Arise, dearest Mary, before it be late.

The sweet-scented blossom is cover'd with dew;
The flowers of the field are perfumed anew;
The blithe birds are singing on ev'ry green tree;
Arise, dearest Mary, and come unto me.

Thy breath is more sweet than the breeze of the morn;
The lily's pure white doth thy bosom adorn;
Thy look is as bright as the beaming of day;
Oh! come dearest maid, to thy true love away.

Lancashire also sung a sweet and simple melody to words somewhat like the following:

> " I wonder why my love is cold,
>   Whilst I so kind would be?
> I would give hoards of countless gold,
>   To win thine heart from thee.
> To win thy love, my beauteous maid,
>   And find it ever true:
> One thousand jewels, too, were thine,
>   That flash like sun-bright dew."

We breakfasted at Redburn, a small village, which takes its name from a clear, sedgy stream, immortalised by the unfortunate Chatterton, and said, with much probability of truth, to have been reddened with blood at the great battle of St. Albans.

At this place we breakfasted, washed, and made ourselves as decent as we could, preparatory to our entrance into London. O'Connor's legs were swelled, and the chains gave him much pain. A few miles short of London the coach stopped at a road-side publichouse, where, whilst taking a little porter, my companions had an opportunity for conferring, without the immediate presence of our conductors. I then found they were afraid of each other, and that they expected nothing less than a trial, and a conviction on the evidence of some one or two of the party. I endeavoured to unite them, and persuaded them to say as little as possible when examined by the Secretary of State; and at length they agreed to say, that the meetings they had attended were to raise subscriptions for the families of prisoners, and of those who had left the country in consequence of the Suspension Act. This they were to admit and abide by; and each pledged himself to be faithful to the agreement, and then we all went on again with confidence and satisfaction.

We arrived in London about twelve o'clock, and were immediately conveyed to Bow Street, which was filled with people before we could be got off the coach. We were placed in a decent room our irons were immediately removed, and

most of us wrote home to our families. A gentleman named
Capper was introduced, and I thought he seemed to scrutinise
us very much. Sir Nathaniel Conant, an elderly and respectable looking gentleman, also came in, and informed us
that Lord Sidmouth could not see us that day, and that we
should be well provided for at a house in the neighbourhood.
Soon afterwards we were conducted in couples to a room
prepared at the Brown Bear publichouse, opposite; where,
after supper, the doctor amused ourselves and keepers
(who were eight or ten police officers) with several recitations
in his most florid style. Messrs. Williams and Dykes came
and brought with them a friend, and they each seemed much
entertained. Mr. Perry, one of the chief officers at Bow
Street, afterwards entered, and apologised for having to
submit us to what might be a small inconvenience. It was
customary, he said, to secure prisoners during the night
by a chain, and he hoped we should take it as a mere matter
of form; we expressed our readiness to submit to whatever
restraint might be deemed necessary. Small chains being
produced, myself, Lancashire, and Healey were fastened
together, and the other five were in like manner secured, after
which we continued our amusements during an hour or two,
and then went to rest on beds in the same room, still secured
by chains to the bedposts, and to each other.

On the following morning our kind conductors, the
messengers, again came to see us, and furnished some of the
party with clean linen; other articles of dress were not withheld to such as wanted them most. John Lancashire and
the doctor were completely changed in appearance, and came
forth dapper, smart young fellows. To all, except myself and
O'Connor, something was furnished: we were probably
excepted, not because our apparel was better than that of the
others, but because it was in a more careful condition, and we
had also put on clean linen before we left home. The kindness of Messrs. Williams and Dykes made, I am sure, a
strongly grateful impression on the minds of the whole of their
prisoners; and I may also add that the demeanour of the
Bow Street officers was, without exception, such as might be

expected from men who knew their duty, and had the full power to perform it. It presented a striking contrast to the conduct which was at that time generally practised by men of the same station at Manchester.

CHAPTER XVI.

ABOUT four o'clock in the afternoon we were conveyed in four
coaches to the Secretary of State's office at Whitehall. On
our arrival we were divided into two parties of four and four,
and each party was placed in a separate room. A gentleman
now appeared, who asked severally our names and occupations,
which he wrote in a book, and then retired. In a short time
another person came and called my name, and I rose and
followed him along a darkish passage. I must confess that
this part of the proceedings gave rise to some feelings of incer-
titude and curiosity, and brought to my recollection some
matters which I had read when a boy about the Inquisition in
Spain. My conductor knocked at a door and was told to go
in, which he did, and delivered me to an elderly gentleman,
whom I recognised as Sir Nathaniel Conant. He asked my
christian and surname, which were given : he then advanced
to another door, and desiring me to follow him, he opened it,
and, bowing to a number of gentlemen seated at a long table
covered with green cloth, he repeated my name and took his
place near my left hand. The room was a large one, and
grandly furnished, according to my notions of such matters.
Two large windows, with green blinds and rich curtains,
opened upon a richer curtain of nature—some trees, which
were in beautiful leaf. The chimney-piece was of carved
marble, and on the table were many books; and several

persons sat there assiduously writing, whilst others fixed
attentive looks upon me. I was motioned to advance to the
bottom of the table, and did so: and the gentleman who sat
at the head of the table said I was brought there by virtue of
a warrant issued by him in consequence of my being suspected
of high treason; that I should not be examined at that time,
but must be committed to close confinement until that day
se'nnight, when I should again be brought up for examination.
Meantime, if I had anything to say on my own behalf, or any
request to make, I was at liberty to do so; but I must observe
they did not require me to say anything.

The person who addressed me was a tall, square, and bony
figure, upwards of fifty years of age, I should suppose, and
with thin and rather grey hair; his forehead was broad and
prominent, and from their cavernous orbits looked mild and
intelligent eyes. His manner was affable, and much more
encouraging to freedom of speech than I had expected. On
his left sat a gentleman whom I never made out; and next
him again was Sir Samuel Shepherd, the Attorney-General, I
think, for the time, who frequently made use of an ear trumpet.
On Lord Sidmouth's right, for such was the gentleman who
had been speaking to me, sat a good-looking person in a plum-
coloured coat, with a gold ring on the small finger of his left
hand, on which he sometimes leaned his head as he eyed me
over—this was Lord Castlereagh.

"My lord," I said, addressing the president, "having been
brought from home without a change of linen, I wish to be
informed how I shall be provided for in that respect until I
can be supplied from home?" The Council conferred a short
time, and Lord Sidmouth said I should be supplied with whatever was necessary. I next asked, should I be allowed freely
to correspond with my wife and child, inform them of my
situation, and to receive their letters, provided such letters did
not contain political information?

"You will be allowed to communicate with your family,"
said his lordship; "but I trust you will see the necessity of
confining yourself to matters of a domestic nature. You will
always write in the presence of a person who will examine

your letters; you will, therefore, do well to be guarded in your correspondence, as nothing of an improper tendency will be suffered to pass. I speak this for your own good."

"Could I be permitted to have pen, ink, and paper in prison?" I asked; "and could I be allowed to keep a small day-book, or journal, for my amusement?"

"It is an indulgence," was the reply, "which has never been granted to any State prisoner; and as I do not see any reason for departing from the established rule, I should feel it my painful duty to refuse it."

I said I had heard that the Suspension Act contained a clause securing to State prisoners the right of sending petitions to Parliament; and I wished to be informed if there were such a clause.

His lordship said the Suspension Act did not contain any such clause, but the power to petition would be allowed by his Majesty's ministers, and I should have that liberty whenever I thought proper to use it. I bowed and retired.

The other prisoners were then severally called in and informed of the cause of their arrest, in the same terms that I had been; and that they would be again examined on that day se'nnight. All of them afterwards declared they had not made any statement or disclosure of any description; but that, according to the agreement mentioned, they had remained silent as to the purpose of their meetings. One characteristic incident was, however, said to have occurred before the Privy Council. On the doctor being asked how he spelled his surname, he answered in broad Lancashire, "Haitch, hay, haa, l, hay, y" (H, e, a, l, e, y), but the pronunciation of the e and a being different in London, there was some boggling about reducing the name to writing, and a pen and paper were handed to him. The doctor knew that his *forte* lay not in feats of penmanship any more than in spelling; and to obviate any small embarrassment on that account, he pulled out an old pocket-book, and took from it one of his prescription labels, on which the figures of a pestle and mortar were imposed from a rudely engraved plate, and these words, "Joseph Healey, Surgeon, Middleton. Plase take —— tablespoonfuls of this mixture each —— hours." This he handed to Lord Sidmouth, who, as may be supposed, received it graciously, looked it carefully over, smiled, and read it again, and passed it round the Council table. Presently they were all tittering, and the doctor stood quite delighted at finding them such a set of merry gentlemen. The fact was, the first blank had been originally filled with a figure of two, "Plase take 2 table-spoonfuls," &c., but some mischievous wag had inserted two ciphers after the figure, and made it read "200 tablespoonfuls of this mixture each two hours." However it was, the doctor certainly imbibed a favourable opinion of the Council. The circumstance was supposed to have transpired from his own lips ; and I certainly had seen such a card in his possession before he went to London, but I never saw it afterwards.

In the same vehicle which brought us to the Home Office, we were next taken to the prison at Coldbath Fields, and placed in the inner lodge until a ward could be got ready for our occupation. O'Connor, who was unwell, and whose legs were swollen and painful from the gout and his chains, was taken from us and put into a sick ward, as was also Robert Ridings, who was likewise in delicate health, and who, being already incipiently consumptive, died soon after his return, from colds, as he thought, taken during his journey home-wards.

Whilst we were in the lodge, Evans the younger, one of the London reformers—who, as well as his father, was confined in this prison under the Suspension Act—came to the gate to speak with a friend. Samuel Drummond also, who has been mentioned as being apprehended at the Blanket meeting, was walking in a courtyard, seemingly in good health and spirits.

When our place was ready a turnkey conducted the six of us who remained together through a number of winding pas-sages to a flagged yard, into which opened a good room, or cell, about ten yards in length and three in width. On each side of the room were three beds, placed in what might be termed wooden troughs ; at the head of the room a good fire was burning, and we found a stock of coal and wood to recruit it at our pleasure. There were also a number of chairs, a table, candles, and other requisites; so that, had it not been for the grating at the window above the door, and the arched roof, bound by strong bars of iron, we might have fancied ourselves to be in a comfortable barrack. After surveying the place thoroughly, and striking the walls to ascertain if they were hollow, we stirred up the fire, drew our seats to the hearth, and spent the evening in conversing about our families and friends until the hour of rest, when we concluded by singing " The Union Hymn," which I led for that purpose.

THE UNION HYMN.

Ye bards of Britain, strike the lyre,
   And sing the happy union;
In strains of patriotic fire,
   Oh ! sing the happy union;
Not distant is the welcome day,
When woe, and want, and tyranny,
Shall from our isle be swept away :
The grand epoch of liberty
   Awaits a faithful union.

Oh! worthy is the glorious cause,
   Ye patriots of the union ;
Our fathers' rights, our fathers' laws,
   Await a faithful union.
A crouching dastard sure is he
Who would not strive for liberty,
And die to make Old England free
From all her load of tyranny ;
   Up ! brave men of the union.

Our little ones shall learn to bless
   Their fathers of the union.
And every mother shall caress
   Her hero of the union.
Our plains with plenty shall be crown'd ;
The sword shall till the fruitful ground ;
The spear shall prune our trees around ;
And joy shall everywhere abound,
   To bless a nation's union.

> Then Britain's prince shall truly reign ;
>   His subjects will defend him ;
> And, freed from loath'd corruption's train,
>   Bright honour shall attend him.
> Whilst foreign despots evermore
> Shall venerate Old Albion's shore ;
> And war, with all its crime and gore,
> Forgotten, and for ever o'er ;
>   Shall crown a nation's union.

And now, whilst my fellow prisoners are sleeping—some probably agonised by visions of the scaffold and block, others again winging their souls homeward in sweet dreams—let us, my reader, discuss the spirit of the foregone hymn. If thou sayest it is inconsistent with the advice to contentment which I have already given, I reply that a spirit of humble satisfaction with the good things a man hath, a full appreciation of the blessings he enjoys, is not by any means incompatible with fair means and honourable wishes for the obtainment of other good things which he hath not. That there is a time and a means for all rightfully obtainable things, and that the industrious and patient man will sooner arrive at his ends by a beaten and legalised path, though he advances slowly, than will he who, breaking down all barriers, is himself broken down, as he must be, unless the nation become his pioneer ;— that the industrious and poor man best serves his country by doing his duty to his family at home ;—that he best amends his country by giving it good children, and, if he have not any, by setting a good example himself ;—that he best governs by obeying the laws, and by ruling in love and mercy his own little kingdom at home ;—that his best reform is that which corrects irregularities on his own hearth ;—that his best meetings are those with his own family by his own fireside ;—that his best resolutions are those which he carries into effect for his own amendment and that of his household ;—that his best speeches are those which promote " Peace on earth, and goodwill " towards mankind ;—that his best petitions are those of a contrite heart, addressed to the King of Heaven, by whom they will not be despised, and those to the governors of the earth for the peaceable obtainments of ameliorations for his brother man; and that his best means for such obtainment is the cultivation of good feelings in the hearts and of good sense in the heads of those around him;—that his best riches is contentment;—that his best love is that which comforts his family;—that his best instruction is that which humanises and ennobles their hearts; and that his best religion is that which leads him to "Do justly, to love mercy, and to walk humbly with his God." Would he triumph? let him learn to endure. Would he be a hero? let him subdue himself. Would he govern? let him first obey.

Should my reader, as I may almost expect, especially if he be a young and sanguine politician, feel as if I were presuming too much, let me remind him that at the time I am writing of I was in my thirtieth year, at my present writing in my fifty-third (well and hearty and free of wind and limb, thank God). He may then perhaps allow that a close and somewhat severe experience of twenty-five years (say from 1815) entitles a man to have an opinion of his own, and to express it; if not, he has lived to very little purpose, either for himself or his fellow-beings. May I not then say, in the language of the wise king of Israel, "Wisdom is the principal thing, therefore get wisdom, and with all thy getting get understanding. Exalt her, and she shall promote thee; she shall bring thee to honour when thou dost embrace her. She shall give to thine head an ornament of grace; a crown of glory shall she deliver to thee."

CHAPTER XVII.

DESCRIPTION OF OUR PRISON—OUR FARE—OUR NEXT NEIGHBOURS—OTHER MATTERS.

On the morning following we were aroused from sleep by a loud report of firearms, and soon afterwards the door of our room was opened, and a turnkey saluted us with a "good morning" and a "hope that we had slept well"; we thanked him, assured him we had, and he left us. We now rose and put the place in order, washed ourselves, and took a survey of our department and its premises. The door opened into a flagged yard, about twelve yards in length, by nine in width, and to which we descended by a couple of steps. On the right and the front of the door the yard was bounded by high and strong palisades, beyond which was a large garden, bounded again by a lofty wall, above which we could see upper windows of buildings. On our left we were separated from another yard by a wall about nine feet high; abutting upon it were a sewer, a water tap, and other conveniences. A door was fixed in one corner of the wall, and near it was a second door, which led into the passages of the prison, whilst above our heads and along our front appeared the windows, strongly barred, of numerous cells, and the thoroughfares communicating with them. Such was our position in this place, on viewing which as a prison we saw nothing to complain about.

At breakfast time the turnkey again made his appearance, with another man, who took from a basket six loaves of bread of nearly a pound each, a pipkin containing two pounds of butter, a jar with two pounds of sugar, a canister with one pound of tea, six cups and basins, salt, plates, dishes, half a dozen knives and forks, a kettle, a pan, and other articles to complete a kitchen service, to which were added a wash-basin, soap, and clean towel, so that we began to look a little homely, and soon having the kettle boiling, we sat down to a comfortable cup of tea, wishing that those at home, and all others who deserved it, might have as good a breakfast as ourselves. At noon we dined on a quarter of pork, with potatoes and other vegetables, to dilute which each man was allowed a pot of porter, and pipes and tobacco were added. Our supper was tea and cold meat, and thus, so far as diet was concerned, we lived more like gentlemen than prisoners. I recollect, however, one of the party shaking his head at what appeared to us profusion, and observing that he did not think any better of his own case for all that; "for," said he, "it's always the way here; when they intend to hang 'em, they let 'em have whatever they choose to eat or drink—only they *will* hang 'em at last." This remark made an impression on some of my companions, and most of them seemed to be of opinion that all this kindness would prove only precursory to some terrible act of severity; and the idea was strengthened when, a few days after, on some of us requesting to have books to read, a Bible, a prayer-book, some tracts, and "sermons for persons under sentence of death" were put into our hands.

But long before this one of our men had made a most interesting discovery. He came in with surprise and joy in his countenance, and said "There were women in the next yard." Another followed saying there were women indeed! The question was asked, what sort? and we all ran to ascertain that point according to our several tastes. The oldest man amongst us was speaking to one of them through the keyhole, and he had already commenced a negotiation for a kind of "friendly compact," which was soon agreed upon and ratified by both parties, by mutual congratulations and good wishes expressed through the keyhole. They were, if I recollect aright, just the same number of women as we were of men —six, and they readily undertook to assist us in every possible way within their power. They were to wash and darn whatever small articles we had that required it, and to do all our needlework generally, besides which they were to obtain and transmit to us all the information they could respecting ourselves, and to be faithful and secret in their communications. They vowed, indeed, to be true friends, and we never had cause to doubt their word. On our part we promised to keep faithfully their secret information, and to render them whatever services lay in our power, and we also kept our compact. The signal when either party was wanted was to throw a piece of blue slate (of which several pieces lay in the yard) over the wall, when the other party was to repair to the keyhole and receive the communication. Poor things! tears came into their eyes when we spoke to them in words of confidence and kindness, and they wept bitterly when we touched, as we were almost compelled to do, a more tender chord—when we asked about their former condition in life, and inquired respecting their fathers and mothers, their husbands or their children. Some of our men almost promised to love them (a word of strange power over the heart of woman), and we could see a faint, hopeless smile when the head was turned aside, as if to look back on some recollections of former days.

One alone was of matronly age; the others varied, I should think, from twenty to thirty. Two had infants at the breast, and all of them were widows or married women. Two had lost their husbands, who were officers, in the service of their country, and the husband of a third, also in a military capacity, was absent on a foreign station. One or two had been seduced and deserted, and more than that number had disgusted their connections by becoming intemperate, after which they descended to poverty, crime, and disgrace. All had been condemned to death, or to long terms of transportation, and they severally acknowledged that they narrowly escaped the fulfilment of their sentence only by urgent and powerful interest of most respectable connections. None of them were less than good-looking; some were more than that, and two were remarkably fine women, for we could see their form and stature as they paced the yard at a distance from the door. One of the young ones was a little dimpled, cherry-looking thing, but the melancholy of her eye was strangely at variance with the rosy health of her cheek. One of them would tell of her poor old father in the country—of his ancient mansion, and the servants he had around him; another thanked God that her mother had, by death, escaped the affliction of seeing her disgrace; and another would talk of what her husband (her Henry, I think she called him) would do when he came home—how he would, after all, forgive her, "knowing it was distress," and get her liberated, and how they would be happy again, and she virtuous and ever affectionate. Poor things! with such bright hopes and illusions they would amuse themselves, and they seemed consoled when we talked with them of such matters, and thereby helped them to relief by floods of tears.

We too had our illusions—our thoughts of home, and our hopes, as well as our fears. But our case at present wore a worse aspect than theirs; their periods of imprisonment were definite, and some of them soon to expire, whilst ours were all uncertainty. They knew the worst; we knew nothing, save that we were in the power of those we had made our enemies. Besides, they shook their heads and sighed when we talked about going home soon and leaving them. They had heard us termed "the Lancashire rebels," and that we were to be tried for high treason, and the case was expected to go hard against us.

I may, perhaps I ought to say that their demeanour justified us in crediting their account of themselves. They were very friendly, but nothing more; they never, so far as I could learn, gave encouragement to improper freedom of speech; nor do I believe that any of our men greatly offended in that respect.

After our first dinner we had a decent surplus of meat and vegetables left. One asked, "What shall be done with these?" another said, "It would never do to send them back; if we did we should have so much less the day following." "Cut it up for the women," said a third, and it was done: and we made them up as nice a little dinner as we could. The meat, excellent pork, was reduced to slices, and put on a flat dish; the vegetables and bread, and all our other little trifles, were

similarly disposed on another dish. The slate, the ever
welcome messenger, was then thrown over the wall, and they
were presently at the door. "Will you do us another
favour?" asked our spokesman. "With pleasure," was the
reply. "Look down then, and accept a trifle from our table."
A space below the door admitted this. There was a scream of
delight, and a "hush, hush," and the dishes were hurried
away, emptied, washed, and returned in like manner, with ten
thousand thanks for our remembrance of them. How, indeed,
could we have forgotten them, the poor, lost, cut-off, and
world-despised beings? After tea we did the same; we gave
them plentifully of our stock—our tea, our sugar, our butter—
bread they had. They told us they secreted our gifts until
they were locked up in their house and the turnkeys had
retired for the night, when they set on a pan, brought their
stores from their hiding-place, and had a feast that might have
comforted a queen.

The day following we did the same, and continued it. We
cut them up the remainder of a leg of mutton, weighing
thirteen pounds and a half—with carrots, parsnips, and other
condiments. They informed us that there was astonishment
in the governor's kitchen when the platters with the clean
bones only were returned. It was no wonder, the domestics
said, "that the people of Lancashire rebelled if they were all
starved, as they were sure they must have been, from the
enormous quantities of meat we devoured."

CHAPTER XVIII.

AFTER we had finished our first dinner, and had got seated
with our pipes and allowance of porter, we set about making
regulations amongst ourselves; the principal of which was
that each was to become room's-man for the day, in turn, and,
as such, servant to the others. The reader will recollect that
our party now consisted of James Sellers, Joseph Healey,
John Lancashire, Nathan Hulton, John Roberts, and myself.
I now addressed them, saying I had a matter of some consequence to mention, and hoped they would consider it seriously,
and act in their best discretion. I said they well knew that,
though I had been arrested and confined with them (provi-
dentially, it almost appeared to me), I had not, at any time,
been connected with their secret meetings; and that both
Lancashire and Healey could testify that I had always condemned such meetings—my maxim being, " Hold fast by
the law." That, consequently, I considered myself in small
jeopardy compared with themselves, unless suborned and false
witnesses were brought against me, which, however, the
Government could doubtless procure if it chose. I therefore
viewed myself as standing on much better ground than I did
them; they having been apprehended in the act of carrying on
a secret meeting for unlawful purposes. That such difference,
however, now I was with them, should not prevent me from
doing my best to render them a service, and with that view
giving them my best advice. They should remark, I said, that,

either through the interposition of Providence, or the fatuity
of the Government, they were (O'Connor and Ridings excepted,
neither of whom were deeply versed in their private transactions) all together in one place. That hitherto, as I understood
from their conversations, none of them had been questioned
by the Privy Council ; and that consequently no admissions
or declarations had been made to that body. They all solemnly
declared nothing had escaped from their lips. Then I continued, " the pie-crust is yet whole, and you may keep it so."
I proposed that every day after dinner they should appoint a
chairman, who should put such questions to them as he
considered the Privy Council were likely to do at their next
examination, supposing some one of their body to have given
secret information. That their replies should be deliberated
upon, and determined accordingly ; and those replies should
be committed to memory, and, in substance, strictly adhered
to at their next interview with the ministers. That they
would consequently all give the same account ; all be of one
party and of one mind ; and that if Government brought them
to trial, it would have to unmask its spies and informers,
instead of making them fall by their mutual contradictions,
mistrusts, and jealousies, which, as it seemed to me, the
Government would prefer doing.

They all declared it was the best of advice, and it was
adopted with acclamation. I would have retired, but they
would not suffer me, and insisted that I should become their
questioner. I complied at length—put them through a
catechising according to my poor ability—and established a
set of replies, such as I thought would either answer or ward
off any question they were likely to encounter. The basis of
the old tale was adopted ; their meetings were to devise relief
to persons who had fled from the Suspension Act, and to their
families in their absence. This was to be the skeleton ; we
stuffed and padded it in our own way, and threw over it a
cloak of plausibility, which we thought the devil himself could
not penetrate. And so we continued day by day, catechising
and drilling, until my fellows would, I believe, have stood
before old Rhadamanthus without quail or fear.

We now began to be much better satisfied with ourselves and each other; those thoughtful and suspicious looks which had hitherto indicated fear and mistrust were no longer observable. Our time passed more agreeably; and, striving to amuse each other, we had no lack of songs, hymns, and love and family tales, with scraps of plots and insurrections, and droll blunders, which sometimes caused roars of laughter.

About this time we discovered we had some little attendants upon us which we were extremely desirous to get rid of; how or where we picked them up we could not tell; but every man was infested, and we made it known to our attendant, who informed the governor, Mr. Atkins. A more thorough or speedy removal could not have been effected anywhere; that worthy and humane gentleman immediately caused all our bedding to be taken out, our room to be cleansed, new and clean bedding to be supplied, all our linen to be changed, and our other clothes to be carefully examined, and we felt no more of that nuisance.

On the ninth of April we were conveyed in coaches, as before, to the Home Office, at Whitehall. But let me apprise the reader that, not having the means for writing, and not being able to commit every particular to memory, I cannot pretend to furnish a verbatim report of my examinations, and shall only give the substance of what passed on those occasions.

I was introduced to the Council with the previous formalities, and by the same person, Sir Nathaniel Conant. Lord Sidmouth repeated what he had said on my first examination—viz., that I was arrested on suspicion of high treason, and that they were willing to hear what I had to say in reply. I said I was not conscious of having deserved suspicion of treasonable practices, as, instead of being a promoter of violence and disturbance, I had always been a friend to peace and order; and, with that purpose, had used my little influence to the utmost amongst my neighbours. That if his lordship was as well acquainted with the situation of the working people as I was, and with the conduct which I had pursued amongst them, he would see the justice, as well as the policy, of restoring me to my family. I acknowledged I was a Parliamentary reformer, and always should be so until reform was obtained—that no circumstance or situation whatever could induce me to disavow my opinions—nay, I considered it as the pride and glory of my life to have, in some degree, merited the name of a reformer; but I never advocated its obtainment by violence. That I had trusted, and endeavoured to inspire my neighbours with the like confidence, that when our grievances and sufferings were properly made known to Parliament, attention would be paid to them; that we had petitioned, but were not listened to. That I could not tell how to account for this neglect, save by crediting the existence of corruption in the honourable House; but still I would not recommend its removal by violent means. That I firmly believed reform would ultimately take place; circumstances occurring in their own due time which would induce his Majesty's ministers and Parliament to take the measure into consideration. That I had always been an enemy to private meetings—had deprecated them as much as possible, believing that reform did not require privacy; and, finally, that, in my opinion, nothing save reform could preserve the country from revolution. No questions were asked, and I was re-conducted as before.

When the other prisoners had been severally introduced, we were conveyed to our old quarters; and the day following James Sellers was taken from our party, and put, as we understood, into the deputy-governor's house.

In the course of this week we were visited by the magistrates appointed to examine the prison. I was room's-man for the day, and was stripped, with sleeves rolled up, and washing some pots which had been used at our mess when the gentlemen entered the room, preceded by Mr. Beckett, the deputy-governor of the prison. They bade us "good morning," and asked if we were comfortable. We answered in the affirmative, at which they expressed satisfaction. One of them, an elderly gentleman (Mr. Sketchly, I believe), asked Mr. Beckett, "which is Bamford?" and Mr. Beckett pointed me out. The gentleman was pleased to compliment me, and said he understood I was a poet. I thanked him for his favourable opinion, but disclaimed being a poet; I was only a country rhymester, I said, just capable of throwing a few doggerel verses together. He asked how I received my education, as he understood I was but a poor man. I said I did not pretend to much education—my father did, however, send me to school, where I was taught to read; I first began to write at a Sunday school, kept by the Methodists, and I afterwards went to other schools; but what little information I was possessed of had been chiefly acquired by my own reading and study. He said he was sorry to see us in our present situation; it was a pity men should be so deluded. I replied that we did not consider ourselves to be deluded men. I, at any rate, did not suppose myself to be one. I had not done anything to repent of. I had not said anything that I would not repeat again under the circumstances. How was it possible, he asked, that we could be dissatisfied with the taxes. Poor people paid no taxes; how could taxation operate on them? I said, " Suppose a tax were laid upon land, or on the landlord. As his leases expired the rents of his farms were advanced to meet the tax, and the farmer was obliged, in order to meet the advance, to lay an additional charge on the produce of the farm. The shopkeeper who purchased from the farmer then advanced to his customer, and the poor man, being a customer as well as others, paid the advanced price for so much as he consumed; and that was the way in which taxation operated on the poor." To this there was no reply; and soon after our visitors took their departure.

Bad as our case was (and we supposed we should have a long imprisonment of some years at least), there were others in this place, besides our women friends, whom we could pity. For two hours every forenoon a low, dark-complexioned man, with somewhat of a military carriage, took his walk to and fro under the garden wall, at the greatest allowable distance from, but parallel with our yard. He was an object of interest to us, and we often bowed to him, which he always politely returned. He had been, we were informed, a long time in this prison, and likely to remain much longer, being entirely at the disposal of the Secretary of State. He had once or twice annoyed the Prince Regent by obtaining access to his presence and demanding payment of a large sum of money, which he asserted the Prince owed him, he being "The King of Denmark." He had been imprisoned before for such annoyances; and soon after his liberation he went again, and attempted to ride into the palace of Carlton House, for the purpose of obtaining "his money" from "his cousin," the Regent of England. He was said to be perfectly sane in all matters except these—viz., that he was the King of Denmark, and that our King owed him a great sum of money. The elder Evans, one of the London prisoners, a wordy and intemperate man, was also allowed his stated walks in the garden, but he never ventured to exchange a word with us.

On Tuesday, the 16th of April, we were again taken to the Home Office. John Roberts was called in first, Hulton second, Healey third, and myself the fourth, when Lord Sidmouth thus addressed me:—"Mr. Bamford, the persons who have been examined to day are committed to prison, from whence they will not be liberated except by a due course of law. From the information received respecting you, his Majesty's ministers would not be justified in adopting the same course towards you; you will therefore be brought up for another examination, which will take place this day week." I then retired.

The day following Roberts, Hulton, and the doctor were taken out of our ward and sent to different prisons. Roberts, with John Bagguley, before mentioned as an orator at the Blanket meeting, were consigned to Gloucester Gaol. Hulton and Sellers were sent to Exeter; whilst John Johnstone, of Manchester, also before mentioned, Samuel Drummond, of the same place, and our friend the doctor, were conveyed to Dorchester.

The day after their departure George Plant, of Blackley, William Kent, of Chadderton, and James Leach, of Spotland, who were apprehended at the Plot meeting at Ardwick, and had remained in the New Bailey since, arrived in London; and after passing in review before the Privy Council, as we had done, were brought to this general *depôt* for all dangerous and suspected characters. Kent, who had a lame arm, was placed in the hospital ; Leach was put in the outer yard ; and Plant was locked up with Lancashire and myself.

My new comrade was, I should suppose, about twenty-five years of age ; he was a weaver, and had left a wife and one or two young children, at Crab-lane-head, in Blackley, near Manchester. He was fully as tall as myself; thin, very pale, with black hair, black eyes, thick lips, big white teeth, a kind of stiffness, and a stoop in the shoulders. He was indeed, in person, rather an oddity; but I believe as simple and innocent intentioned a man as could be produced. He related some curious particulars of the conduct adopted towards him by the police of Manchester, during his detention at the New Bailey.

He said that Joseph Platt, one of the police beadles, who had formerly known him, and whose parents were then neighbours to Plant, came to him one night in his cell, and, after reminding him of old acquaintance and expressing much friendship towards him, said he had obtained permission to make a proposal, and it would be his fault if he did not take advantage of it for his own good. Two of the persons already sent to London, he continued, had offered, on condition that their lives were spared, to disclose the whole of the Manchester plot, and to give details of the proceedings of the conspirators at their several meetings. These discoveries, he said, would place all the rest in jeopardy, and they might think well if they got off with transportation for life. He added that, knowing Plant, and having a great respect for him, and a kind feeling towards his family, he had, as a great favour, obtained permission from the magistrates to mention the thing to him, and to say that if he (Plant) would come forward and give a statement of all he knew about the conspiracy he should have the first chance of becoming King's evidence, and of thereby saving his life, procuring his freedom, at any rate, and very likely of getting something handsome in the way of a provision afterwards.

George assured me that his only reply to this—which was

repeated on a second visit—was, that "he knew nothing, and could not, therefore, tell anything"; that such had been his constant answer, that he never in the least varied it, and that at length his friend Platt gave him up, and resigned him, as he said, to the scaffold or to perpetual chains abroad.

If such was his answer to Platt—and I never had any reason for doubting it—he certainly gave the true one. He had never been at a plot-meeting before the one at Ardwick, and the proceedings at that had scarcely commenced when the police arrived and took the whole party into custody.

CHAPTER XIX.

THE BOTANIST—THE BIRD CATCHER AND THE LOVER— THEIR AGREEMENT.

AND now, reader, the natural current of my story leads us from this prison to the deep woods, sombre shades, and bare wilds of Lancashire, to speculations and ceremonials founded on superstitions of the rural population, and to beings and appearances, a thorough belief in which does even in the present day retain its place amongst the undeniable evidences narrated by the dwellers of the glens and moorlands of the county. At the time I am writing of, such opinions were still more prevalent than at present; when I was a child, a disbelief of them was looked on as an almost impious exception; they are now quickly departing from amongst us, and in another twenty years will probably be entirely ranked amongst the obsolete superstitions of a benighted age.

But, to be more explicit, know that my friend Plant was a firm believer in ghosts, witches, and hobgoblins, in the virtues of herbs under certain planetary influences, and in the occult mysteries of Culpepper and Sibley. He was entirely self-taught; had been a great reader, knew something of arithmetic, was a botanist, and a dreary-minded wanderer in lonely dells, on moors and heaths, searching after herbs of surpassing virtue, of mysterious growth and concealment, and of wonderful and unaccountable power.

How a man of his tastes and pursuits became induced to resign them for the culture of unpoetic politics it might perhaps be interesting to inquire. Possibly he was drawn into the vortex by the force of example amongst his numerous class. Possibly, being a knowledge seeker, he might wish to learn something of the new doctrine—the great political "Heal-all." Possibly his little learning was flattered, and latent ambition urged him to seek distinction; or, assigning higher motives, he might really wish to render a service to his country. However it was, he proved unfortunate ; his first experiment in the political line was also his last.

One night after we were locked up, having drawn near the fire and lighted our pipes, we entered as usual into conversation, which he soon led to his favourite subject—botany. We discussed the occult virtues of herbs, and their connection with the spiritual and planetary worlds, in which he believed as firmly as in his own existence. I did not dispute with him, but was rather an inquirer and a listener ; and as he narrated, in perfect assurance of their realities, the visionary experiments he had made, and their strange and fearful results, I enjoyed the illusions of the superstitions of my childhood which now recurred, as it were, like a tide after a long ebb, with double force. I felt interested, encouraged him to continue, and he finished by recounting an attempt in which he was once concerned, to take and carry off " Saint John's Fern seed."

He said that in one of his, " Yarbin Eawts," as he termed his rambles after herbs, he was in Guestless, or more properly, Griselhurst Wood, in Birkle, when a storm induced him to seek shelter in a cottage which he had observed at no great distance from the wood-side. He was made welcome, and pulled off his coat and hung it to dry before the fire, which the good woman improved by adding coal and root-stocks to the blazing heap. She was a widow about middle age, and had an only child, a son, a decent-looking youth, who sat mending her clogs beneath the window. He might be from eighteen to twenty years of age, very fair for a country lad, with light red, or " gowden-coloured," hair ; tall, and of a thoughtful way of speaking. The room was barely furnished but clean, and the articles were well arranged. There was a bread-flake covered with oak cakes, a bit of nice bacon, part of a sack of potatoes, and a " drink mug, " reaming with ale ; and he was given to

understand that "decent, honest foke" were sometimes accommodated there both with meat and drink; that, in short,
it was a "hush shop." He accordingly ordered a jug of ale,
and cut a rasher of bacon, which he was roasting on a fork,
when the door opened, and a short, broad-set, and dark-
visaged man entered, carrying two cages, with each a gorse-
cock, a pot with some bird-lime and water, and a number of
limed twigs.

"Hallo, Chirrup," said the young man, "I thowt if th'
storm didno' send thee fro' th' hillside, summut wud be op."
"Why, indeed, it's likely to be a weet afternoon; an' th'
brids are o' away to th' covers, an' th' twigs are weet an'
winno howd iv owt coom, an' th' wynt makes sitch a din, at
no gorse-cock can be yerd ogen it; an' I've had quite enoof for
to-day, for I've seen that at I shall never forget to th' last day
o' my life." "Wot wur it, Chirrup?" said the young man,
laying down the clog, and looking earnestly at the bird-catcher,
for such he was. "Bangle, my lad, it wur th' bonnyist brid at
ever flew o' wings." "Well, then, it wur nother gorse-cock,
ouzle, nor dunnock, at any rate; an' yo'd no coers to catch it
wi'. But wot wur it like; wot kullur wur it?" "It wur as
fair a gowden yallo' as ever glizzent; wi' white wings o'th'
untherside." "That wur indeed a strange brid," said Bangle;
"but wot mickle wur it, and wot wur it like i' shap?" "It
wur as like an ouzle as owt as ever theaw seed i' the lyve, o'
but th' kuller," said Chirrup. "An' weer did it come fro', an'
wot becoom on it?" inquired the earnest Bangle. "I seed it
fost ut top ov a stone wall; it wur plumin its wings i'th' sun-
leet, an' it lookt like a thing o' livin gowd—it made my heart
jump. An' then it coom nar th' cages, an' then nar th' twigs;
an' I thowt if ever mon won heaven, I should get that brid;
an' I lee beind th' rush hoyle, panting till I could yer my heart
thump—that bonny innocent brid—I thowt it wur mine, an'
thur coom a glare o' leet at made o' dazzle agen, an' thoose
white wings flash'd, an' away it went i'th' glizzen, an' th'
thunner-din, o'er th' moor." "An' weer wurto when theaw
seed it?" inquired Bangle. "I wurno far off Owd Birkle, an'
just oppo' th' edge o'th' Wilder Moor." "Aye, there's bonny

brids bin seen i' Owd Birkle afore," said the youth, flushing red, and then pale as a sheet. "But the bonnyist it seems hasno' bin taen yet." "Nowe, I wish it wur," interrupted Chirrup; "I'd giv o'th' cocks an' linnits at ever I cag'd, for yon beauty at I've seen an' lost to-day." "Happen not lost," observed Plant; "while there's life there's hope." "Thank yo' for that," said the youth Bangle; "while there's life, there's hope; aye, while there's life, there's hope." "Did I not olis tell the so," said his mother, looking significantly at Plant and Chirrup. "One on yo wants a brid, an' one a bride; but faint heart never won fair lady; an' lyen i' rush hoyles till th' bally warches 'll never catch yallo' wagtails." "It wur as much a wagtail as theaw'rt a dagtail," said Chirrup, "an' theaw'd be pottert iv only body co'd the so." "Wagtail or not," said the woman, "it wur a brid o' some sense, for it chose to fly wi' th' thunner devils sooner nor tarry wi' thy daubing lime twigs. I howd it *wit* good ut ony rate. As for that gawmblin o' mine," she continued, "he met ha' had his coo-dove lung sin, iv he'd nobbut ha' follod th' advice o' Limping Billy at Radcliffe. His feyther, dyed an' gwon as he is, wudno ha' ston sighen' an' yammerin' as this dus; he coom a kworten i'th' owd way, lung dree miles fro' Affeside, an' iv th' dur wurno oppent when he coom, he'd ha' punst it oppen. He didno come glooring at th' chimney reech an' then maunder back again."

The rain having set in dree, and several jugs of ale having been emptied, a free discourse ensued between Plant, Chirrup, and young Bangle, in which the woman occasionally took a part; and it was soon explained to Plant, for Chirrup seemed to have known some of the circumstances before, that the youth was love-smitten, and almost hopelessly so, the object of his passion being a young beauty residing in the house of her father, who held a small milk-farm on the hillside, not far from Old Birkle. The lad was of an ardent temperament, but bashful, as the truest lovers often are. His modest approaches had not been noticed by the adored one, and, as she had danced with another youth at Bury fair, he imagined she was irrecoverably lost to him, and the persuasion had almost driven him melancholy. Doctors had been applied to, but he was no better; philters and charms had been tried to bring down the cold-hearted maid, but all in vain—

> He sought her at the dawn of day;
> He sought her at the noonin';
> He sought her when the evenin' grey
> Had brought the hollow moon in.
>
> He called her on the darkest night,
> With wizard spells to bind her;
> And when the stars arose in light,
> He wandered forth to find her.

At length sorcerers and fortune-tellers were thought of, and Limping Billy,* a noted seer, residing at Radcliffe Bridge, having lastly been consulted, said the lad had no chance of gaining power over the damsel unless he could take Saint John's Fern seed; and if he but secured three grains of that he might bring to him whatever he wished, that walked, flew, or swam.

"Iv that's so," said Chirrup, on hearing the last, "I'd goo to th' seet o' devil-dom to win yon brid." "I'd goo to th' smell on't to win mine," said young Bangle. "An' I'd go to th' leet on't," said Plant, who had been listening with much interest to the conversation, and who had for years been wishful to engage companions for trial of that mysterious experiment. He then opened to them his lore in botany, telling them of wonderful herbs and sympathies and cures, and concluded by saying that he knew where the finest clump of fern in the country grew, and offered to conduct them to it at the proper time, viz., on the eve of Saint John the Baptist. It was agreed; and meantime Chirrup was to get particular instructions from Limping Billy for taking it; and so, night approaching, and the rain having abated, the three separated, and Plant and Chirrup went to their several homes.

* See Vol. I. p. 171.

CHAPTER XX.

BOGGART, OR FEYRIN-HO—FEYRIN-HO KLOOF—ST. JOHN'S FERN.

On the left hand, reader, as thou goest towards Manchester, ascending from Blackley, is a rather deep valley, green swarded, and embowered in plantations and older woods. A driving path, which thou enterest by a white gate hung on whale-jaw posts, leads down through a grove of young trees, by a modern and substantial farmhouse, with green shutters, sashed windows, and flowers peeping from the sills. A mantle of ivy climbs the wall, a garden is in front, and an orchard redolent of bloom, and fruit in season, nods on the hill-top above. Here, at the time Plant was speaking of, stood a very ancient house, built partly of old-fashioned bricks, and partly of a timber frame, filled with raddlings and daub (wicker-work, plastered with clay). It was a lone and desolate-looking house indeed, misty and fearful, even at noon-day. It was known as "Boggart-ho," or "Feyrin-ho"; and the gorge in which it is situated was and still is known as "Boggart," or "Feyrin-ho' Kloof," "the glen of the hall of spirits." Such a place might we suppose Milton had in contemplation when he wrote the passage of his inimitable poem—

> " Tells how the drudging goblin sweat,
> To earn his cream-bowl, duly set,
> When, in one night, ere glimpse of morn,
> His shadowy flail had thrash'd the corn
> Which ten day-labourers could not end ;
> Then lies him down, the lubber fiend ;
> And, stretch'd out all the chimney's length,
> Basks at the fire his hairy strength,
> And cropful, out of door he flings,
> Ere the first cock his matin sings."

By the side of the house, and through the whole length of the valley, wends a sickly, tan-coloured rindle, which, issuing from the great White Moss, comes down, tinged with the colour of its parent swamp. Opposite the modern house a forbidden road cuts through the plantation on the right towards Moston Lane. Another path leads behind the house, up precipitous banks, and through close bowers, to Booth Hall; and a third, the main one, proceeds along the kloof, by the side of the stream, and under sun-screening woods, until it forks into two roads: one a cattle track to "The Bell," in Moston, and the other a winding and precipitous footpath to a farmhouse at "Wood End," where it gains the broad upland, and emerges into unshaded day.

About half way up this kloof is an open cleared space of green and short sward: it is probably two hundred yards in length, by sixty in width, and passing along it from Blackley a group of fine oaks appear on a slight eminence, a little to the left. This part of the grove was, at the time we are concerned with, much more crowded with underwood than at present.* The bushes were then close and strong; fine sprouts of " yerth-groon " hazel and ash were common as nuts, whilst a thick bush of bramble, wild rose, and holly, gave the spot the appearance of a place inclosed and set apart for mysterious concealment. Intermingled with these almost impervious barriers were tufts of tall green fern, curling and bending gracefully, and a little separate from them, and nearer the old oaks, might be observed a few fern clumps of a singular appearance, of a paler green than' the others, with a flatter and a broader leaf, sticking up, rigid and expanded, like something stark with mute terror. These were "Saint John's Fern," and the finest of them was the one selected by Plant for the experiment now to be described.

A little before midnight, on the eve of Saint John, Plant, Chirrup, and Bangle were at the whale-jaw gate, before mentioned, and, having slightly scanned each other, they pro-

---

* Those oaks have been felled, and the kloof is now comparatively denuded of timber; the underwood on the left side is also nearly swept away. Sad inroads on the ominous gloom of the place! (*Bamford.*)

ceeded, without speaking, until they had crossed the brook at
a stepping-place opposite the old Feyrin-ho'. The first word
spoken was, " What hast thou ? "

" Mine is breawn an' roof,'

said Plant, exhibiting a brown earthen dish. " What hast
thou ? " he then asked.

" Mine is breet enough,"

said Chirrup, showing a pewter platter ; and continued,
" What hast thou ? "

" Teed wi' web an' woof,
Mine is deep enough,"

said Bangle, displaying a musty, dun skull, with the cap sawn
off above the eyes, and left flapping like a lid, by a piece of
tanned scalp, which still adhered. The interior cavities had
also been stuffed with moss and lined with clay, kneaded with
blood from human veins ; and the youth had secured the
skull to his shoulders by a twine of three strands of unbleached
flax, of undyed wool, and of woman's hair ; from which also
depended a raven black tress, which a wily crone had procured
from the maid he sought to obtain.

" That will do,"

said a voice, in a half whisper, from one of the low bushes
they were passing. Plant and Chirrup paused ; but Bangle,
who had evidently his heart on the accomplishment of the
undertaking, said, " Forward, if we turn now a spirit hath
spoken, we are lost. Come on," and they went forward.

A silence, like that of death, was around them as they
entered on the open platting. Nothing moved either in tree
or brake. Through a space in the foliage the stars were seen
pale in heaven ; and a crooked moon hung in a bit of blue,
amid motionless clouds. All was still and breathless, as if
earth, heaven, and the elements were aghast. Anything
would have been preferable to that unnatural stillness and

silence—the hoot of the night owl, the larum of the pit sparrow, the moan of the wind, the toll of a death bell, or the howl of a ban-dog would, inasmuch as they are things of this world, have been welcome sounds amid that horrid pause. But no sound came, no object moved.

Gasping, and with cold sweat oozing on his brow, Plant recollected that they were to shake the fern with a forked rod of witch hazel, and by no means must touch it with their hands; and he asked in a whisper if the others had brought one. Both said they had forgotten, and Chirrup said they had better never have come; but Plant drew his knife, and stepping into a moonlighted bush, soon returned with what was wanted, and they went forward.

The green knowe—the old oaks—the encircled space—and the fern—were now approached; the latter stiff and erect in a gleamy light.

"Is it deep neet?" said Bangle.

"It is," said Plant.

> " The star that bids the shepherd fold,
>   Now the top of heaven doth hold."

And they drew near. All was still and motionless.

Plant knelt on one knee and held his dish under the fern.

Chirrup held his broad plate next below, and

Bangle knelt, and rested the skull directly under both, on the green sod, the lid being up.

Plant said—

> " Good Saint John, this seed we crave,
>   We have dared; shall we have?"

A voice responded—

> " Now the moon is downward starting.
>   Moon and stars are all departing;
>   Quick, quick; shake, shake;
>   He whose heart shall soonest break
>   Let him take."

They looked, and perceived by a glance that a venerable form, in a loose robe, was near them.

Darkness came down like a swoop. The fern was shaken, the upper dish flew into pieces, the pewter one melted, the skull emitted a cry, and eyes glared in its sockets; lights broke, beautiful children were seen walking in their holiday clothes, and graceful female forms sung mournful and enchanting airs.

The men stood terrified and fascinated; and Bangle, gazing, bade " God bless 'em." A crash followed, as if the whole of the timber in the kloof was being splintered and torn up, strange and horrid forms appeared from the thickets, the men ran as if sped on the wind—they separated and lost each other. Plant ran towards the old house, and there, leaping the brook, he cast a glance behind him, and saw terrific shapes, some beastly, some part human, and some hellish, gnashing their teeth, and howling and uttering the most fearful and mournful tones, as if wishful to follow him, but unable to do so.

In an agony of terror he arrived at home, not knowing how he got there. He was, during several days, in a state bordering on unconsciousness ; and when he recovered he learned that Chirrup was found on the White Moss, raving mad, and chasing the wild birds. As for poor Bangle, he found his way home over hedge and ditch, running with supernatural and fearful speed—the skull's eyes glaring at his back, and the nether jaw grinning and jabbering frightful and unintelligible sounds. He had preserved the seed, however, and having taken it from the skull, he buried the latter at the cross-road from whence he had taken it. He then carried the spell out, and his proud love stood one night by his bedside in tears. But he had done too much for human nature; in three months after she followed his corpse, a real mourner, to the grave !

Such was the description my fellow prisoner gave of what occurred in the only trial he ever made with Saint John's Fern seed. He was full of old and quaint narratives and of superstitious lore, and often would beguile time by recounting them. Poor fellow ! a mysterious fate hung over him also. After his return from London, which was in a few days, he seemed to have become disgusted by the levity of his young and handsome but thoughtless wife. In a short time he suddenly disappeared from the country, and has not been heard of since.

CHAPTER XXI.

AUTHOR'S FOURTH APPEARANCE BEFORE THE PRIVY COUNCIL—A
MOTHER'S LAMENTATION FOR HER CHILD—A PAIR OF COCK-
NEYS—FIFTH ATTENDANCE BEFORE THE PRIVY COUNCIL, AND
AUTHOR'S DISCHARGE.

IT was, I think, on the 23rd of April that I was taken to
the Home Office, with George Plant, for my fourth examination. Having been introduced in the customary way, Lord
Sidmouth said, "Mr. Bamford, the information which we
expected to have received respecting you is not yet arrived;
therefore you will be remanded for another examination,
which will take place next week." To which I replied, "My
lord, if you think proper to wait for information which will
establish a charge of high treason against me, your lordship
may wait for ever, as I am certain that no such information
will arrive. I also went on to state that my conduct had
been quite opposed to treason, that I had certainly done all
which lay in my power to promote the cause of Parliamentary
reform, but I had always acted openly, and I trusted legally,
that I did not think his Majesty's ministers were fully acquainted with the state of the country and the condition of
the people; nor did I perceive how they could be, considering
the partial source from whence their information must be
derived; that the gentry, or what were called the higher
classes, were too proud or too indifferent to examine minutely
the abode of the poor and distressed; and that the interests of
many, as well as their want of accurate knowledge, tended to
elicit from them distorted or partial statements of facts. The
poor, I said, would be content could they only procure the

common necessaries of life by hard labour, but they could not even do that; and if ministers were thoroughly acquainted with the distress of the people, they would be almost surprised that the country was not a scene of confusion and horror, instead of being, as it was, peaceable though discontented. I said more than this, to the same purport; but the above are the principal heads on which I touched. The Council, as they always did, listened to me with patience and attention; and whatever I said was written down by gentlemen who appeared to be clerks or secretaries. I was then reconducted, and I and Plant were lodged in our old quarters; the day following he was discharged, and I was left alone.

One evening, as I was pacing my yard thoughtfully, and somewhat touched by that "hope deferred which maketh the heart sick," I was startled, astonished, and affected by a sudden burst of the most mournful and woe-fraught cries that ever struck my ear or moved my heart. At first it was a wild and agonised scream, intense and full, as if the soul was coming forth in unspeakable woe. It was a long time ere I could distinguish words amid that pity-moving cry; at length I heard a name and words of endearment. "My Ann," "my love," "my child." It was the name of my own child; and I must leave to parents who have known separation from their homes and their offspring, the task of appreciating my feelings, whilst, transfixed and listening, I caught the name of one so dear, accompanied by the most heart-broken lament that I had ever heard from human suffering. "My Ann!" "my love!" "my child!" "my beauty!" "my lost love!" and so she continued, raising and lowering her voice in an almost musical though entirely unartificial cadence, and in the simplest utterance of soul affliction. The mourner was a female convict, and the tidings had been brought to her in her cell that her child was dead.

Poor thing! I then felt that others might be more unhappy than myself, that I had still something to be thankful for, that I had yet a dove-nest in reserve at least—I so hoped—to which I could return after the present storm had blown over; and I retired to my ward for the night, contented with my lot, and entirely cured of the melancholy of "hope deferred." But the tones of that poor woman still rung in my ears; and I either dreamt of, or heard her cries, mingled with the night-wind, and resounding through the corridors of the prison.

On the 29th of April I was again introduced to the Privy Council. Lord Sidmouth said, "Mr. Bamford, I hope you are now before me for the last time. You will be discharged on conditions which will be read over to you: the same conditions which others of your fellow prisoners who have been discharged have accepted. I assure you I feel great pleasure in thus restoring you to your family." I said I hoped nothing would be proposed to me which was at variance with my political principles, as I could not consent to forego any rights to which, as an Englishman, I was entitled. His lordship could not desire me to give up the only right I had exercised— namely, the right of petition. His lordship said:—"Nothing will be proposed to you which an honest and a good man need object to. We are not averse to the subject petitioning for a redress of grievances; it is the manner in which that right has been exercised which we condemn; a right may be exercised in such a way that it becomes a wrong, and then we must object to it. Mr. Bamford, there are three things which I would have you to impress seriously on your mind. The first is, that the present distress of the country arises from un-avoidable circumstances; the second, that his Majesty's ministers will do all they can to alleviate such distress; and thirdly, no violence, of whatever description, will be tolerated, but it will be put down with a very strong hand. I wish you well; I assure you I wish you well, and I hope this is the last time I shall ever see you on an occasion like the present." I sincerely thanked his lordship for his good wishes and con-descension, and expressed my gratitude for the kindness I had experienced whilst his lordship's prisoner; and having asked, and very obligingly obtained, permission to have my liberty the following morning until the coach started, I bowed to his lordship and the Council and retired.

I was next conducted to the private office of Sir Nathaniel

Conant, which was in a lower room in the same building, where, in the presence of Sir Nathaniel and a clerk, I gave my personal bond in the sum of a hundred pounds, to be levied on my goods and chattels, " if, within twelve months from that day, I appeared in his Majesty's Court of Justice at Westminster."

CHAPTER XXII.

FURTHER KINDNESS FROM THE KING'S MESSENGERS—A GLIMPSE
AT THE "INFERNALS" — DEPARTURE FROM PRISON —
ARRIVAL AT HOME.

I MUST own that I did not clearly comprehend the meaning of
this bond. I could not guess at the reason why I was not to
"appear in his Majesty's Court of Justice at Westminster"
as well as any other British subject, and I could only account
for the exception by supposing it was the common form—a
mere official ceremony; indeed, Sir Nathaniel intimated as
much, and Lord Sidmouth had said it was only what the
others had agreed to. I afterwards, however, had reason to
suppose that it was intended to deter me, should I become so
disposed, from commencing an action in the above Court for
false imprisonment, which I could have done, the Indemnity
Bill not having then passed. I should imagine, however,
that my bond could hardly have kept me out of court * unless
the law could be made to commit *felo de se;* unless it could be
made to forbid a subject from claiming the law. But these
questions I must leave to those who are learned in such
matters.

On returning from Sir Nathaniel's office to the messengers'-
room, I was warmly congratulated by Mr. Williams, one of
the kind messengers who brought myself and companions from
Manchester. He cautioned me in a friendly manner as to my
future interference in politics, and concluded by inviting me to
his house the morning following, and soon after I stepped into
the coach and was conducted to my old quarters for the night.

* Certainly not as a plaintiff. He had merely been required to enter into
his own recognisances to keep the peace for twelve months.

After breakfast on the succeeding morn I collected every
article I had left in the provision and grocery line, and conveyed them under the door to the women, and bidding them
farewell I told them to keep up their spirits and mind their
good resolutions, and with a thousand thanks and their best
wishes I left them, and passed into the inner yard of the
prison. Here I encountered my fellow captive, James Leach,
from Rochdale. He was much affected, and expressed great
anxiety as to the duration of his imprisonment, and whether
it were likely to end in a capital charge, or be merely detention as a State prisoner. I consoled him as well as I could,
and told him I now thought it would be imprisonment only,
and that not of long duration. He sat down on a stone and
shed tears. I was grieved to see him so much depressed, and
did all in my power to cheer him, promising also to go over
and see his mother and other relatives, and inform them of his
actual condition and future prospects, and so I left him.

On arriving at the outer gates I found one of the turnkeys
smartly dressed, and ready to accompany and conduct me; for
I was a stranger to the town, and could not, therefore, have
readily found my way; neither was I to be lost sight of until
carried off by the coach. He first took me to Mr. Williams's,
I think, in Jermyn Street. We were received with much
kindness, and after partaking a lunch that gentleman made
me a handsome present of clothes. He also consigned to my
care as a present from Mr. Dykes, his fellow messenger, a
stock of clothes for the doctor and some money for his wife ;
and I must say that the kindness of these two gentlemen to
myself, and to my less fortunate comrades, was such as will,
whilst we live, deserve our warmest gratitude.

My conductor, as may be supposed, was rather well acquainted with the town, and with those descriptions of its
residents who were most frequently under the cognisance
of the police. He asked if I should like, before I quitted
London, to look into one or two of the "flash cribs,"
"shades," and "infernals," as he called them, and I assented. He led me then through lanes and alleys and sombre
courts, where our fellow-beings, both male and female, young

and old, appeared in squalid misery; and where a disgusting odour came reeking from the doors and windows of every habitation. I mentally ejaculated—

> "Oh! let me live afar from scenes like these,
> Where the winds bend the giant armed trees;
> Bask on my own dear banks of new-blown flowers,
> When thirsty Sol hath supp'd the morning showers."

The dens we visited were indeed horrid and murky shades. But it was morning, and the thieves and their "pals," as he termed the repulsive females, seemed drowsy and almost as blind as owls in sunshine. He showed me some characters who had already figured conspicuously at the Old Bailey, and one or two he pointed out who were to be had up again in a short time.

These revelations, the objects they distinguished, and the mode of life they illustrated, were almost wonders to me, and my conductor seemed to enjoy my surprise. I could almost write a book on the scenes and characters I noticed in the course of two hours. But such a production is the less necessary, inasmuch as a clever writer of the present day has, in his life and adventures of a famous housebreaker,* disclosed quite as much as it is either requisite or agreeable to know of such characters and their modes of life.

After visiting many other places, and gratifying my curiosity as well as the time would permit, I returned to the prison and dined. After again seeing James Leach, and bidding him good-bye, I took leave of Mr. Atkins, the governor, and of Mr. Beckett, the deputy-governor, whose behaviour to me had been uniformly kind, and leaving the prison with my morning's conductor, I mounted the coach at "The Peacock," Islington, and, quitting London, I arrived at home on the morning of the 2nd of May.

Having taken an early opportunity for delivering to Healey's wife the presents for her husband and herself, I afterwards, in conformity with my promise to James Leach, visited his mother and other relatives at Spotland Bridge, near Rochdale.

* Harrison Ainsworth's "Jack Sheppard."

To these poor but industrous and respectable people I gave a faithful account of the situation in which I had left him; told them all about our imprisonment and the treatment we had experienced, and concluded with as consoling a prospect for the future as I thought the facts justified. I felt great pleasure in this latter part of my mission, because I wished to soothe the old woman's uneasiness on account of her son, and I came away with the agreeable assurance that I had contributed to make this family happier than I found it.

I now went to work, my wife weaving beside me, and my little girl, now become doubly dear, attending school, or going short errands for her mother. Why was I not content? Why was not my soul filled and thankful? What would I more? What could mortal enjoy beyond a sufficiency to satisfy hunger and thirst, apparel, to make him warm and decent, a home for shelter and repose, and the society of those he loved? All these I had, and still was craving—craving for something for "the nation," for some good for every person, forgetting all the time to appreciate and to husband the blessings I had on every side around me; and, like some honest enthusiasts of the present day, supervising the affairs of the nation to the great neglect of my own, of my—

" Hours more dear than drops of gold."

But it was not with us then as it is now; and we have that excuse to plead. We had none to direct or oppose us, except a strong-handed Government, whose politics were as much hated as their power was dreaded. We had not any of our own rank with whom to advise for the better, no man of other days who had gone through the ordeal of experience, and whose judgment might have directed our self-devotion, and have instructed us that, before the reform we sought could be obtained and profited by, there must be another, a deeper reform, emerging from our hearts, and first blessing our households by the production of every good we could possibly accomplish in our humble spheres, informing us also, and confirming it by all history, that governments might change from the despotic to the anarchical, when as surely as death would come the despotic again; and that no redemption for the masses could exist save one that should arise from their own virtue and knowledge; that king tyranny and mob tyranny, the worst of all, might alternately bear sway; and that no barrier could be effectually interposed save the self-knowledge and self-control of a reformed people.

But, as I said, we had none such to advise. Our worthy old major * was to us a political reformer only; not a moral one. His counsels were good so far as they went, but they did not go to the root-end of Radicalism. He seemed to have forgotten, in the simplicity of a guileless heart, good old man as he was, that the people themselves wanted reforming, that they were ignorant and corrupt, and that the source must be purified before a pure and free government could be maintained.

In the absence therefore of such wholesome monition—in the ardour, also, and levity of youth—and impelled by a sincere and disinterested wish to deserve the gratitude of my working fellow countrymen, it is scarcely to be wondered at that I soon forgot whatever merely prudential reflections my better sense had whispered to me whilst in durance, and that, with a strong, though discreetly tempered zeal, I determined to go forward in the cause of Parliamentary reform.

And so, as it were, like another Crusoe, I lay with my little boat in still water, waiting for the first breeze to carry me again to the billows.

* Cartwright.

CHAPTER XXIII.

SOON after my return I found that a secret influence had
been at work during my absence exciting to and carrying on
private meetings and suspicious intrigues in our neighbourhood; and that one of my neighbours in particular, whom I
wished better, had been so deluded as to give his attendance
at one or two meetings of a suspicious character which had
been held in Yorkshire. I became aware also, though my
information was not very distinct, that my old acquaintance,
Joseph Mitchell, and another person, a stranger whom I did
not know, were the chief movers in these proceedings, that
the stranger had made frequent inquiries after me since my
return, and that I might expect to hear shortly of a decisive
blow being struck for " the liberties of the country."

I treated these reports with contempt or reprehension, as
might be requisite at the time. The enunciation of Mitchell's
name certainly did not awaken confidence on my part; nor
did the intelligence that he was moving about with a well-
dressed and apparently affluent stranger at all tend to repress
certain forebodings which had begun to arise in my mind.

One day, when I was at work, a message was sent requesting
me to step over to the Dog and Partridge publichouse, which
was opposite to where I lived. I went, and found an aged,
grey-headed man, stooping beneath probably seventy years,
his venerable locks hanging on his shoulders, and having in

one hand a stick, and on the other arm a basket containing
rolls of worsted and woollen yarn, and small articles of hosiery,
which he seemed to have for sale. On looking at him more
steadfastly I recognised him as my old co-delegate to London,
from the town of Derby, Thomas Bacon, and I shook him
heartily by the hand and sat down beside him. With him was
a tall, decent-looking young man, much like a town's weaver,
wearing a blue coat, and with a clean white apron wrapped
about his waist. After a civil salutation to him also, I
addressed friend Bacon, and asked what particular business
might have brought him to our part of the country, so far
from his residence. With a smile he pointed to his wares,
but almost immediately gave me to understand that he carried
them only as a disguise to his real business. He said a delegate meeting was to be held in Yorkshire, which would cause
a finishing blow to be levelled at the boroughmongers, as I
should shortly hear ; and that a man from Middleton, whose
name he gave, and who attended several previous meetings,
was particularly wanted on the present occasion ; and he
concluded by asking me to direct him to that man.

I paused, as if striving to recollect the person, repeating the
name, and considering meantime what might be the consequences to my neighbour if I sent the unconscious emissary
to his house, and I finished by declaring there was no such
man, and that the name must be a fictitious one. I then
took the opportunity to caution my old friend against forming
connections so liable to abuse, and so dangerous and unwise,
as well as hurtful to the country, directed, as they were,
against a strong Government, and for the overthrow, by force,
of a national order of things. The old man seemed struck by
what I said about the delegate from Middleton having given
a false name ; but he huff'd at my advice, and said I should,
notwithstanding there might be a traitor or two, soon learn
something which I at present little understood. I reminded
him I had but just returned from a Government prison, and
told him that from what I had observed, or been able to
gather in various ways, I was sure no force would avail in
overturning the present state of things, that I believed

ministers had eyes to see and ears to hear and tongues to whisper whatever occurred; and that he might depend on it neither he nor any persons with whom he might be connected could take one step beyond the pale of the law, without being instantly in the gripe of the executive. I entreated him to consider these things, to pause, and not to be led away and lead others at his time of life.

He drank his beer rather hastily, took up his basket, thanked me for my good wishes, but declined my advice, saying he was " too old a politician to be counselled by one so young as myself"; and so, motioning his companion, they both went down the street, and, to my satisfaction, took the road back towards Manchester.

This pertinacious old man was, in a few weeks after, arraigned for high treason at Derby, and pleading guilty, was, with fourteen others, transported for life : whilst the young man, who was one of the Turners, was hung and beheaded, with the equally unfortunate Brandreth and Ludlam. The stranger whom Joseph Mitchell had so assiduously introduced amongst the discontented classes of Lancashire, Yorkshire, and Derbyshire, first inveigled them into treasonable associations, then to armed insurrections ; he got them to arm as has been done in the present day, and then betrayed them. How one, if not more, of my neighbours at Middleton escaped has just been shown. I thought it no dishonour to deny a person and a name when apprised that their discovery would probably lead to the ruin of the parties sought after, if not of many others.

That stranger, that betrayer, was Oliver the spy.

It may perhaps not be amiss to refer to a few of the more prominent national events which occurred in the year 1817, after my liberation from prison. On June 13th the Habeas Corpus Act was further suspended. On the 16th Sir Francis Burdett's motion relative to the conduct of Oliver the spy, who had consummated his villainies, and had been accidentally unmasked, was made in the House of Commons. On the 4th of October there were great disturbances at Worcester. On the 18th Jeremiah Brandreth was tried, and found guilty of high treason, and on the 22nd was sentenced, with Turner and Ludlam, to be executed. On the 5th of November the Princess Charlotte died, lamented by the whole nation; and it was expected, that now the hand of death had struck within the Prince Regent's threshold, his heart would be moved, and he would respite the prisoners under sentence at Derby; especially when he considered that they had been instigated to crime by a Government agent—Oliver the spy. But his heart was untouched, and the day after that on which his daughter expired, they were brought forth and executed. On the 28th of January, 1818, a Bill was introduced into Parliament to restore the Habeas Corpus Act; and on the 10th of March an Indemnity Bill passed.

By this time all the State prisoners had been released, and had arrived at home. My friend Healey returned quite an altered man; instead of being flattish in front, and somewhat gaunt looking, he came home plump and round, and genteelly dressed, with one or two large boxes, a rather heavy purse, and his finger bedizened by a broad gold ring, which he said he had received for an " extraordinary operation on the teeth of a great lady of Devonshire."

James Leach also arrived in Middleton about the same time, on his way home. I went to see him at the public-house where he stopped, and found him also much altered in outward appearance and manner. Instead of the simple-minded and soft-hearted lad I had left at Coldbath Fields, I now found a person smartly attired, and with some cash in his pockets. I perceived also that he affected superiority, and was somewhat distant, and that my neighbours took notice of this. But, as I despised all affectation, and not the less because he displayed it, and as I cared nothing about his motives for coolness, I did not trouble him with any questions on either subject, but merely remarked them, and he went his way.

I found afterwards that this young man and his relatives had been secretly propagating reports that I had acted as a spy for the Government; that I had become that being most abhorrent to my soul; and had, in fact, purchased my own liberation from prison by betraying this James Leach and my companions.

This was a sore blow to my feelings,—heavier from not being expected, and coupled as it was with deep ingratitude. I had the consolation, however, to know that I had not deserved this at their hands, that I had merited the very reverse of detraction, and that their best good offices would not have been more than equivalent to the entire good faith with which I had served them in their hour of humbled sorrow. But why should I expect them, or their like, to reciprocate with me? Because I judged of them as was then my wont with respect to nearly all mankind, that their sentiments were as disinterested as my own, and that they were worthy of friendship because they stood in need of it When, however, I found out my error, the pride of an indignant though wounded spirit was my solace, and I looked with serene contempt above the calumny and the calumniators, leaving to time the obliteration of the injury, and the infliction of shame on my detractors.

The principal of these is now reputed to be wealthy. With the aid of political friends he entered the provision line, soon after his return from prison. He has maintained *his* distance and *his* superiority ever since, and he is welcome to both, and his riches to boot. He has, however, never yet found an opportunity to acknowledge the service I formerly rendered him; and it was not until one of the late elections for Rochdale that I obtained distinct evidence of the part he had been playing, though I knew as much; I then, however, sent for him into a public company, where his words were repeated to his face, and, not being able to deny them, or to prove anything against me, he acknowledged the letter, and so I left him, and have ever since held him at *his* distance, and in *his* unenviable superiority.

Healey also scarcely acted the part of a friend in these matters. He heard the slanders, and conveyed them to me by hints and half-sentences—a line of conduct which I should not now tolerate for one moment—but he never spoke out candidly, nor disclosed his authors. He, however, had his reward. I did that for him which I would have done at the time for the other, or for any friend in need. He became ill of the typhus fever, and when he sent for me he was fast sinking under the worst symptoms of the disorder. He took medicines, but they seemed of no avail, and he expressed his belief that he should die. May I be forgiven, for I swore he should not ! and I got a large tub in which I placed him, and his wife filled it nearly to the brim with water as hot as he could bear. I washed and laved him all over, and then lifted him out, and rubbed him with a cloth till his skin burned, and then I put him into bed, and covered him well up ; he fell into a sound sleep, awoke streaming with perspiration, and from that time he began to get better.

CHAPTER XXIV.

WITH the restoration of the Habeas Corpus Act, the agitation for reform was renewed. A public meeting on the subject was held at Westminster, on the 28th of March and in June; Sir Francis Burdett's motion for reform was negatived in the House of Commons.

Numerous meetings followed in various parts of the country; and Lancashire, and the Stockport borders of Cheshire, were not the last to be concerned in public demonstrations for reform. At one of these meetings, which took place at Lydgate, in Saddleworth, and at which Bagguley, Drummond, Fitton, Haigh, and others were the principal speakers, I, in the course of an address, insisted on the right, and the propriety also, of females who were present at such assemblages voting by a show of hand for or against the resolutions. This was a new idea; and the women, who attended numerously on that bleak ridge, were mightily pleased with it. The men being nothing dissentient, when the resolution was put the women held up their hands amid much laughter; and ever from that time females voted with the men at the Radical meetings. I was not then aware that the new impulse thus given to political movement would in a short time be applied to charitable and religious purposes. But it was so; our females voted at every subsequent meeting; it became the practice, female political unions were formed, with their chairwoman, committees, and other officials; and from us the practice was soon borrowed, very judiciously no doubt, and applied in a greater or less degree to the promotion of religious and charitable institutions.

Amongst the meetings for reform held in the early part of the summer of 1819 were the one which took place on Spa Fields, London, at which Mr. Hunt was chairman, and another held at Birmingham, at which Major Cartwright and Sir Charles Wolseley * were elected to act as legislatorial attornies for that town in Parliament.

It would seem that these movements in the country induced our friends at Manchester to adopt a course similar to that at Birmingham, and it was accordingly arranged that a meeting for that purpose should be held on St. Peter's Field on the 9th of August. But the object of that meeting having been declared illegal by the authorities, it was countermanded, and another was appointed to be held on the 16th of the same month.

It was deemed expedient that this meeting should be as morally effective as possible, and that it should exhibit a spectacle such as had never before been witnessed in England. We had frequently been taunted by the press with our ragged, dirty appearance at these assemblages ; with the confusion of our proceedings, and the mob-like crowds in which our numbers were mustered ; and we determined that, for once at least, these reflections should not be deserved—that we would disarm the bitterness of our political opponents by a display of cleanliness, sobriety, and decorum, such as we never before had exhibited. In short, we would deserve their respect by showing that we respected ourselves, and knew how to exercise our rights of meeting, as it were well Englishmen always should do, in a spirit of sober thoughtfulness, respectful, at the same time, to the opinions of others.

" Cleanliness," " sobriety," " order," were the first injunctions issued by the committee, to which, on the suggestion of Mr. Hunt, was subsequently added that of " peace." The fulfilment of the two first was left to the good sense of those who intended to join our procession to this " grand meeting"; the observance of the third and

---

* Sir Charles Wolseley, Bart., of Wolseley, Staffordshire.

of the last injunctions—order, peace—were provided for by general regulations. Order in our movements was obtained by drilling; and peace, on our parts, was secured by a prohibition of all weapons of offence or defence, and by the strictest discipline, of silence, steadiness, and obedience to the directions of the conductors. Thus our arrangements, by constant practice and an alert willingness, were soon rendered perfect, and ten thousand men moved with the regularity of ten score.

These drillings were also, to our sedentary weavers and spinners, periods of healthful exercise and enjoyment. Our drillmasters were generally old soldiers of the line, or of militia, or of local militia regiments; they put the lads through their facings in quick time, and soon taught them to march with a steadiness and regularity which would not have disgraced a regiment on parade. When dusk came, and we could no longer see to work, we jumped from our looms and rushed to the sweet, cool air of the fields, or the waste lands, or the green lane-sides. We mustered, we fell into rank, we faced, marched, halted, faced about, countermarched, halted again, dressed, and wheeled in quick succession, and without confusion; or, in the grey of a fine Sunday morn, we would saunter through the mists, fragrant with the night odour of flowers and of new hay, and ascending the Tandle Hills, salute the broad sun as he climbed from behind the high moors of Saddleworth. Maidens would sometimes come with their milk-cans from the farms of Hoolswood or Gerrard-hey, or the fold near us; and we would sit and take delicious draughts, new from the churn, for which we paid the girls in money, whilst a favoured youth or so might be permitted to add something more—a tender word or a salute—when, blushing and laughing, away would the nymphs run for a fresh supply to carry home.

Next would follow a long drill in squads; and so expert were the youths that they would form a line and march down the face, or up the steep, or along the sides of the Rushpenny, and, suddenly halting, would dress in an instant in a manner which called forth the praises of the old campaigners. Then, when they broke for a little rest, would follow a jumping match, or a race, or a friendly wrestle, or a roll down the hill amid the laughter of others sitting in the sun. Some would be squatted on the lee of a bush of gorse or tall fern; some reading, some conversing in earnest discussion on the state of trade or national affairs, or on their own privations or those of their neighbours—for few secrets were kept of those matters— some would be seen smoking their pipes, kindled by burning-glasses; and so till the bugle sounded to drill, and after that, away to breakfast.

Such was one of our drilling parties. There were no arms— there was no use for any, no pretence for any, nor would they have been permitted. Some of the elderly men, the old soldiers or those who came to watch, might bring a walking staff, or a young fellow might pull a stake from a hedge in going to drill or in returning home; but assuredly we had nothing like arms about us. There were no armed meetings, there were no midnight drillings. Why should we seek to conceal what we had no hesitation in performing in broad day? Such as I have described were all our drillings, about which so much was afterwards said. We obtained by them all we sought or thought off—an expertness and order whilst moving in bodies; and there was no hyper-bole in the statement which a magistrate afterwards made on oath, that "the party with the blue and green banners came upon the field in beautiful order!" adding, I think, that "not until then did he become alarmed."

Some extravagancies, some acts, and some speeches better left alone certainly did take place. When the men clapped their hands in "standing at ease," some would jokingly say it was "firing," whilst those who were sent to observe us (and probably we were seldom unattended by such), and who knew little about military motions, would take the joke as a reality, and report accordingly; whence probably it would be surmised that we had arms, and that our drillings were only preparatory to their more effective use.

On the afternoon of Friday, the 13th of August, I saw Mr. Hunt, at the residence of Mr. Johnson, at Smedley. Tuke, the painter, was amending Mr. Hunt's portrait, as indeed it wanted. In the course of conversation Mr. Hunt expressed himself as apprehensive lest the people from the country should bring arms to the meeting on the following Monday ; and he desired me to caution those from Middleton against so doing. He also showed me a letter on a placard, addressed to " The Reformers of Manchester and its Neighbourhood," wherein he entreated them to come to the meeting " armed only with a self-approving conscience." He said that if the soldiers did attack the people, and take their caps of liberty and their banners, still he hoped they would proceed to the meeting, and not commit any violence.

I must own that this was new and somewhat unpalatable advice to me. I had not the most remote wish to attack either person or property, but I had always supposed that Englishmen, whether individually or in bodies, were justifiable by law in repelling an attack when in the King's peace, as I certainly calculated we should be, whilst in attendance at a legally constituted assemblage. My crude notions led me to opine that we had a right to go to this place, and that, conse- quently, there would not be any protection in law to those who might choose to interrupt us in our right. I was almost certain there could be no harm whatever in taking a score or two of cudgels, just to keep the specials at a respectful distance from our line. But this was not permitted.

Still I scarcely liked the idea of walking my neighbours into a crowd both personally and politically adverse to us, and without means to awe them, or to defend ourselves. Was it not a fact that a numerous body of men had been sworn in to act as special constables ?—was not an armed association formed at Manchester ? and had not weapons been liberally distributed ? and what could we do, if attacked by those men, with nothing to defend ourselves ? But Mr. Hunt combated these notions. " Were there not the laws of the country to protect us ? would not their authority be upheld by those sworn to administer them ? And then was it likely at all that magistrates would permit a peaceable and legal assemblage to be interfered with ? If we were in the right, were they not our guardians? If wrong, could they not send us home by reading the Riot Act? Assuredly, whilst we respected the law, all would be well on our side."

But on the Sunday morning a circumstance occurred which probably eradicated from the minds of the magistrates, and our opponents generally, whatever sentiments of indulgence they might have hitherto retained towards us. It is set forth in the following document:—

"Examination of James Murray, of No. 2, Withy Grove, Manchester, Confectioner, who, on his Oath, saith that on Sunday last, the 15th instant, he was at White Moss, near Middleton, about five miles from Manchester, between three and four o'clock in the morning, and saw there assembled between fourteen and fifteen hundred men, the greatest number of whom were formed in two bodies, in the form of solid squares; the remainder were in small parties of between twenty and thirty each; there were about thirty such parties, each under the direction of a person acting as a drill serjeant, and were going through military movements; that Examinant went amongst them, and immediately one of the drill serjeants asked him to fall in. He said he thought he should soon, or gave some such answer; he then began to move away, upon which some persons who were drilling cried out, 'Spies!' This Examinant, and William Shawcross, and Thomas Rymer and his son (all of whom had accompanied this Examinant from Manchester) continued to retire; the body of men then cried out, 'Mill them!—murder them!' Near one hundred men then pursued this Examinant and his companions; they overtook them near a lane-end, at the edge of the Moss, and began to pelt them with clods of earth. They at last came up to the Examinant and his companions, and beat them very severely. Examinant begged they would not murder him; but the general cry was, 'Damn him! kill him! murder him!' Examinant said, 'You treat me very differently to what nations treat each other's prisoners when they are at war. Suppose that I am an enemy, you ought to treat me as a prisoner.' They said, 'How will you treat us if you take us prisoners when we come to Manchester?'

"Examinant knew at the time that a meeting was appointed for the next day (Monday) at Manchester.

"The men kept beating Examinant all the time; at last they debated among themselves whether they would kill Examinant or forgive him, and they determined to forgive him provided he would go down upon his knees and beg pardon to them, and swear never to be a king's man again, or to mention the name of a king. Examinant complied to save his life, they standing over him with sticks, as he apprehended, to murder him, provided he had objected. They afterwards went away. Examinant was not previously acquainted with any of the persons assembled that he saw, but is certain that he should know again two of those who beat him.

"The greatest part of the number assembled had stout sticks from three to four feet long.

"In consequence of the ill-treatment received by Examinan as above, he was confined to his bed for three days.

"Sworn at Manchester before me, this 21st day of August, 1819. } JAMES MURRAY.

"RA. FLETCHER."

Some years afterwards a young man named Robert Lancashire informed me that the detection of, and assault on, these parties happened as follows :—

He said he was coming from his work at Manchester, late on Saturday night, when he fell into company with some men whom he did not know, but who proved to be Murray and his companions. The men began to converse with him chiefly on the state of the country, and, as he was of a communicative turn, they questioned him about the drilling parties, and particularly those which were said to frequent the White Moss ; and he told them all he knew about such parties. The people at the "White Lion" at Blackley were up, and they all went into the house and had something to drink, during which he promised to show the men into the road leading to the Moss. He also heard them use expressions to each other which convinced him they were sent by the police to watch the drillers ;

and, as they were going to take advantage of others, he determined to do the same by them. He accordingly put them into a road which led to the Moss, and afterwards, taking a shorter way over the fields, he apprised the drillers of the sort of persons who were coming, and the consequence was that they were set upon and beaten, as described by James Murray.

This circumstance, as before intimated, was unfortunate for us. On the return of Murray and his companions to Manchester they were visited by some of the authorities, to whom their statements were given. A special meeting was held at the police office the same forenoon; and it is probable that, at that meeting, it was determined to return a full measure of severity to us on the following day, should any circumstance arise to sanction such a proceeding.

CHAPTER XXV.

THE same forenoon we had a meeting in Langley Dingle, a
pleasant and retired spot, where was a sheltered bank sloping
towards the sun, with plenty of bushes and dry grass, and a
rindle tumbling at our feet. Here—whilst some were sitting,
some lying, and some pacing to and fro—we discussed and
arranged our plans for the succeeding day.

All allowed that the occurrence at the White Moss was an
unfavourable one; and I, now more than ever impressed with
the belief that we should meet with opposition of some sort,
proposed that a party of men with stout cudgels should be
appointed to take care of the colours, in order that, at all
events, they might be preserved. This was discussed at some
length, but the more confiding views of my neighbours, together with Mr. Hunt's admonition, prevailing, my suggestion
was overruled, and we shortly afterward separated.

I may say that, with myself, the preservation of our colours,
under any circumstances, was a point of honour worth any
sacrifice. Fortunately, more placid views than mine prevailed;
and if an aspect of entire confidence could have disarmed
party feeling, it would have been done the following morning.
But such is seldom the case; and it was not so in the present
instance, as will soon appear.

By eight o'clock on the morning of Monday, the 16th of
August, 1819, the whole town of Middleton might be said to

be on the alert: some to go to the meeting, and others to see the procession, the like of which, for such a purpose, had never before taken place in that neighbourhood.

First were selected twelve of the most comely and decent-looking youths, who were placed in two rows of six each, with each a branch of laurel held presented in his hand, as a token of amity and peace; then followed the men of several districts in fives; then the band of music, an excellent one; then the colours: a blue one of silk, with inscriptions in golden letters, "Unity and Strength," "Liberty and Fraternity"; a green one of silk, with golden letters, "Parliaments Annual," "Suffrage Universal"; and betwixt them, on a staff, a handsome cap of crimson velvet with a tuft of laurel, and the cap tastefully braided, with the word "*Libertas*" in front. Next were placed the remainder of the men of the districts in fives.

Every hundred men had a leader, who was distinguished by a sprig of laurel in his hat; others similarly distinguished were appointed over these, and the whole were to obey the directions of a principal conductor, who took his place at the head of the column, with a bugleman to sound his orders. Such were our dispositions on the ground at Barrowfields. At the sound of the bugle not less than three thousand men formed a hollow square, with probably as many people around them, and, an impressive silence having been obtained, I reminded them that they were going to attend the most important meeting that had ever been held for Parliamentary Reform, and I hoped their conduct would be marked by a steadiness and seriousness befitting the occasion, and such as would cast shame upon their enemies, who had always represented the reformers as a mob-like rabble; but they would see they were not so that day. I requested they would not leave their ranks, nor show carelessness, nor inattention to the order of their leaders; but that they would walk comfortably and agreeably together. Not to offer any insult or provocation by word or deed; nor to notice any persons who might do the same by them, but to keep such persons as quiet as possible; for if they began to retaliate, the least disturbance might serve as a pretext for dispersing the meeting. If the peace officers should come to arrest myself or any other person, they were not to offer any resistance, but suffer them to execute their office peaceably. When at the meeting, they were to keep themselves as select as possible, with their banners in the centre, so that if individuals straggled, or got away from the main body, they would know where to find them again by seeing their banners; and when the meeting was dissolved, they were to get close around their banners and leave the town as soon as possible, lest, should they stay drinking, or loitering about the streets, their enemies should take advantage, and send some of them to the New Bailey. I also said that, in conformity with a rule of the committee, no sticks, nor weapons of any description, would be allowed to be carried in the ranks; and those who had such were requested to put them aside, or leave them with some friend until their return. In consequence of this order many sticks were left behind; and a few only of the oldest and most infirm amongst us were allowed to carry their walking staves. I may say with truth that we presented a most respectable assemblage of labouring men; all were decently, though humbly attired; and I noticed not even one who did not exhibit a white Sunday's shirt, a neck-cloth, and other apparel in the same clean, though homely condition.

My address was received with cheers; it was heartily and unanimously assented to. We opened into column, the music struck up, the banners flashed in the sunlight, other music was heard, it was that of the Rochdale party coming to join us. We met, and a shout from ten thousand startled the echoes of the woods and dingles. Then all was quiet save the breath of music; and with intent seriousness we went on.

Our whole column, with the Rochdale people, would probably consist of six thousand men. At our head were a hundred or two of women, mostly young wives, and mine own was amongst them. A hundred or two of our handsomest girls, sweethearts to the lads who were with us, danced to the music, or sung snatches of popular songs; a score or two of children were sent back, though some went forward; whilst on each side of our line walked some thousands of stragglers.

And thus, accompanied by our friends and our dearest and most tender connections, we went slowly towards Manchester.

At Blackley the accession to our ranks and the crowd in the road had become much greater. At Harpurhey we halted, whilst the band and those who thought proper, refreshed with a cup of prime ale from Sam Ogden's tap. When the bugle sounded every man took his place, and we advanced.

From all that I had heard of the disposition of the authorities, I had scarcely expected that we should be allowed to enter Manchester in a body. I had thought it not improbable that they, or some of them, would meet us with a civil and military escort; would read the Riot Act, if they thought proper, and warn us from proceeding, and that we should then have nothing to do but turn back and hold a meeting in our town I had even fancied that they would most likely stop us at the then toll-gate, where the roads forked towards Colly-hurst and Newtown ; but when I saw both those roads open, with only a horseman or two prancing before us, I began to think that I had over-estimated the forethought of the authorities, and I felt somewhat assured that we should be allowed to enter the town quietly, when, of course, all probability of interruption would be at an end.

We had got a good length on the higher road towards Colly-hurst, when a messenger arrived from Mr. Hunt with a request that we would return, and come the lower road; and lead up his procession into Manchester. I at first determined not to comply. I did not like to entangle ourselves and the great mass now with us in the long hollow road through Newtown, where, whatever happened, it would be difficult to advance or retreat or disperse, and I kept moving on. But a second messenger arrived, and there was a cry of " Newtown," " Newtown," and so I gave the word, " left shoulders forward," and running at the charge step we soon gained the other road, and administered to the vanity of our "great leader," by heading his procession from Smedley Cottage.

A circumstance interesting to myself now occurred. On the bank of an open field on our left I perceived a gentleman observing us attentively. He beckoned me, and I went to him. He was one of my late employers. He took my hand, and rather concernedly, but kindly, said he hoped no harm was intended by all those people who were coming in. I said "I would pledge my life for their entire peaceableness." I asked him to notice them, "did they look like persons wishing to outrage the law? were they not, on the contrary, evidently heads of decent working families? or members of such families?" "No, no," I said, "my dear sir, and old respected master, if any wrong or violence take place, they will be committed by men of a different stamp from these." He said he was very glad to hear me say so; he was happy he had seen me, and gratified by the manner in which I had expressed myself. I asked, did he think we should be interrupted at the meeting? he said he did not believe we should; "then," I replied, "all will be well"; and shaking hands, with mutual good wishes, I left him, and took my station as before.

At Newtown we were welcomed with open arms by the poor Irish weavers, who came out in their best drapery, and uttered blessings and words of endearment, many of which were not understood by our rural patriots. Some of them danced, and others stood with clasped hands and tearful eyes, adoring almost, that banner whose colour was their national one, and the emblem of their green island home. We thanked them by the band striking up, "Saint Patrick's day in the morning." They were electrified; and we passed on, leaving those warm-hearted suburbans capering and whooping like mad.

Having squeezed ourselves through the gully of a road below St. Michael's Church, we traversed Blackley Street and Miller's Lane, and went along Swan Street and Oldham Street, frequently hailed in our progress by the cheers of the towns-people. We learned that other parties were on the field before us, and that the Lees and Saddleworth Union had been led by Doctor Healey, walking before a pitch-black flag, with staring white letters, forming the words, "Equal Representation or Death," "Love"—two hands joined and a heart; all in white paint, and presenting one of the most sepulchral looking objects that could be contrived. The idea of my diminutive friend leading a funeral procession of his own patients, such it appeared to me, was calculated to force a smile even at that thoughtful moment.

We now perceived we had lost the tail of our train, and understood we had come the wrong way, and should have led down Shudehill, and along Hanging Ditch, the Market-place, and Deansgate ; which route Hunt and his party had taken. I must own I was not displeased at this separation. I was of opinion that we had tendered homage quite sufficient to the mere vanity of self-exhibition, too much of which I now thought was apparent.

Having crossed Piccadilly, we went down Mosley Street, then almost entirely inhabited by wealthy families. We took the left side of St. Peter's Church, and at this angle we wheeled quickly and steadily into Peter Street, and soon approached a wide unbuilt space, occupied by an immense multitude, which opened and received us with loud cheers. We walked into that chasm of human beings, and took our station from the hustings across the causeway of Peter Street, and so remained, undistinguishable from without, but still forming an almost unbroken line, with our colours in the centre.

My wife I had not seen for some time ; but when last I caught a glimpse of her, she was with some decent married females ; and thinking the party quite safe in their own discretion, I felt not much uneasiness on their account, and so had greater liberty in attending to the business of the meeting.

In about half an hour after our arrival the sounds of music and reiterated shouts proclaimed the near approach of Mr. Hunt and his party ; and in a minute or two they were seen coming from Deansgate, preceded by a band of music and several flags. On the driving seat of a barouche sat a neatly dressed female, supporting a small flag, on which were some emblematical drawings and an inscription. Within the carriage were Mr. Hunt, who stood up, Mr. Johnson, of Smedley Cottage ; Mr. Moorhouse, of Stockport ; Mr. Carlile, of London ; Mr. John Knight, of Manchester ; and Mr. Saxton, a sub-editor of the *Manchester Observer.* Their approach was hailed by one universal shout from probably eighty thousand persons. They threaded their way slowly past us and through the crowd, which Hunt eyed, I thought, with almost as much of astonishment as satisfaction. This spectacle could not be otherwise in his view than solemnly impressive. Such a mass of human beings he had not beheld till then. His responsibility must weigh on his mind. Their power for good or evil was irresistible, and who should direct that power? Himself alone who had called it forth. The task was great, and not without its peril. The meeting was indeed a tremendous one. He mounted the hustings; the music ceased; Mr. Johnson proposed that Mr. Hunt should take the chair; it was seconded, and carried by acclamation; and Mr. Hunt, stepping towards the front of the stage, took off his white hat, and addressed the people.

Whilst he was doing so, I proposed to an acquaintance that, as the speeches and resolutions were not likely to contain anything new to us, and as we could see them in the papers, we should retire awhile and get some refreshment, of which I stood much in need, being not in very robust health. He assented, and we had got to nearly the outside of the crowd, when a noise and strange murmur arose towards the church. Some persons said it was the Blackburn people coming, and I stood on tip-toe and looked in the direction whence the noise proceeded, and saw a party of cavalry in blue and white uniform come trotting, sword in hand, round the corner of a garden-wall, and to the front of a row of new houses, where they reined up in a line.

"The soldiers are here," I said; "we must go back and see what this means." "Oh," some one made reply, "they are only come to be ready if there should be any disturbance in the meeting." "Well, let us go back," I said, and we forced our way towards the colours.

On the cavalry drawing up they were received with a shout of good-will, as I understood it. They shouted again, waving their sabres over their heads; and then, slackening rein, and striking spur into their steeds, they dashed forward and began cutting the people.

" Stand fast," I said, " they are riding upon us ; stand fast."
And there was a general cry in our quarter of " Stand fast."
The cavalry were in confusion · they evidently could not,
with all the weight of man and horse, penetrate that compact mass of human beings ; and their sabres were plied to
hew a way through naked held-up hands and defenceless
heads ; and then chopped limbs and wound-gaping skulls
were seen ; and groans and cries were mingled with the
din of that horrid confusion. " Ah ! ah ! " " for shame ! for
shame ! " was shouted. Then, " Break ! break ! they are
killing them in front, and they cannot get away ; " and there
was a general cry of " break ! break." For a moment the
crowd held back as in a pause ; then was a rush, heavy
and resistless as a headlong sea, and a sound like low thunder,
with screams, prayers, and imprecations from the crowd-
moiled and sabre-doomed who could not escape.

By this time Hunt and his companions had disappeared
from the hustings, and some of the yeomanry, perhaps less
sanguinarily disposed than others, were busied in cutting
down the flag-staves and demolishing the flags at the
hustings.

On the breaking of the crowd the yeomanry wheeled, and,
dashing whenever there was an opening, they followed,
pressing and wounding. Many females appeared as the crowd
opened ; and striplings or mere youths also were found.
Their cries were piteous and heart-rending, and would, one
might have supposed, have disarmed any human resentment :
but here their appeals were in vain. Women, white-vested
maids, and tender youths, were indiscriminately sabred or
trampled ; and we have reason for believing that few were the
instances in which that forbearance was vouchsafed which
they so earnestly implored.

In ten minutes from the commencement of the havoc the
field was an open and almost deserted space. The sun looked
down through a sultry and motionless air. The curtains and
blinds of the windows within view were all closed. A gentleman or two might occasionally be seen looking out from one
of the new houses before mentioned, near the door of which a

group of persons (special constables) were collected, and apparently in conversation; others were assisting the wounded or carrying off the dead. The hustings remained, with a few broken and hewed flag-staves erect, and a torn and gashed banner or two dropping; whilst over the whole field were strewed caps, bonnets, hats, shawls, and shoes, and other parts of male and female dress, trampled, torn, and bloody. The yeomanry had dismounted—some were easing their horses' girths, others adjusting their accoutrements, and some were wiping their sabres. Several mounds of human beings still remained where they had fallen, crushed down and smothered. Some of these still groaning, others with staring eyes, were gasping for breath, and others would never breathe more. All was silent save those low sounds, and the occasional snorting and pawing of steeds. Persons might sometimes be noticed peeping from attics and over the tall ridgings of houses, but they quickly withdrew, as if fearful of being observed, or unable to sustain the full gaze of a scene so hideous and abhorrent.

Besides the Manchester yeomanry, who, as I have already shown, did "the duty of the day," there came upon the ground soon after the attack the 15th Hussars and the Cheshire yeomanry; and the latter, as if emulous of the Manchester corps, intercepted the flying masses, and inflicted some severe sabre wounds. The hussars, we have reason for supposing, gave but few wounds, and I am not aware that it has been shown, that one of those brave soldiers dishonoured his sword by using the edge of it. In addition to the cavalry, a strong body of the 88th Foot was stationed at the lower corner of Dickinson Street: with their bayonets at the charge, they wounded several persons, and greatly impeded the escape of the fugitives by that outlet. Almost simultaneously with the hussars, four pieces of Horse artillery appeared from Deansgate, and about two hundred special constables were also in attendance; so that force for a thorough massacre was ready, had it been wanted.

On the first rush of the crowd I called to our men to break their flag-staves and secure their banners, but probably I was not heard or understood, all being then inextricable confusion. He with the blue banner saved it, the cap of liberty was dropped and left behind—indeed, woe to him who stopped, he would never have risen again; and Thomas Redford, who carried the green banner, held it aloft until the staff was cut in his hand, and his shoulder was divided by the sabre of one of the Manchester yeomanry.

A number of our people were driven to some timber which lay at the foot of the wall of the Quakers' meeting house. Being pressed by the yeomanry, a number sprung over the balks and defended themselves with stones which they found there. It was not without difficulty, and after several were wounded, that they were driven out. A heroine, a young married woman of our party, with her face all bloody, her hair streaming about her, her bonnet hanging by the string, and her apron weighed with stones, kept her assailant at bay until she fell backwards and was near being taken; but she got away covered with severe bruises. It was near this place and about this time that one of the yeomanry was dangerously wounded and unhorsed by a blow from a fragment of a brick; and it was supposed to have been flung by this woman.

On the first advance of the yeomanry, one of the horses plunging at the crowd, sent its fore-feet into the head of our big drum, which was left near the hustings, and was irrecoverable. Thus booted on both legs at once, the horse rolled over, and the drum was kicked to pieces in the *mêlée*. For my own part, I had the good fortune to escape without injury, though it was more than I expected. I was carried, I may say almost literally, to the lower end of the Quakers' meeting house, the further wall of which screened us from observation and pursuit, and afforded access to some open streets. In my retreat from the field a well-dressed woman dropped on her knees a little on my left: I put out my hand to pluck her up, but she missed it, and I left her. I could not stop; and God knows what became of her. Two of the yeomanry were next in our way, and I expected a broken head, having laurel in my hat, but one was striking on one side, and the other on the other, and at that moment I stepped betwixt them and escaped.

After quitting the field, I first found myself in King Street, and passing into Market Street and High Street, I more leisurely pursued my way, taking care, lest some official should notice me, to remove the laurel from the outside to the inside of my hat. I was now unhappy on account of my wife, and I blamed myself greatly for consenting to her coming at all; I learned, however, when in St. George's Road, that she was well, and was on the way towards home; and that satisfied me for the time.

Having met with an old neighbour, we agreed to go round past Smedley Cottage, to learn what intelligence had arrived there. We descended the hill at Collyhurst, and on arriving at the bottom we espied a party of cavalry, whom from their dress I took to be of the Manchester yeomanry, riding along the road we had quitted towards Harpurhey. One of them wore a broad green band, or sash, across his shoulder and breast; I thought from its appearance it was a fragment of our green banner, and I was not mistaken. They were traversing the suburbs to reconnoitre and to pick up any person they could identify (myself, for instance, had I then been in their way), and the inglorious exhibition of the torn banner was permitted for the gratification of the vanity of the captor. This party rode forward a short distance, and then returned, without making any prisoners from our party.

At Smedley Cottage we found Mrs. Johnson, her two children (I think two), her maid-servant, and Mr. Hunt's groom, who had just come from the town, and had brought the information that Mr. Hunt, Mr. Johnson, Knight, Moorhouse, and several others, were prisoners in the New Bailey. I was touched by the lady's situation, though she bore the trial better than I could have expected. We gave her some particulars of the meeting, to which she listened with a manner mournfully thoughtful, occasionally shedding tears, and her features pale and calm as marble. She spoke not much: she was evidently too full to hold discourse, and so, with good wishes and consoling hopes, we took our departure.

We now called at Harpurhey, and found at the public-house, and in the road there, a great number of the Middleton

and Rochdale people, who had come from the meeting. My
first inquiry was for my wife, on whose account I now began
to be downright miserable. I asked many about her, but
could not hear any tidings, and I turned back toward Manchester, with a resolution to have vengeance if any harm had
befallen her. But I had not gone far ere I espied her at a
distance, hastening towards me; we met, and our first
emotions were those of thankfulness to God for our preservation. She had been in greater peril and distress of mind, if
possible, than myself: the former she escaped in a remarkable
manner, and through the intervention of special constables,
to whom let us award their due. She afterwards heard, first,
that I was killed, next, that I was wounded and in the
Infirmary; then, that I was a prisoner; and lastly, that she
would find me on the road home. Her anxiety being now
removed by the assurance of my safety, she hastened forward
to console our child. I rejoined my comrades, and forming
about a thousand of them into file, we set off to the sound of
fife and drum, with our only banner waving, and in that form
we re-entered the town of Middleton.

The banner was exhibited from a window of the Suffield
Arms publichouse. The cap of liberty was restored to us by
a young man from Chadderton, who had picked it up on the
outskirts of the field; and now we spent the evening in
recapitulating the events of the day, and in brooding over a
spirit of vengeance towards the authors of our humiliation
and our wrong.

CHAPTER XXVI.

AUTHOR'S OBSERVATIONS AT MANCHESTER—REDFORD AND HIS
MOTHER—LUNCH AT THE "TEMPLE"—ARMING AT MIDDLETON.

THOMAS REDFORD, who, as before stated, had been wounded,
was going to Manchester the following morning to visit his old
mother, and I chose to go with him. At the house of an
acquaintance of his, where we first called, we found means to
procure a disguise for me, as I was desirous to move about
without exciting particular notice. My hat was accordingly
changed for an old slouched felt; my lapelled coat for an
'ancient-looking long-waisted surtout, with broad metal
buttons; a handkerchief was tied over my mouth, a stick was
in my hand, and a wig concealed my hair; and so attired I
walked slowly forth, a tall, pale, and feeble, elderly man—
indifferent health had then rendered me pale. I passed many
persons, some of the police, who in my ordinary dress would
have known me, but they all seemed quite engaged and in a
hurry; and so, confident in my disguise, I made my observations at leisure.

All seemed in a state of confusion; the street were patrolled
by military, police, and special constables; the shops were
closed and silent; the warehouses were shut up and pad-
locked; the Exchange was deserted; the artillery was ready;
and it was reported that thousands of pikemen were on the
way to Manchester, from Oldham, Middleton, and other surrounding districts. I entered publichouses, called for my
squib of cordial, and listened, saying nothing. I overheard
the groups in the streets, and the general opinion was that the
authorities were stunned, and at a loss how to proceed; that

many of the wealthy class blamed them, as well for the
severity with which they had acted, as for the jeopardy in
which they had placed the lives and property of the towns-
people ; whilst all the working population were athirst for
revenge, and only awaited the coming of the country folks to
attempt a sweeping havoc.

Some proposals which I heard assented to filled me with
horror. The immolation of a selected number of the guilty
ones might have been discussed before God and man, but
what these men sought would not do ; and I retired and put
off my dress, more thoughtful than when I took it up. I found
Redford's mother bathing his wound with warm milk and
water, and to please her he said it was easier. It was a clean
gash of about six inches in length and quite through the
shoulder blade. She yearned, and wept afresh when she saw
the severed bone gaping in the wound. She asked who did
it, and Tom mentioned a person ; he said he knew him well ;
and she, sobbing, said she also knew him, and his father and
mother before him ; and she prayed God not to visit that sin
on the head of him who did it, but to change his heart and
bring him to repentance. That prayer had well-nigh touched
my heart also, but Tom rapped out one of another sort, to
which I incontinently, as may be supposed, added my
" Amen." The wound having been linted, and bound with
sticking-plaster, Tom put on his clothes, the slash in his coat
having been sewed, and the blood sponged off by a young
woman. His mother then, with many prayers and much good
advice, resigned him, as she said, " to the guidance of God,
through a wild and weary world." We called at Smedley
Cottage, but nothing had been heard of the prisoners since the
day preceding.

On arriving at the end of the lane, before descending past
Smedley Hall, we met two men with a covered basket, and
they asked us to go with them. They both knew me, and one
of them I knew well : he was a staunch Radical, and an
influential one as I supposed ; his name was Chadwick, and
he was a shawl weaver, latterly of Stockport. They had got a
good lump of a nice leg of roasted veal, and some ham to match

it, and were going to the "Temple" bowling-green to meet some friends, and to discuss their grievances and their viands over a bottle or two of porter. They had taken the meat from a public dinner table in George Leigh Street the day before. A feast had been provided by the reformers for the evening's solacement. After the catastrophe anything, it would seem, was law that could be done, and a band of hungry constables and police hastened to seize the meat; but the reformers, hearing of their intention, removed some of the best joints, and left them to devour the remainder, which they did on the spot, and never paid for it. Such was the account these friends gave of their lunch, and their motive for coming out of town.

We went with them, and met some half dozen others; and a discussion ensued on the state of affairs, and the course that should be taken by the reformers. At last it was agreed to hold a larger meeting the day following on the Tandle Hills, and with mutual pledges to be punctual we separated.

I found when I got home that there had been a general ferment in the town. Many of the young men had been preparing arms, and seeking out articles to convert into arms. Some had been grinding scythes, others old hatches, others screw-drivers, rusty swords, pikels, and mop-nails—anything which could be made to cut or stab was pronounced fit for service. But no plan was defined, nothing was arranged, and the arms were afterwards reserved for any event that might occur.

The day following I attended on the hills with a trusty friend. Notices had been sent to Oldham, Rochdale, Bury, and some other places, but at the time appointed no one appeared. We waited for hours, until the afternoon waned, but no one came; and then we went down to Royton, to ascertain the disposition of the reformers of that place. Some had been severely wounded, but most of the people were carousing, and there did not appear to be any disposition to retaliate the outrage we had suffered by force of arms. I called on William Fitton, but he gave no encouragement to such an idea. I went to John Kay, in Royley Lane, but he was, as usual, im-

perturbably placid. He was one of the least impassioned men
I ever knew.

After introducing the cause of my visit I asked his opinion,
and in order to obtain it frankly I spoke the more so. "If
the people were ever to rise and smite their enemies, was not
that the time? Was every enormity to be endured, and this
after all? Were we still to lie down like whipped hounds,
whom nothing could arouse to resistance? Were there not
times and seasons, and circumstances, under which the
common rules of wisdom became folly, prudence became
cowardice, and submission became criminal? and was not
the present one of those times and seasons?" It was astonishing that men could eat and sleep, that "the voice of their
brothers' blood crying from the ground did not make them
miserable."

"It does make them miserable," said this philosopher, for
he was one if ever such existed in humble life, and we are
taught to believe as much—"it does make them miserable,
and on account of this affair neither you nor I are happy, but
our oppressors are wretched. We, according to the impulse
of our nature, wish to avenge that outrage. Let us be quiet,
it is already in the course of avengement. Those men would,
even now, shrink out of existence if they were only assured of
getting to heaven quietly. They are already invoking that
obliviousness which will never come to their relief."

"Again, if the people took vengeance into their own hands,
where would they begin? where would they end? Would
they denounce all Manchester and the whole country?"
"No, no, the authors and perpetrators only." "But how
could they be got at? Would we descend to assassination?"
"No, no!" "To indiscriminate massacre, like that we had
witnessed?" "Oh, no, no!" "Could we march against
an army?" "We had no thought of doing so, we had no
thought of anything save avenging in some way our slain
and imprisoned fellow-beings." "Then," he said, "we had
best remain as we were; we should hear of a sensation
in many parts which would forward our cause, but the
least outrage on ours would only strengthen the aggressors,

and create that plea of justification which alone could mitigate their remorse." They would exclaim, "See, these are the men who came with peace on their lips; behold now the violence of their hearts—what would they not have done had we not put them down—and so, claiming merit for what they had done, they would next arraign their captives, our friends, and have them executed." Such was the substance of the arguments of our friend John Kay. His reasons had at all times some weight with me; on this occasion they were conclusive.

Several persons from Middleton came to me whilst at Royton. They said that a number of men, representing themselves as deputies, had arrived, and were at the "Suffield Arms." On going there I found persons from Manchester, Rochdale, and Blackburn. My heart recoiled from one of the former. He was one of those whose atrocious conversation the day before had filled me with disgust. I told them briefly that I would not take any part in a delegate meeting to discuss the taking up of arms; that I saw not any prospect of succeeding, and if I did they were not the men with whom I could act. I had sent for men whom I knew, but they came not; strangers came whose faces I had never seen before, and I would not act with such, neither was it to be expected that I should. I then recapitulated the arguments of my friend John Kay, and advised them to return from whence they came, and they soon after did so. The day following there was another attempt to get up a delegate meeting—the Manchester people seemed determined to have one—but it met with the same fate, and the men, about half a dozen in number, separated without doing any business.

Some days after I was informed of the arrest of Joseph Healey, at Lees. I began to expect something of the sort myself, and told our constable that if he got a warrant, and would let me know, I would go with him any day or night to Manchester, and there should be no fuss, no one should be the wiser. He said he would take that course should he have a warrant, and I attended to my business as usual.

As a narrative collateral with these passages, the account

given by my dear wife of her attendance at the meeting on
Saint Peter's Field, and of some incidents which befel her,
may not be devoid of interest to the reader, and certainly will
not be out of place if introduced here.   She says:—

"I was determined to go to the meeting, and should have
followed, even if my husband had refused his consent to my
going with the procession.   From what I, in common with
others, had heard the week previous, ' that if the country
people went with their caps of liberty, and their banners, and
music, the soldiers would be brought to them,' I was uneasy,
and felt persuaded, in my own mind, that something would be
the matter, and I had best go with my husband and be near
him, and if I only saw him I should be more content than in
staying at home.   I accordingly, he having consented after
much persuasion, gave my little girl something to please her,
and promising more on my return, I left her with a careful
neighbour woman, and joined some other married females at
the head of the procession.

"Every time I went aside to look at my husband, and that
was often, an ominous impression smote my heart.   He
looked very serious I thought, and I felt a foreboding of something evil to befal us that day.   I was dressed plainly as a
countrywoman, in my second best attire.   My companions
were also neatly dressed as the wives of working men.   I had
seen Mr. Hunt before that time ; they had not, and some of
them were quite eager to obtain good places, that they might
see and hear one of whom so much had been reported.   In
going down Mosley Street I lost sight of my husband.   Mrs.
Yates, who had hold of my arm, would keep hurrying forward
to get a good place, and when the crowd opened for the
Middleton procession, Mrs. Yates and myself, and some others
of the women, went close to the hustings, quite glad that we
had obtained such a situation for seeing and hearing all.   My
husband got on the stage, but when afterwards I saw him leap
down and lost sight of him, I began to be unhappy.   The
crowd seemed to have increased very much, for we became
insufferably pressed.   We were surrounded by men who were
strangers, we were almost suffocated, and to me the heat was

quite sickening; but Mrs. Yates, being taller than myself, supported it better.

"I felt I could not bear this long, and I became alarmed. I reflected that if there was any more pressure I must faint, and then what would become of me? and I begged of the men to open a way and let me go out, but they would not move. Every moment I became worse, and I told some other men then, who stood in a row, that I was sick, and begged they would let me pass them, and they immediately made a way, and I went down a long passage betwixt two ranks of these men, many of them saying, 'make way, she's sick, she's sick, let her go out,' and I passed quite out of the crowd, and, turning to my right, I got on some high ground, on which stood a row of houses—this was Windmill Street.

"I thought if I could get to stand at the door of one of those houses I should have a good view of the meeting, and should perhaps see my husband again; and I kept going further down the row until I saw a door open, and I stepped within it, the people of the house making no objections.

"By this time Mr. Hunt was on the hustings addressing the people. In a minute or two some soldiers came riding up. The good folks of the house, and some who seemed to be visitors, said 'the soldiers were only come to keep order, they would not meddle with the people;' but I was alarmed. The people shouted, and then the soldiers shouted, waving their swords. Then they rode amongst the people, and there was a great outcry, and a moment after a man passed without a hat, and wiping the blood off his head with his hand, and it ran down his arm in a great stream.

"The meeting was all in a tumult; there were dreadful cries; the soldiers kept riding amongst the people and striking with their swords. I became faint, and turning from the door I went unobserved down some steps into a cellared passage; and, hoping to escape from the horrid noise, and to be concealed, I crept into a vault and sat down, faint and terrified, on some firewood.

"The cries of the multitude outside still continued, and the people of the house, upstairs, kept bewailing most pitifully.

They could see all the dreadful work through the window, and their exclamations were so distressing, that I put my fingers in my ears to prevent my hearing more ; and on removing them, I understood that a young man had just been brought past, wounded. The front door of the passage before mentioned soon after opened, and a number of men entered, carrying the body of a decent, middle-aged woman, who had been killed. I thought they were going to put her beside me, and was about to scream, but they took her forward and deposited her in some premises at the back of the house.

"I had sat in my hiding-place some time, and the tumult seemed abated, when a young girl, one of the family, came into the vault, and suddenly crouching, she bumped against my knee, and starting up and seeing another dead woman, as she probably thought, she ran upstairs, quite terrified, and told her mother. The good woman, Mrs. Jones, came down with the girl and several others, and having ascertained that I was living, but sadly distressed, she spoke very kindly, and assisted me to a chair in her front room. She offered me refreshment, and would have made tea, but I declined it. I was too unhappy to take anything except a little water. I could not restrain my feelings, but kept moaning and exclaiming, 'My lad—my poor lad!' They asked if I was married, and I said I was, and had lost my husband in the crowd, and was afraid he was killed. Those good people did all they could to comfort me. They asked where I came from, and my husband's name; and I told them I came from Middleton, but evaded mentioning his name, lest, on account of his being a leader, I should be put in prison; for though they had behaved most kindly, I doubted whether they would continue to do so if they knew whose wife I was.

"I now became wishful to go, and Mrs. Jones called a special constable, and requested he would see me into Market Street, from whence I could find my way. The man very civilly took my arm, and led me over the now almost deserted field. I durst not look aside lest I should encounter some frightful object, and particularly that which I most dreaded to see, the corpse of my husband, being almost assured he was dead or wounded. I only looked up once, and then saw a great number of horses at rest, and their riders dismounted. I durst scarcely open my eyes; and hurrying with the constable over that dreaded place, we were soon in Market Street, where, thanking my conductor for his civility, he returned, and I hastened towards Shudehill, where I met one of our people who had heard that my husband was killed. Afterwards I was informed that he was in the Infirmary; another said he was in prison; and then I heard that he was gone home; and soon after I had the pleasure of again rejoining him at Harpurhey, for which mercy I sincerely returned thanks to God."

CHAPTER XXVII.

AUTHOR'S SECOND ARREST ON A CHARGE OF HIGH TREASON.

About two o'clock on the morning of Thursday, the 26th of August—that is, on the tenth morning after the fatal meeting—I was awoke by footsteps in the street opposite my residence. Presently they increased in number, and came nearer, and from the manner in which they collected and approached the place, I was convinced a sore trial was at hand for the little woman who lay asleep on my arm, and I felt more concern on her account than on my own.

Bang! bang! came the blows on the door. "Hallo! who's makin' that din at this time o' neet?"

My wife was crying, and all in a tremor, but I cheered her, and told her to be quick, and I would keep them in talk whilst I put on a few things of my own.

"Open the door," said a voice, authoritatively.

"Open the door"—imitating the voice—"an' hooa arto 'at I should oppen my dur to thee? Theawrt sum drunken eawl or other, or elze theaw wud no' come i' that way."

"Open the door, or I'll break it," said the same person.

"Break it wilto? An' hooa art theaw ot tawks o' breakin' into foke's heawses ot dyed oth neet? Theaw'd better not break it, unless theaws an eyyron pot o' the yed."

There was another bang, and a stout push at the door, but they might as well have shoved against the Rock o' Gibraltar; the door had been firmly propped to prevent a too sudden surprise.

"Will you open the door, man?" said another voice.

"Well, but hooa ar yo' and wot dun yo' want? for thurs moor nor won I yer."

"We are constables, and we want you," was the reply.

"Oh! that's a different thing quite: iv yoar constables yo' shan com in by o' myens. Why didno yo' tell me so at forst?"

By this time both my wife and myself were decently attired, and advancing to the door I took away the prop and shot the bar, and bid them come in, and not soil the silk work in the looms.

A crowd of men entered; it was quite dark, but I learned from the sound of gunstocks on the floor that we had soldiers. My wife was terrified and clung to me. I told her to get a light, and she went towards the door for that purpose, but shrunk back on running against a musket as she groped her way: the constables also repulsed her. They said she must not go out; they would get a light themselves; and in a short time Joseph Platt, one of my former conductors to London, appeared with a candle.

I now perceived that my visitors were a strong posse of police, some soldiers of the 32nd Regiment; Mr. Nadin, the deputy-constable of Manchester; and several officers of infantry and hussars. These seemed interested by the proceedings, and were attentive observers of what took place. The military force consisted of a company of Foot, and as I afterwards learned, a troop of hussars. The officers were no doubt surprised that such a parade should have been deemed requisite for the apprehension of a poor weaver in his cellar. "Well, Mr. Nadin," I said, laying aside my vernacular and speaking common English, "and what may be your pleasure with me now?" He informed me in his usual dogged way, striving to be civil, that he had a warrant against me for high treason. I said if that was the case I was ready to accompany him; but he would never convict me, and if he did, my blood would kill him. He and his assistants then commenced searching the place, for arms, as I thought, on which I ridiculed their simplicity, saying, "And do you think I should keep my depôt here?" One of the men laid hold of a sugar cane, and asked what that was? I said he might surely see it was a pike shaft, but the head I had removed to another place. I had been expecting them, I said, seven or eight days, and, of course, had made the place as clear as I could for their reception.

The drawers were rummaged; my oaken box was explored; a shawl was spread on the floor, and all my books and papers were bundled into it; there was not, however, anything of consequence; some poems in manuscript had been deposited elsewhere. I took up some of my printed poems, "The Weaver Boy," and would have presented a copy to each of the officers, but Mr. Nadin would not permit me; he took the books and threw them on the heap, and I thought the officers seemed displeased. He then bade one of his men to handcuff me. "Nay, Mr. Nadin," I said, "can this be necessary? I give you my word of honour not to attempt an escape." With a profound oath he bade the man do his duty, and I was chained.

The order was then given to move; my wife burst into tears. I tried to console her, said I should soon be with her again; and bestowing a kiss for my dear child when she came in the morning, I ascended into the street, and shouted, "Hunt and liberty." "Hunt and liberty," responded my brave little helpmate, whose spirit was now roused. One of the policemen, with a pistol in his hand, swearing a deep oath, said he would blow out her brains if she shouted again. "Blow away," was the reply; "Hunt and liberty. Hunt for ever."

Nothing further was said. The soldiers shouldered arms, and the word "March" being given, the prisoner and his escort tramped down the street.

"I thought you very foolish," said a young hussar officer, in a friendly tone at my left elbow. "Why so?" I asked; but before he could reply he was interrupted, and I had not an opportunity for speaking to him again: I supposed he meant something about the books. "Well, but how is this?" I said to Mr. Nadin. "You know I am not in the habit of walking on these excursions; I must have a coach." And

scarcely had we gone many yards ere we came to a coach
with the door open, the steps down, and a file of hussars on
each side of the road. I stepped into the vehicle, followed
by Nadin, one of his men, and a boy; the door was
closed and we drove off, accompanied by the trample of
horses and the clatter of arms.

With reference to this transaction the London *Times*
newspaper—whose information would seem to have been
derived from some one upon the spot—said, "The party
sent to arrest him consisted of a troop of horse, a detachment
of infantry, and a *posse* of constables. To such a formidable
force no resistance was offered, nor was there any apparent
inclination to resist. The alleged traitor was called up from
his bed about four o'clock in the morning, when he little
expected to be honoured by such visitors; but he manifested
no symptoms of confusion, displeasure, or alarm. He was
even good-humoured and jocose with the officers, inspiring
them at the same time with a high idea of his talent,
coolness, and presence of mind. He first asked why he had
been so waited upon, and was told by Nadin that he had
a warrant to arrest him. 'On what charge,' he rejoined.
'On charge of having committed a capital felony.' 'Ah,' he
replied, 'you will never convict me; my blood would poison
you, man; it is as black as a bull's blood.' Seeing the officers
search the house for pikes, or pikeheads, he remarked upon
their suspicious simplicity, saying, 'And do you think that
I would keep them here?'"

As if this were too good a thing to be given unmutilated, to
one of my station, the same paper, as a kind of qualifier, says
in another place: "BAMFORD, THE REFORMIST!—This individual, who is now in confinement, charged with seditious
practices, was formerly an actor of very considerable repute
at Liverpool and other places, and was then in flourishing
circumstances. He has since, we understand, procured a
scanty subsistence by writing comic songs, and occasionally
jeux d'esprit, and by trifling benefactions from actors who had
formerly known him."

This, I need not inform my Lancashire readers, was as

unfounded as it was absurd. A hand-loom weaver metamorphosed into " an actor of considerable repute," and then
" living by writing comic songs and *jeux d'esprit*," and by
" trifling benefactions from actors ? " That would indeed have
been worse than weaving !

Who ever heard of a play actor becoming a patriot ? the
one all reality, the other all imitation ; the one a reflector only,
the other the thing reflected. The writer of that paragraph
knew but little of human nature.

As we were ascending the brow at Alkrington, I remarked
that it would seem as if Mr. Nadin and myself were destined
to be fellow travellers ; this was the second trip I had taken
with him.

It was, he said ; but we should not travel often.

How so ? What did he mean ?

It was my last journey with him, probably.

Did he think so ?

Yes. He was nearly certain I should never return from
whence I was going.

Indeed ! Why not ? What was to be done with me then ?
" Thou'll be hanged," he said. " Hanged ! " shall I ?
" Aye ! thou'll be hanged at this hurry ! Thou'll never come
back alive ! " Might there not be a small misreckoning in
that hanging matter ? I said, No ! Speaking seriously, he
did not think there would. Well ! I was not of his opinion.
He would find himself mistaken ere long. Did I expect to
get off then ? I had no doubt about it. And if I did he
would give me credit for greater cleverness than he thought I
possessed or ever should. He had been in the fish market at
Manchester, of course ? He had. And had seen live snigs
there ? He had. And had seen them glide out of the rude
grasp of the fishwomen ? He had seen that. " Well ! " I
said, " I am like one of those snigs. I shall slip through your
hands this time, whether you will or not : and I hope to do
more." What was that ? " To assist in bringing to condign
punishment some dozen or so of your Manchester magistrates
and yeomanry " Psha ! I need not speculate on such an
event. This would be my last journey up that hill.

The coach stopped at Sam Ogden's at Harpurhey. Nadin got out, and left me, the man, and the boy, guarded by the hussars. After sitting some time the foot soldiers came up; a person or two dressed as gentlemen also appeared. One of them said, " Where is the villain ? " The door was opened and I was asked to step out. I did so, and in passing forward to the lobby a blow, or severe push in my neck, nearly flung me on my face. I turned, and saw Mr. Thomas Andrew, of Harpurhey, in an attitude of menace ! I shall not repeat the terms in which I addressed him ; but I told him that no man, much less a gentleman, would descend to outrage a person in chains—that he had disgraced himself ; and that it was well for him—a circumstance he no doubt had calculated on—that my hands were confined. The lobby was filled with soldiers and police, and some one said, " No one should touch the prisoner." Probably it was one of the military, who knew not that this person was brother to the head constable of Manchester.

I was next shown into the kitchen, and took my seat in an old armed chair, in the farther corner near the fireplace. On each side of me was seated a policeman with a pistol in his hand. The infantry piled arms in two or three stacks, and the hussars came in, in turn, whilst others remained on guard. Half a dozen tables were quickly surrounded, and as soon plentifully supplied with oat cake, cheese, and ale ; to which the men set with right good will. I told them to make play, and spare nothing, and if no one else would pay the shot I would. They laughed, said I was a hearty fellow, and they wished they might take such a one every night. Of course I and my two policemen replenished to our liking ; but our ale was eightpenny, and of a prime tap.

The large bread-flake in the kitchen was speedily unthatched, and about half of a large old cheese disappeared. Pipes were then lighted, more ale was brought, and, being willing to improve our acquaintance, I sung, in my way, that fine old piece known as " General Wolfe's Song," beginning—

" Why, soldiers, why—
Should we be melancholy, boys ? "

The jugs were again replenished, the soldiers were becoming good company, and I said if they were all of my mind we would not march so long as old Sam would chalk up, either for King George or myself. The soldiers asked me to drink with them ; I did so, and gave them a toast. Soon after I was sent for into the bar parlour, and there found the military officers, Mr. Nadin, Mr. Jonathan Andrew, the head constable of Manchester, and his brother. Speaking to the officers, I said they would excuse me, but there was a person in that room to whom no deference whatever would be shown by me, and therefore I should take the liberty to be seated. A few questions were asked, some conversation of no consequence passed, and it seemed to me as if I were sent for more for the purpose of observation than any other thing. At length I was reconducted, and the ale being finished, of which my especial guards had freely partaken, the word to fall in was given, and in a short time we were clattering through the drowsy streets of Manchester. I was first taken to the police office in King Street, and from thence to the prison in Salford. The turnkey appeared, in temper crusty, and half awake ; the door opened and banged to behind me, and the next moment I was ushered into one of the lock-ups.

A close, warm air, tainted with an abominable odour, was the first thing that saluted my senses on entering this wretched place. It was a small cell, perhaps four or five yards in length, by two or three in width, and probably as lofty as it was long. Opposite the door was an aperture to let in a stinted quantity of air ; on two sides of the room were two benches fastened to the wall ; in the centre was a stove with a fire in ; and at a corner on the right was a convenience, from which emanated the disagreeableness first mentioned. Two or three fellows were stretched on the benches ; one was doubled up in a corner, and one lay coiled up like a dog on the floor before the stove ; one of them opened it, flung in some slack, and stirred it, and a light flashed out that showed every corner of that noisome crib, and the persons I was now associated with.

" In the name of the devil," demanded he who stood with

what served as a fire-poker in his hand, "what comes here."

" He's e'en a lang un like teseln," said another, a Yorkshireman. " A flash cove," said a third ; " he's a smart shirt on ! " " He's a fence, or a devout smasher," exclaimed another. " Come, friend, let's have a word of exhortation." " Nay," said one," "that leathern skull-cap looks too priggish. That'll pray none ; he'll rap out when he's been afore the beak." " Come, friend, let's be knowing what thou'rt here for," said he with the poker, " we jolly boys, who give life to these palace halls, keep no secrets." " Then let me know my company," I said ; " what art thou here for ? " " Knives and forks—third appearance—I'm lagged this time." " And what art thou down for ? " addressing another. " Oh ! mine is only bail, or good behaviour. I knocked a fancy pal down, and thrashed her bully." " And what art thou for ? " I asked a third. " Mutton," he said ; " a leg of mutton, but it was all a mistake." " Who'll believe it," exclaimed he in the corner ; " thou was near being lagg'd last time, and thou goes it now, old boy · we'll both sail together ; then it'll be—

> " Suppose the duke be short of men,
> What would old England say ?
> They'd wish they had those lads again,
> They'd sent to Botany Bay."

He who sung this catch was accused, he said, " of grabbing a purse " ; but it was all a mistake, as Bill there said, about the mutton ; only who'd believe it, when they couldn't find the other man as did it. " My case, then, is worse than any of yours," I said. " Ah ! ah ! 'flimsies,'" was the remark— " notes, man, don't you know the proper names of notes ? you've been in the note business, I suppose ? " " Oh, no, nothing of that sort." " A little in the crack line, perhaps ? " " Housebreaking," said another. " No, not that ! " " Not on the road, surely ?—not in the collecting way ?

> ' With your loaded pop in hand.' "

"No, not an highwayman either, if that is what you mean?" "What the devil are you? Have you robbed a church, and killed a man?" "Worse than either, as the law says." "What have you done?" several now asked in surprise. "My crime is honoured, if it succeed, and the most dreadfully punished if it fail. Hanging, drawing, and quartering is my doom, I understand." "Oh! high treason; aye, high treason; are you one of those Peter's Field pikemen then?" "That is what they say."

One of them now produced an old stump pipe, another some tobacco; they smoked round; their conversation turned on their own affairs; and, becoming drowsy, I stretched myself on one of the benches, and was soon asleep.

When I awoke a peep of dull light was gleaming through the lofty and grated aperture. My companions were, some huddled in drowsiness; others pacing backwards and forwards wearily, breathing the muddled and tainted air; aye, as wearily as do those unfortunate fishes which are doomed to paddle around glass vials, through thick and sickening water, as an ornament to parlour windows; or for the amusement of the lady and her visitors, and the improvement of the young "prodigies" in the study of natural history.

I admire not that philosophy which would go in a coach to see Africa in the next field, nor that religion which requires the wonders of other lands to direct it to "nature's God," which crieth, "bring hither all things, that *I* may learn to adore the Creator;" nor that civilisation which is for ever catching, and caging, and immuring, and tormenting God's noble creatures, and robbing them of their inheritance in the wilds of air, earth, and ocean, for the gratification of a selfish and indolent curiosity, for the promotion of a knowledge which availeth little, and is obtained at the expense of humanity.

Towards noon we were called out of this odious place and taken into the court above for examination, or rather recognition, before the magistrates. My companions were placed in the box commonly allotted to the jury, whilst I was seated at a small desk near the dock, generally occupied by the governor or an assistant.

The magistrate on this occasion was Mr. Norris.

The felony cases were first disposed of, and it went hard against some of my late fellows. One man was afterwards committed for trial for drilling, and several were required to find bail, or sureties, for assaults and other minor offences.

My case, Mr. Norris said, was a most serious one; the charge against me was nothing less than that of high treason. The evidence would not be gone into at present, and I should be brought up for a future examination. I asked, might I be allowed to put a question or two. Certainly. I wished to know who was my accuser? and on what information I had been deprived of my liberty? Mr. Norris said that would be made known to me in due time. I said Mr. Nadin had seized a number of papers and political tracts at my house, and I begged to know who held them, and from whom they would be recoverable? Mr. Norris said the constable who seized them would be responsible: they might become necessary to the ends of justice. That did not satisfy me, I replied. It was possible that other papers might be introduced amongst them, and I wished them to be sealed up, and deposited with a party beyond all suspicion. I was told to be silent; if I uttered any more impertinence I should be committed. I said I understood I was committed. No; I was remanded, and would be brought up on a future day for final examination. The turnkey then tipped me on the shoulder, and I followed him.

My prison was now a pleasant one, compared with the cell I had quitted. To be sure, except my bed, everything around, beneath, and above was of iron or stone, and those are cold comforts; yet on the whole I was agreeably disappointed in the change which had taken place. The walls were very white, the floors were well stoned, my bed seemed very clean, and there was a free current of air, as good as any gentleman in the neighbourhood breathed; and, contrasting this place with the lock-up, I thought I could not wish a better if I were a king. I had also a long airy passage to walk in during the day; and there, pacing backwards and forwards—sometimes studying, sometimes whistling, and sometimes singing—I contrived to pass the hours much more pleasantly

than if I had been locked up with my cell companions. A
thinking mind tranquillised by fortitude, with some book
reminiscences, especially poetic ones, and some cheerful
thoughts of the world outside, need not, indeed never will,
give itself up to unavailing regrets because the earthly form
which it directs has become circumscribed in its whereabouts.
Nature, seeking its ever destined change, through life to
death, and through death to another life, must necessarily
become aware of the drag on existence which a prison
imposes; it cannot be insensible to that, and it will doubtless
wish it were removed, but a mind thus constituted need not
descend to frivolous complaints.

I might perhaps have some gifts and resources not common
to others; and if I had, I made good use of them in my
solitary hours; and, grateful for their bestowal, I derived
solacements commensurate with their exercise.

I happened to have a kind turnkey here: I think he had
formerly known me; he was a Rochdale man, and his name
was Grindrod. He found that I was unwell, having a cough,
and fulness of the chest; and instead of the prison gruel, he
brought me up a basin of warm tea or coffee, morning and
evening, from his own table; my dinners were of the prison
allowance. Once or twice also my fellow prisoner, James
Moorhouse, sent me a little fruit, which I was allowed to
receive. My kind gaoler never hinted at remuneration, and it
was not without difficulty that, on my going away, I prevailed
on him to accept a small gratuity as an acknowledgment of
my gratitude.

On the morning of our final examination, which was Friday,
the 27th of August, my wife and Joseph Healey's wife came
to the prison to see us, if they might be allowed. Mr. Andrews,
the late deputy-constable of Bury, with whom I previously had
some acquaintance, was at that time connected with the
Manchester police, and was on that day in attendance at the
New Bailey on business. He saw the two women standing in
the crowd outside the gates, and beckoning my wife, asked her
if she was come to see me. She said she wished to do
so and her companion, who was Healey's wife, wished

also to see her husband. He accordingly took them into a room upstairs, where there was a comfortable fire, seats, and a table. A number of soldiers' wives were about their business, and foot soldiers were walking sentry. Amongst those of the soldiers who passed to and fro was John Hall, a Middleton man, formerly a neighbour of ours, and then a private in the 31st Regiment of Foot. He conversed with them a short time and left them, and soon after reappeared, and set before them a dinner of excellent steak and porter, which was very acceptable at the time. They were, however, not the less unable to account for this, as the table was set out in a style which could not be within the means of a private soldier; but John said nothing: he refused to receive any gratuity, and, having removed the things, he went about his business. They were afterwards ushered into the public court, but it was so crowded as to be insufferable, and, after exchanging a few looks and mute gestures with me and Healey, who were in the dock, they were glad to escape from the crowd and await our disposal in the room they had quitted.*

From the bar I was conducted to the yard of my former cell, where I was joined by several of the other prisoners, and we were taking what should have been our dinners, when an order suddenly came that we were to prepare to set off for Lancaster Castle. Our meal was soon despatched, and we quickly bundled up our few things. We were then taken to the turnkey's lodge, and each hand-chained, after which we were placed on a four-horse coach, in the inside of which were Mr. Hunt, Mr. Knight, Saxton, and Nadin. The outside party consisted of myself, Swift, Wilde, Healey, and Jones, with a number of constables armed with pistols; we were also escorted by a strong detachment of hussars, and thus, amid the huzzas of an immense multitude, we drove off.

* At this point Bamford inserts in his narrative an account of the proceedings before the magistrates, taken from the *Times* of August 30, 1819. The Government abandoned the charge of high treason and prosecuted for conspiracy. On this charge the accused were committed, but bail was allowed, Hunt and Johnson each in £1,000, and two sureties in £500; Bamford and the rest in £500, and two sureties of £250. Johnson and Moorhouse found bail at once. Bamford then resumes his narrative.

Proceeding at a rapid pace, we soon left the dim atmosphere, and crowded streets of Manchester and Salford behind. The populous thoroughfares of Pendleton were next traversed, and a pleasant ride of twelve miles brought us to the large town of Bolton, where we changed horses, amid a throng of people, which the hussars found some difficulty in keeping at a distance. But their expressions of sympathy and goodwill were not to be restrained, and their loud shouts of " Hunt for ever!" " Never mind 'em, lads!" " Down with the tyrants!" and a general huzza, with waving of hats and handkerchiefs, and clapping of hands, when we drove off, added to the cheerfulness of our party.

Soon after leaving Bolton darkness came on, and we had scarcely cleared the moors of Horwich, when the coachman, who knew not the way, drove upon a piece of new road, and, endeavouring to extricate himself, the coach began to heel on one side, and we should have gone over—constables, prisoners, and all—had not the pole broken, on which the horses were steadied, and we dismounted, and being most carefully looked to by the constables and soldiers, we walked down to the village of Lower Darwen, and were all snugly counted into a public house there. The poor Jehu, whose mistake had led to the misadventure, then got a large dividend of devil's blessings from our conducting constable.

At this place Mr. Hunt refused to partake of any vinous or fermented liquor, and out of compliment to him most of us did the same. Saxton, however, whose fiery visage told of the indulgence he loved, took brandy and water, and candidly declared that he would not attempt to carry into effect Mr. Hunt's rule of temperance. He would attend a meeting at any time he said, or make a speech, or move or second a resolution for parliamentary reform; but a resolution for a personal reform in the matter of a little cordial he neither could nor would entertain. A discussion ensued which caused some laughter, in which Mr. Hunt joined; and having sat about an hour, the pole was repaired, and we drove into Blackburn, where we left the coach, the driver, and the hussars, and went on with a fresh vehicle and guards.

At Preston we stopped at the head inn, and took supper in a large room, to the lower end of which a number of respectable-looking persons were admitted. These genteel visitors seemed not to have the smallest idea that their presence might be disagreeable to men in our situation, and that a plea of curiosity was likely to seem but an ungracious excuse for coming to view us as they would wild beasts, "at feeding time." The streets here, as at every other town where we stopped, were crowded, and we set off amid loud cheers.

Morning broke betwixt Garstang and Lancaster, and the first challenge of "John O'Gaunt's tower," as it stood out before us in the mild sunlight, excited our attention. It looked indeed like the stern and lordly keep of an old baron, and a small exercise of imagination was sufficient to place in our mind's eye its powerful chieftain, waiting in helmet, cuirass and glaive, beneath its portcullis.

We passed quickly along the streets of the town, the hussars came trotting dusty and choked and weary behind us. It was about five o'clock; few people were stirring, and the clatter of our cavalcade aroused many from their peaceful slumbers. We dismounted at the foot of the castle steep, and walked up accompanied by our guards, and took our station beneath the arch of the grim old gate, the boldness and strength of its masonry attracting our admiration. A blow from the ponderous knocker made the place resound, and in a few minutes the wicket was opened, and we were prisoners in Lancaster Castle.

And now friend reader, since thou hast accompanied me to this my fourth place of confinement, instead of contemplating the repulsive walls, and the dungeon towers, and the massive keep, for which there may be time hereafter, let us, from the eminence of this

" Wide water'd shoie,"

mentally cast back our eyes and survey the course by which we have arrived at so undesirable a place. And in doing this, let us not be blind to our own faults, but be simply just towards ourselves as we have been to others. Let us not spare ourselves the humiliation of blame when deserved, though it do humble our self-esteem, though we have to declare, " this hand hath offended."

In our progress now retrospectively scanned, how great was the portion, as we perceive, of folly which accompanied our good intentions ! Groping in a mental and political twilight, we stumbled from error to error, the dim-eyed calling on the blind to follow ; we fell as a natural consequence, and a happy circumstance would it have been had our fall served in these later times as a warning to others, but it has not.

"For a nation to be free, it is sufficient that she wills it," and we may add that a nation cannot be free unless she does will it. We thought the will to be free already existed— foolish though—we looked for fruit ere the bloom was come forth ; we expected will when there was no mind to produce it, to sustain it ; for rational will is the result of mind, not of passion ; and that mind did not then exist, nor does it now.

The agitators of the present day, Radicals I may not call them, have suffered greater humiliations than we did. With the example of our disasters before them, they have not avoided one evil which we encountered, nor produced one additional good. On both occasions there was too much of the " sounding brass and tinkling cymbal," but latterly it has been varied by dark counsels and criminal instigations from their own authorised ones. Then followed delegations, and the silly egotism of portraits, and mock-solemn conventions, and formal self-displaying orations, and words and phrases bandied beyond all human entertainment. Next came multitudes deserted of leaders—who stood at a safe distance—and they drove before them a cloud and a whirlwind of terror and confusion, through which were seen flashes, and conflagrations, and blood-streaks ; and when it had passed all had vanished, and there remained dungeons, beside whose open gates were weeping wives and children, and prisoners, some victims to their own folly, and some to the wickedness of others, were marching in, chained by scores.

On no ! the still small voice of reason has not been listened to now, more than it was formerly. It speaks a language too pure, too unassuming, too disinterested, for any human crowds that have yet appeared. It requires great sacrifices for the obtainment of great results, a stripping of all vanity, an abandonment of all self, and a cleansing from all lucre. Its appeal could be understood by rare minds only, and they have not been found.

CHAPTER XXVIII.

OUR arrival seemed scarcely to have been expected so early as
it took place, for it was not until we had waited some time
between the inner and outer gates that a young man, who we
afterwards found was the governor's son, made his appearance
without coat, and with other indications of a hurried dressing.
Having perused the documents presented by Nadin, and cast
a hasty but observant glance at his prisoners, he conducted us
into the debtors' yard, where we were greeted with a shout and
many good wishes and shaking of hands by some debtors who
were abroad.   A very brief reconnoitre was sufficient for the
settlement of any doubts as to the place being a most excellent
one for safe detention.   All around were high and frowning
barriers of masonry, and we felt as completely shut in from
the world as if we were at the bottom of a great well, where
neither force, nor art, nor supplication, were of any avail.   On
our right were high and smooth walls, capped by movable
spikes, threatening impalement to any wight whom a desperate good fortune enabled to ascend there.   At regular distances were strong prison towers containing sleeping cells ;
a little more in our front stood the huge gloomy mass known
as " John O'Gaunt's tower," which looked like a pile hewn
square from the solid rock.   At the top of the yard, and on

our left, were the habitations of the debtors, with their small windows all looking down into the great well; whilst from the casements and crib-looking loop-holes some of the poor fellows stood clapping hands and waving night caps, as if they really thought that a welcome to such a place must be as gratifying as to any other, and that a welcome was a compliment anywhere.

We were conducted from hence to the first criminal ward on our right, the tower of which is, I believe, called the round tower. Here we found several prisoners, and amongst them an attorney from Manchester, and his clerk, who had each been sentenced to three years' imprisonment for falsely swearing to a debt against my former fellow prisoner, Joseph Sellers. Their time was nearly out, but the old attorney was apparently hastening fast to another world. He lay in one corner on the floor doubled up, and in dreadful agonies from pains in his bowels and limbs; the latter caused by rheumatism. This place was very inconvenient, cold, and comfortless. A continued draught of wind brought the smoke down the chimney, and we were all coughing and nearly blinded. Soon after we were removed into the next ward but one, towards the round-house, and there we were comparatively at home, having a much better day-room and yard, and besides those amendments we were all together, without any admixture with other prisoners, and were consequently at liberty to converse freely amongst ourselves.

There were a good kettle and pan in the day-room, and good water in a pump in the yard; we sent into the town for other kitchen requisites, as plates, knives, forks, and such articles; also for bread and butter (until our prison allowance was given us), tea, coffee, and other grocery matters, and having a fire in the place, we soon contrived to make a good breakfast, and were quite merry over it. At dinner we fared no worse; we sent out for whatever we wanted, ales and liquors excepted; the prison allowance of vegetables and soup was in part used by us, and the remainder we gave to a felon, who was allowed to come in and clear our day-room and cells every morning. The day passed off pretty agreeably, but

towards evening Hunt gave way to fits of impatience because
no one appeared to bail him. He in particular inveighed
against Johnson for having, as he said, invited him down to
Manchester, got him into that trouble, and then abandoned
him. Sooner, he said, than he would have done as Johnson
had done by him—sooner than he would have walked home at
liberty, and left his friend and guest in prison—he would have
had his arm torn from his body. Mr. Hunt generally made
use of the strongest terms he could at the moment command,
and to those of us who had frequently been in his company,
exhibitions of violent feeling were by no means new. He had
not the candour to reflect that Mr. Johnson could not better
serve us than by first securing his own liberty, as a means
towards furthering ours, which in this case I believe he did.

Night came, and the rattle of keys informed us that we
were about being introduced to our sleeping berths. We had
our choice, and Mr. Hunt took the cell next the door. I, at
his desire, went to the next, as he said he could call to me if
he should be unwell, and John Knight went into the third;
the others of our party were lodged in the cells above. During
the day, which turned out rather fine and clear, I had imbibed
a favourable opinion of this prison. The day-room and yard
were clean and airy, and whilst the attendant was sweeping
out the cells and making the beds, I had gone in and found
them with their doors all open, lighted with the forenoon sun,
and as white and sweet as a constant application of quick-
lime could make them. The cells were perhaps eight feet in
width, by ten or twelve in length, and seven or eight upwards.
Over a very strong door of wood—I think with clamped nails
—was a square aperture for the admission of air; on the other
side the door was the passage—beyond it again was a massive
iron grating, and the entrance to the passage was also secured
by another door, of, I think, iron. At the head of the cell
was an iron slab, full of perforations, and resting on projec-
tions from the wall; a sack with straw in, a couple of blankets
or so, and a good horse-rug, made up our bed, and the whole
being apparently clean, I promised myself a sleep as sound as
a king could enjoy in his cups. A capital prison thought I,

and a strong one too, and though it kept one from rambling
out, it would also keep the storms from coming in, as I should
find should I have to spend a winter or two within its shelter.
Besides, I had heard that these felon-dungeons were constructed under the direction of the celebrated " humane
Howard," therefore they must be the very best for comfort
as well as security, and, as I said before, I, from their daylight appearance and these considerations, thought well of my
domicile. But in those days I always looked at things on
their brightest side.

We turned in, and my door had not been many minutes
closed ere I began to feel as if I were being smothered. My
old complaint on the lungs had gone with me to this place,
and though I constantly was cheerful, very stubborn fits of
coughing had convinced me that I was far from being well. I
now began to feel as if I was closed up in a coffin, and not a
breath of air above and around me. How dreadful were my
sensations! I can never forget them. My chest heaved for
air, but the cooling, life-giving stream came not, and I stood
leaning on my bed, pumping and gasping in the close, suffocating den. I thought of the Black Hole of Calcutta, and
concluded that the fate of its sufferers would be mine. I
thought of getting up to the air-hole, but it was above my
reach, and there was not anything in the place I could put my
feet upon, else I should have deemed it luxury to have stood
inhaling the blessed fluid all night. Oh! humanity, humanity,
I thought, what is the humanity which builds prisons on such
plans as these? I endeavoured to tranquillise my mind for
the sustainment of this trial, and I found the effort was not
made in vain. I was now coughing, and had burst into a
profuse perspiration, and sitting on my bed, I felt a breath of
air waft coolly and gratefully on my dewy forehead. I then
knelt on the bed, and being more on a level with the air-hole,
I thanked God for the relief afforded by a more plentiful
supply of the heaven-breathed element. Soon after I got
cooler my coughing became less frequent, and I lay down on
the bed with my clothes on, promising myself a sound repose
during the remainder of the night. I had not dropped asleep

when the rattling of keys was again heard, the outer door was
unlocked, lights glanced in the lobby, and the names of Hunt
and Knight were pronounced ; bail had arrived for them, they
were called from their cells, and Hunt bidding me " good
night," and saying he would be with us again in the morning,
the door was banged to and locked, the light departed, and I
was soon in a peaceful sleep.   I afterwards, so long as I continued here, slept in Hunt's cell, but it was no better than the
others ; all were exactly the same as to dimension and the too
great exclusion of air.

The doors were thrown open in good time the next morning,
and after we had all washed at the pump we were subjected
to the prison rule of examination as to whether we were
infected by cutaneous disease.   Some of our party felt indignant at this, considering it a degradation; but I, who remembered the unpleasant discovery at Coldbath Fields, approved
of it, reflecting that it was impossible to keep the inmates of a
large prison in a clean and healthy state without daily examination.   Our breakfast consisted of milk, coffee, and bread-
and-butter, and I may as well mention here that the prison
allowance of gruel, bread, potatoes, soup, and butcher's meat,
were henceforward regularly dealt out to us ; a small quantity
of butter, I think to each man, was also given us twice a week
in common with the other prisoners, but half of this was
afterwards disallowed and cheese substituted, by order of the
visiting magistrates.

The daily routine of a pent-up life such as we led could not
afford much variety of incident.   We were all—now that
Hunt and Knight were gone—young men and full of life and
spirits.   We chatted, sung, told stories, had hopping and leaping matches, and walked in the yard ; we sometimes also
wrote letters, and when one arrived from a wife or a friend
the lucky wight would retire aside and read it by snatches and
morsels, lest it should be too soon done ; newspapers were also
permitted to pass, and we received one or more daily.   Hunt
and Knight also came to the round-house the morning after
they were bailed, and then set off for Manchester to make
preparations against the day on which we should have to plead.

Meantime we continued to make ourselves as easy as possible. The doctor came to see me and gave me a mixture, which did me some good, but I obtained the greatest relief at night by standing or kneeling on my bed, and inhaling the stream of air as it flowed in. On some nights, when my cough was rather merciful, I found amusement in composing, as at Coldbath Fields, bits of rude verse, like the following :—

> " Here is no repining,
> Every heart is true and steady.
> Here is no declining,
> Still for England's service ready.
> Here is not a tear shed,
> Such a weakness we disdain it.
> Here is not a bow'd head,
> Sign of sorrow, we refrain it.
> The more the cruel tyrants bind us,
> The more united they shall find us."

This verse pleased my companions exceedingly, and it afterwards became of some celebrity amongst the reformers.

One day James Murray, who was so dreadfully beaten at the White Moss, and one Heiffor, a barber from Manchester, were introduced into our yard by one of the turnkeys. They came for the purpose of looking us over, and identifying any of us who might have been present at that outrage, but, fortunately, none of our party happened to be on the Moss that morning, and none of us were ever sworn to as having been there ; at least neither of these two visitors swore to any of us. After viewing us some time, during which not a word was interchanged, they went away. We remarked that persons frequently came upon the round-house and on the great tower to look at us, and as we knew some of them were not our friends we afterwards made it a rule to walk into the day-room and shut the door the moment we noticed any such observers. We also made it a rule to sing "The Lancashire Hymn" every evening before locking-up time. We closed the door of our day-room during this piece of devotion—for we always sung in the true spirit of devotion—and surprised, at first, our almost insensible turnkeys by the awakening of tones of sublime and

heart-stirring music. We were sometimes taken out to pump
water, and that was a little variation from our dull life; it
afforded us opportunities for practical joking and some
laughter. We went to chapel on prayer days and Sundays,
and were also pleased with a trip to the great tower, where
our heights were taken by a standard measure, and a description of our hair, eyes, complexions, and external marks, was
carefully noted down in a book, and may there, probably, be
found to this day should any of my learned and searching
readers wish to consult it.

One morning Sir Charles Wolseley, Hunt, Mr. Thomas
Chapman, of Manchester, and other friends, called us down
to the round-house, and after some congratulations, and
hearty shaking of hands, they informed us that several bills
of indictment which had been presented against certain
individuals of the Manchester yeomanry corps, had been
thrown out by the grand jury, whilst all the indictments
preferred against our party had been returned true bills.
They also informed us that the proceedings of the magistrates
and yeomanry at Manchester had caused a strongly indignant feeling throughout the nation; that the public press had
very handsomely taken up the affair; and that we needed
not to fear being deserted in our struggle, for friends were
coming from all parts to give bail for us. Mr. Hunt put into
my hand a copy of the London *Times*, in which was set forth
an account of my arrest at Middleton, as already quoted. Sir
Charles had also seen my dear wife and child, and in compliment to the spirited conduct of the former, on the above
occasion, he had made her a present of a one pound bank-note,
for which kindness I sincerely thanked him, and felt relieved
from some apprehensions lest they might be distressed whilst
I was at this place; indeed, we were all tranquillised by an
assurance that our families would be protected during our
absence from home. This, if I recollect aright, was the first
time I had ever exchanged a word with Sir Charles, and it
seemed I was destined to know him only for his kindness,
many instances of which he afterwards gave me, as will
probably appear in the course of this my narrative. He was

one of the few who dared to be honest in the worst of times, who marched with the van of freedom against English misrule. May happiness attend his latest moment of consciousness, and may his name be ever cherished in many hearts as it is in mine!

Mr. Harmer, solicitor, of London, with Mr. Dennison, of Liverpool, also called to see us. Mr. Pearson, who, as we understood, was to be our legal manager in the case, was frequently at the gate, and what with the attentions of friends, and our own resources, we contrived to lead a much more worldly mannered life than might have been thought possible in such a place.

One day the iron gate at the round-house was thrown open, and a number of gentlemen entered and walked up the yard into the day-room, where most of us were at the time; we were given to understand they were "the grand jury," the same men who had found the indictments true against us, and had cut those against the magistrates and yeomanry. They looked at the place and at us some time, but mostly at us; we also eyed them pretty closely, but no civilities passed; in truth, we had none to spare; and it was quite as much as we could do to refrain from reproaching them in words. That, to be sure, would have been a sad breach of the irresponsibility which hedges our English juries, but it would have been quite natural, and might have come with a not monstrously bad grace from men in our situation, and treated as we had been. There was perhaps enough said in our looks; they gazed at us till I suppose they could guess what we would say, and then they went back, and in reply they stopped half our butter! One of our young fellows, Swift, I think, was devouring a wedge of bread-and-butter when they entered, and as he had not the manners, or the cunning, to put it aside, but kept biting and chewing, and anon looking most wolfishly towards their honours and worships, that circumstance perhaps suggested the propriety and the expediency and the "high and imperative duty" of "stopping our butter."

When the time comes that the grand jury system shall be abolished, or greatly modified in England, the conduct of these gentlemen in the bills affair—not the butter—will be quoted as one very strong authority for the change.

At length the day came when we were to appear before the court, to plead to the indictments found against us. The turnkeys conducted us through the round-house, through another yard, through a part of the great tower and into a long room at the back, which at this time was lighted by a lamp or two, casting a pale but distinct gleam through the place. Here we were told to wait, and there being a bench or two in the place, we were at liberty to sit if we chose it. I, however, preferred looking about me, and soon espied a man, not of our party, who was seated on one of the benches. This room, I should inform my reader, was, as I afterwards learned, termed " the sweating-room "; it was the room in which prisoners waited until called for trial, and to which they were, in the first instance, conducted after trial; it was therefore indeed fitly named. How many hundreds of victims—some doubtless innocent—had there sweated until their hearts were sick ? The one before me was an example to the point ; he sat near the light and I remarked him well. His dress and general appearance were those of a respectable country shopkeeper or small farmer. He seemed to be about forty years of age, his hair a little grey, and smoothed decently, but not affectedly, on his brow. His coat was drab and of the plain country cut ; one of those good but old-fashioned purple and spotted silk handkerchiefs was around his neck, and his shirt collar, which was turned down, looked so plain and white, that my imagination reverted to his comfortable country home. He sat with his hands clasped betwixt his knees, and his looks directed intensely, but calmly, towards a door in another part of the room. The sweat stood in big, bright drops on his forehead, so big, that they broke into each other and trickled down his face. Then he would wipe his brow, and soon again it would be clustered with the perspiration. He came from some country place near Bolton, and had just been tried for the then capital crime of passing forged bank-notes, and acquitted ; another indictment, however, lay against him, and he was waiting to be again conducted into court.

"He is an old offender," said our turnkey, "and if it goes against him this second time he may say his prayers—nothing can save him."

"But surely," I said, "if he only escapes this once more, he will never give you a chance of having him here again?"

"I rather think he will get off," he said; "the old judge seems not very fond of these things; but then he'll be here again, he's well known, he cannot keep out of it."

"Has he ever been taken before?" I asked. "No," replied the turnkey; "but they have had their eyes on him some time, and it's well known he's done a deal in the note line. He might as well go up and be cast now," he continued—"it will only give us trouble another time. We're sure to have him. When once they get properly into the note business, they never give over till it's too late."

The door from the interior opened, a person entered, and speaking to our conductor, we were motioned to go forward. We descended some steps, and passed along a subterranean passage, nearly dark, at the further end of which the light increased, and we could hear voices, and a kind of confused hum above. In a few minutes a man was handed down some steps into the passage by another, who held his arm; the former appeared to be in distress. They passed to the room from whence we had come, and our guide motioning us to advance, we mounted the steps, and found ourselves in an oblong box or compartment, mounted by iron spikes, in a large crowded place, lighted by numerous lamps and chandeliers, and with hundreds of eyes gazing upon us. The spectacle was certainly calculated to inspire us with awe and alarm; our sudden transition from a scene of gloom and wretchedness to one of light and splendour produced a momentary confusion of mind—a vacant wonder and uncertainty as to what all this could mean. One moment, however, and a glance around was sufficient to recall the mind to its duty; and then, whilst the ear was listening, the eye was observing, and the memory receiving impressions which have never yet been erased.

In the box where we stood were, besides ourselves, several

officers of the prison ; the deputy-governor—the young gentleman who received us at the gate—stood in a small space on
one side ; behind us, but separated from our box, was a
packed mass of human beings, with javelin men in their
liveries, and their glittering weapons. On our right was a
large pew or compartment, crowded with well-dressed persons;
before us, and somewhat elevated, sat the judge, a man of
venerable years, clothed in a long robe of bright scarlet and
ermine, with a flowing white wig, and a countenance of rough,
blunt mould; a look like that of a surly old lion, at once stern,
wilful, and magnanimous—this was the venerable Baron Wood.

On the bench with him were several gentlemen and ladies,
probably the sheriff and his friends ; all the space on the left
was equally crammed, and the galleries on each side were
crowded with elegantly attired females, who, I flattered myself,
seemed generally to be prepossessed in our favour. On the
floor, betwixt us and the judge, was a large table, covered
with green cloth, on which lamps were burning, and books,
papers, and writing apparatus were confusedly distributed;
around the table were a number of barristers in their costume:
some writing, some conversing, and others observing us.
Hunt, Moorhouse, Johnson, and Knight, were in the space
near the table, on the judge's right. Sir Charles Wolseley,
Mr. Chapman, Mr. Harmer, Mr. Dennison, Mr. Pearson, and
a number of other friends, were near them, and every other
inch of the floor was occupied. A number of reporters for the
metropolitan and county press were also there, plying their
ready pencils ; and it is probable that the description of this
scene, which some of those gentleman sketched on the spot,
might, if now consulted, display a more correct and striking
picture of the group than the present one drawn from memory
alone.

Mr. Littledale, who on this occasion acted for the Government, requested that the indictment might be read, and it
was accordingly read by the clerk of the arraigns. It stated
that the prisoners, being persons of a wicked and turbulent
disposition, did on the first day of July, conspire and agree
together to excite tumult and disturbance : and that they did,

on the 16th day of August, unlawfully, maliciously, and sedi-
tiously, assemble together, and cause others to assemble, to
the number of sixty thousand, in a formidable and menacing
manner, with sticks, clubs, and other offensive weapons ; with
banners, flags, colours, and placards, having divers seditious
and inflammatory inscriptions, and in martial array ; and did
on the said 16th of August, make great tumult, riot, and disturbance ; and for half an hour unlawfully and riotously did
continue assembled, making great tumult and disturbance,
contrary to the peace of our Sovereign Lord, the King, &c., &c.

Each of us pleaded " Not Guilty," and elected to traverse
until the next assizes. The judge proposed naming the
amount of our bail in a few days ; but after being respectfully
urged, with sundry good reasons, for an immediate determination, he mentioned ourselves in £200, and two sureties, each
in £100, as the amount of recognisance which would be
required on behalf of us who were in custody. We were
then re-conducted to our old quarters, and our fellow defendants on bail departed into the town with their friends.

I may as well mention that the poor fellow we had seen in
the sweating-room was again put to the bar the same night,
to answer an indictment for uttering another note of the
same parcel as the one for which he had been acquitted
belonged to, but in consequence of the strong observations of
the worthy judge, who held this was a part of the transaction
for which he had been already tried, the man again got off. I
believe no evidence was tendered. If I am not mistaken in the
person, however, he was soon after apprehended for a like
offence, and the predictions of the turnkey were verified.

On Tuesday, the 17th of September, we were again brought
up to put in bail. Hunt, Knight, Johnson, and Moorhouse,
were each bound in £400, and two sureties, in £200 each ;
and the conditions were that we should severally appear on
the first day of next session of Oyer and Terminer, to
answer the indictment which had been read. All the required
forms having now been complied with, Sir Charles Wolseley
and Mr. Chapman becoming my sureties, we were discharged
from custody ; and after some show off by Mr. Hunt, without

which indeed he scarcely knew how to get out of any matter,
we left the dock, and went with our friends to an inn in the
town, where we took a frugal repast, and remained for the
night.

The observant reader will have noted that we were sent
from the New Bailey to Lancaster Castle, because we had not
sureties ready to give bail with us. Now suppose a catastrophe like that of St. Peter's Field was by any means to take
place in Manchester in these days, does not the reader feel
assured that no ten honest labouring men would be allowed to
be dragged off for want of bail? I am of opinion that now
gentlemen in great numbers and of vast wealth would come
forward without the slightest appeal from the prisoners, and
tender themselves as sureties for the fulfilment of the law.
Such, if my view be correct, is the great change which has
taken place since the year 1819; and should not this change,
which is only one of many that are and have been working
vast alterations for the better in men's thoughts and feeling,
encourage us to hope that even without tumult, or violence,
or destruction of property, or oppression of person, all that is
requisite for the redemption of our native country will in due
time be ours if we can only have patience to rest upon reason,
and eschew violence? Some are in the habit of shouting " No
Surrender!" but I say we should all surrender; we should
surrender our passions, and our prejudices, and our uncharit-
ableness towards others. We should seek to win as much as
we can from the common humanity of our adversaries. The
good and the wise will pursue this course, and they will
succeed, whilst the treacherous, the arrogant and the intoler-
ant will dwindle far behind in the march, and will perish of
self-contention, instead of coming up to win the laurels.

It had been arranged that we should all travel the country
back from Lancaster in a four-horse stage coach. One
belonging to Moorhouse, which had conveyed some of our
friends to Lancaster, was accordingly selected, and in it and
upon it we left Lancaster on the morning after our liberation.
Some very inflated and bombastic accounts of this progress, if
I may so call it, appeared in several publications of those

times, but, as it is not my wish either to give a reprint of
exaggerations, or to detract from the real honour of our
triumph by a wreath of tinsel, I must leave such statements
as I find them in the prints of the day. The morning turned
out to be as fine a one as any holiday folks could wish. We
were cheered by rather large crowds in the streets of
Lancaster, breakfasted at Garstang, and on approaching
Preston, we fell in with multitudes of people, numbers of
whom carried handsome flags and banners, some with the
words, " Hunt and Liberty," and various other matters. From
Preston to Blackburn the crowds increased, and our passage
through the latter town was more prolonged, and the shouts
louder than before. From Blackburn to Bolton we were, I
believe, drawn the whole of the way, and the honest and
simple-hearted country weavers seemed to think no labour, no
distinction too great for the persecuted travellers. At Bolton
we were similarly welcomed ; Mr. Hunt and Mr. Pearson
each addressed a dense crowd from the windows of the Swan
Inn. We stopped at Bolton all night, and went towards
Manchester on the morning of Thursday, the 9th of September.
On arriving at Pendleton the crowds became immense, and
we approached the town at a very slow pace. Several stand
coaches, containing friends who had come out to meet us,
here joined the procession. The spectacle now was calculated
to produce feelings of surprise, and perhaps of pleasure ; but
any feelings of that sort were saddened in my breast by seeing
all this fine energy cast like flowers at the feet of one who I
now began to suspect was excessively egotistical ; and I
almost doubted whether he who loved himself so well could
ever really love his country for its own sake ; whether one of
such a nature could be expected to remain faithful, if, from
any change of circumstances, his country no longer yielded
the incense to his self love, for which his whole heart seemed
to beat. But I was amused, as well as a little humiliated, by
what was continually occurring near me. Hunt sat on the
box-seat; I sat immediately behind him, and the other
defendants were disposed of as suited convenience. Moorhouse stood on the roof of the coach, holding by a rope which

was fastened to the irons at each side. He had kept that
position all the way from Bolton, I am not quite certain
whether or not from Blackburn. Hunt continually doffed his
hat, waved it lowly, bowed gracefully, and now and then
spoke a few kind words to the people ; but if some five or ten
minutes elapsed without a huzza or two, or the still more
pleasing sound, " Hunt for Ever ! " " Hunt for Ever ! " he
would rise from his seat, turn round, and, cursing poor Moorhouse in limbs, soul, or eyes, he would say, " Why don't you
shout man ? Why don't you shout ? Give them the hip,
—— you, don't you see they're fagging ? " Moorhouse
himself was fagging ; he would, however, wipe his forehead
and face, which were as red as a kiln, and waving his hat,
and raising his voice, now become perfectly hoarse, he would
" hip, hip," and the third " hip," was generally drowned in a
loud huzza, accompanied by the afore-mentioned exclamation,
now become so grateful to the ears of our leader. He would
then resume his seat, the bowing and hat-waving went on as
before ; we had a little calm, and advanced a short distance ;
Moorhouse was again reminded, and the many-throated voice
again yielded the words of acclamation. At times I had some
difficulty to avoid laughing in Hunt's face ; at times I was
vexed at being a party in such a piece of little vanity ; I con-
trasted all this glare and noise with the useful results of calm,
sober thought, and silent determination, and I made up my
mind that, when once out of this, I would not in future be any
party in such trumpery exhibitions, in the unworthy setting
up of the instrument instead of the principle of a great cause.
To this resolution I have, I think, been faithful ; and though
I have been, and still may be blamed, it is not likely that I
shall ever depart from the rule.

We arrived at Smedley, and were all hospitably received by
Mr. and Mrs. Johnson. At length I got away, and with my
wife on my arm, and my little girl holding my hand, I was
once more happy in traversing by hedge-sides, with their
autumnal hues, towards that lowly home from which
thirteen days before I had departed under such different
circumstances.

CHAPTER XXIX.

OLDHAM INQUEST—REPORTERS EXCLUDED—PETER FINNERTY—
CONDY, ROSS, AND OTHERS—AUTHOR CORRESPONDS WITH
THE PRESS.

I SHALL not pretend to enter into anything like a general history of those times, but shall content myself with stating events which more or less affected my own concerns. The inquest on John Lees, at Oldham, commonly called the Oldham inquest, was the next transaction of importance, as connected with our unfortunate meeting. I was without work, and so I put a pencil and some paper into my pocket and went to Oldham, with a view to copy such parts of the evidence as, in my opinion, might be useful in the ensuing trial in which I should have to take a share. The inquest was held in the large room of the Angel Inn. The reporters for several London journals had been put out of the room for persisting in furnishing daily reports contrary to the coroner's order, and a rather strict supervision was held over the other reporters, both for the London and provincial press, lest they should trespass in like manner; a few reporters only were therefore admitted, and I took my seat beside them, and noted down very expertly, for a first effort, a good deal of the evidence which was given on that day. At one time there was a general clearing out amongst the reporters—several had got in, and were taking notes as usual; the coroner therefore ordered them out, and Mr. Barnes, editor of the *Times*, Mr. Ross, and Mr. Condy were expelled, as was also Mr. Finnerty, of the *Morning Chronicle*. The coroner asked who I was, and on my explaining to him my motive for attending and taking notes, he said no more, and I remained one of the privileged few. A short time before this, whilst perambulating the streets of Manchester in search of work, I was going down Bridgewater Place, when a gentleman threw up a window of the Bridgewater Inn, then the head inn of the town, and called me by name. It was Mr. Pearson, our attorney, and he, finding I was at liberty for a short time, asked me in and introduced me to Mr. Finnerty, who was stopping there; and thus I became personally known to that rather remarkable man. I had previously learned somewhat of his history from several passages in "Cobbett's Register." He had suffered under the government of Castlereagh in Ireland, had been convicted of a libel in England, and had gone through a long imprisonment for it in Lincoln Castle.

When I came out of the room at the inquest Mr. Finnerty, profiting by his accidental knowledge of me, asked me into a room, and with much ease and perfect self-possession—in neither of which was he seldom deficient—he inquired what I had been doing at the inquest, and on my producing my notes he slapped me on the shoulder, and continued, "Ah! Bamford, my dear fellow, you must let me have the loan of those notes. You will, I know—won't you, now?" I said I could not spare them; they would be of service to me on my trial. "Ah! and is it the thrial you're dreaming about? Niv'r disthress yourself on that account, man: you'll all be well taken care of. Why, isn't there Harmer here, and Pearson, our friend, and Hunt, himself a host? Ah! my dear friend, you needn't be bothering your head about the thrial yit. You could let me have the notes, you know, and get them back in print—they'll do you honner, boy! and, hear ye now, I'll pay you for your throuble." I refused to part with my notes, to the evident chagrin and disappointment of my new friend, who eyed me with his peculiar owl-like squint and paraded to and fro in fretful mood. I, however, kept my writings, and went home; and in a day or two I received a note requesting me to call on him at the Bridgewater Arms. I did so, and the result was that I agreed to attend the inquest on his account, and to furnish him with notes and verbal communications for the *Morning Chronicle*.

I accordingly attended at Oldham during several days, and afterwards at the Star Inn, Manchester, until the proceedings were quashed on the alleged ground of an improper interference with the jury. And thus commenced my first correspondence with the public press.

Mr. Hunt, it would seem, had been taken with a horror of Lancashire juries and Lancashire gaols. Nothing would satisfy him save a removal of the trial to another county, and in accordance with his pressing solicitations myself and the other co-defendants joined him in an application for a removal; and, after a hearing before the judges, the application was acceded to, and the cause ordered for trial at the next Spring Assizes at York.

Seeing, as I suppose, that I was pretty active with my pen, and had, besides, rather more than a mere countryman's share of ready information, Mr. Finnerty intimated that if I were in London he could procure an engagement for me at the *Morning Chronicle* office. Mr. Pearson approved of the idea, and was almost sure that something for my advancement in society would offer if I were only at the metropolis. Sir Charles Wolseley entirely coincided, but, whether I went to London or not, he should be glad at any rate to have me as his guest during a week or fortnight at Wolseley Bridge. These flattering prospects determined me, and a day or two after Mr. Finnerty had left Manchester I arrived by the coach at Wolseley Arms Inn, Wolseley Bridge. During the supper, which the coach passengers took together, a London reporter before mentioned and a tradesman from Manchester, who shortly afterwards became bankrupt, made, as I thought, some too-free allusions to the parts which Sir Charles Wolseley and Mr. Finnerty had been acting in the Manchester affair, and to their political conduct generally. I remained silent some time, until I perceived a look directed towards me. I then said it was a pity the two gentlemen they had been making free with were not present, but if they would stop whilst a message was sent to the hall I had no doubt they would soon come over and give the talkers whatever explanation they chose to ask to their face. My sentiment was approved of by several at the table, and especially by one gentlemanly looking man, who I thought would have been with the other party. "John," I said to the waiter. "Yes, sir." "Can you step to the hall, and——" "Coach, gemmen! Coach, coach!" said the driver at the door; and in a trice the two respectable backbiters had left the room, when I and several other of the passengers enjoyed a laugh at their expense.

The next morning I went over to the hall, and found Finnerty quite comfortably domiciled. Lady Wolseley was in the straw upstairs, so that Sir Charles had much of his own way below. Friend Finnerty, now that he had the run of a splendid suite of apartments, attendance of servants, and all hospitalities, was also somewhat changed in his manner. His place was in the parlour with Sir Charles; mine in the housekeeper's room, with the occasional company of that amiable, respectable, and well-informed lady. I dined with her in the servants' hall, and took my other meals in her apartment, in company with her, the lady's maid (a joking, smiling, and modest young girl), and a Monsieur something, the French cook. I lived pretty agreeably amongst my kindhearted new acquaintance, yet at times I could not prevent gloomy sensations from pressing on my mind. Finnerty had become quite condescending, for which I could not prevail on myself to feel thankful. Sir Charles was always kind and affable, without pretension, but still I could not but feel that in his house I was only a very humble guest. I had read how "an Ayrshire ploughman" had once been deemed good company for a Scottish duchess, but I found that the barriers of English rank were not to be moved by "a Lancashire weaver," though he could say, "I also am a poet," and, quite as much as the Scottish bard, a patriot also. I lodged at the inn, and often on mornings would I stroll out solitarily to look at the deer on the moorlands. Those majestic and beautiful animals would toss their proud antlers, gaze a moment in surprise, as if they also knew I was a stranger, and,

> "Stretching forward free and far,
> Seek the wild heaths."

Sometimes I rambled through the town of Rugeley, but I knew not any one there, nor did any one know me, and my visits consequently yielded but little social intercourse. Often would I saunter through the secluded and quiet village of Colton, but I knew not then that such a man as Walter Savage Landor existed, and if I had I am not certain that I should have ventured to knock at his door. The little village of College, or Col-edge, with its church, the banks of the Trent, and the grounds about Wolseley Hall, were often the objects of a contemplation which was continually wandering to other scenes. Several times I went with Monsieur to shoot rabbits, but I killed none, and was more likely to be shot myself; twice I walked across my comrade's fire, and the pellets came peppering about my legs. I was thinking of other things, wearied, but not ungrateful, out of place, and "out of gearing," as the mechanists would say.

At length the glad morning came when an end was to be put to this. I was to go with Finnerty to London, with a gig and horse, which Charles Pearson had left at Stafford, I think, on his way down to Lancashire. Sir Charles made me a present of two pounds; Finnerty took the whip, and bidding good morn to our worthy host, we drove slowly from Wolseley Hall.

We passed through Rugeley, Mavesyn Ridware (Malvoisin, one of the heroes of "Ivanhoe"), and along a rural country of farm-steads, clustered cottages, and other sights of profitable industry. I soon thought Finnerty was but an indifferent driver, he could not get the mare to go; he kept lashing, stamping on the bottom of the gig, hissing, and calling "go-'long," but the tit did not quit the ground. She would trot a little down a slope or on a short level; but there was no speed nor any continuation. I often got out to ease her on the ascents, for I did not like to have my weight lashed out of her, but still there was little amendment; she could not get to a pace much more keep one; in fact she spoke by her manner, as plainly as a dumb beast could speak, "I cannot do it, gentlemen,—I would freely, if I could, but I have not the work in me. I am done, I am old!" I soon framed this address for her in my mind, and repeated it to my fellow traveller, who said it was not so ; she had been starved by some rascally ostler, and a warm mash or two would bring her round. He, however, withheld his whip rather more, until her pace became a creep, when again he would give her a cut or two, stamp, hiss, and lash again, and make up the lost lashes by as many imprecations against the "scoundrelly ostlers." I was right, however; had she been fit for work it is not likely that Charles Pearson would have left her.

I began to be amused by the manner of my fellow traveller, and I thought better of him for laying the blame anywhere save on the dumb beast. I soon found that he wished me to be a useful companion on the road that is, a kind of half cad, and half comrade, and, as I really thought he had much goodness at heart, I felt disposed to humour him in all his bearable caprices.

At Litchfield, Finnerty spent an hour in looking at the cathedral, whilst I looked after the mare at the inn. At Birmingham, which we reached tardily, we dined, gave the mare a good feed, and after resting two hours my friend, un-expectedly by me, gave the word to proceed, and, with reluc-tance on my part, for I thought the beast had done enough for that day, we went on to some road-side inn, about nine miles further, where we got down and the jaded thing was released and put into a warm stable. On looking over the luggage, it was discovered that a new silk umbrella, which Finnerty had bought at Manchester, was missing. He went into a passion, and stormed with all the wordiness and gesticulation for which his countrymen are remarkable ; whilst I, sometimes provoked, sometimes amused, sat coolly and smoked a pipe until supper was ready. He laid all the blame on me ; he expected I would have seen that the luggage was safe ; he had trusted all to me, and was thus disappointed, like a fool as he was, for troubling himself about other people's welfare. He was sure it had been left at Birmingham, and it was my neglect in not putting it in the gig ; and then again he repeated what it had cost him—two pounds, I think.

When I could get a word in, I reminded him of its being in

his hand at a certain part of the road we had just come, on which he acknowledged that it was so ; but he said he put it in on my side, and I, no doubt, had suffered it to slip down by the apron. I was of the same opinion, that it had slipped out of the gig, but I defended myself from all blame as to its loss, proffering, however, to go back in the morning, and see if I could find it. This rather pacified him, and we got supper, but his philosophy had been too sorely tested, and when we parted for the night he was in very bad humour. I got up early next morning, and went back on the road about four miles, looking at every rut by the way, but nothing could I see of the umbrella ; as I returned I inquired at several places, but nothing could I hear of it. He was at breakfast when I got to the inn, and on making known the bad result of my search the " fat was in the fire " again, and we yoked up, and went forward mutually dissatisfied.

At Stratford-on-Avon he had come to a little, for I also had been knitting my brows. He went to see Shakespeare's monument, and I the house in which the poet resided, a dilapidated place, the walls covered with the names of persons who had visited, and I added mine.

At an ascent betwixt Stratford and Shipton, I must drive and Finnerty would walk, for the once. He got out encumbered with his top and box coats, and began to ascend a narrow track which I saw would lead him from the road, and not to it again ; as he had not, however, of late, paid much respect to my opinions, I thought I might as well not obtrude them just at that moment, and so I kept moving forward, leaning on the gig-side, and keeping an eye towards my blusterous friend. He mounted to some height, when, looking up, he perceived his dilemma, and then, with a twist and a jerk, expressive of impatience, he descended the way he had gone up. I laughed until tears came into my eyes, and had with difficulty composed myself, when he having hallooed as loud as he could, and I having stopped, he came up puffing and perspiring, and so we went on.

At Shipton we learned that a coach would pass through the town that night for Oxford, and Finnerty took a sudden, and to me a happy, resolution to proceed by it, leaving me to bring the horse and gig the day following to the Mitre Inn, at Oxford. He intimated that he had a particular engagement to be there next morning; and thus, for the present, I lost the society of my troublesome, querulous, but sometimes amusing companion.

It was a fine morning when, leaving Shipton, I urged the old tit gently on the road to the great seat of learning. Every nook, dell, and hill was new to me; and the men, the women, the children, and the houses were objects for continual observation. The mare had it pretty much her own way; her load was lighter, and she went trotting when she listed, and walked when she had a right to do—namely, up-hill, and it was only when I detected her absolutely crawling that I touched her with the whip. At Chapel House, a large posting establishment, we both breakfasted, and then went on, through Eustone, Kiddington, and to Woodstock, the scene of the tale of Fair Rosamond, which had deeply interested me when a boy. At a respectable looking publichouse, where I stopped, I endeavoured to learn whether there was any tradition as to the probable site of the famous bower of the unfortunate beauty, but the people knew nothing respecting it, I heard enough about Blenheim and its duke, but I should not feel justified in repeating what they said, and the less so because the persons with whom I conversed were strangers to me, and neighbours to the nobleman, and therefore the more likely to remember his failings, and forget his commendable parts.

On entering Oxford I was struck by the noble and venerable appearance of many of its buildings, which I concluded in my own mind must be its churches and colleges. The streets were occupied by a numerous and very respectable looking population, and I was not long in descrying, by the peculiarity of their dress, some of those fortunate and ingenious youths who, "born with silver spoons in their mouths," are, as we are taught to believe, "designed by a wise providence," and are certainly permitted by a wise people (?) to spoon up the riches and superfluities, which else would, by their very grossness, render said people dull of intellect, and sluggish in action ; and yet I didn't think the young fellows looked like " spoonies."

Having been directed to the Mitre Inn, I drove thither, and resigned the horse and gig to the ostler, with a charge to look well to the former. I then inquired at the bar for Mr. Finnerty, and was shown into a very smart room upstairs, where a plain-featured lady beyond the bloom of life, with a bonnet on, dressed in a florid style, and with a deep patten-shoe on one foot, was caressing a fine child that could run about. I paused and held back, the lady was surprised. I apologised and said I understood Mr. Finnerty was there. She said he was, and asked me to take a seat, he was in another room, and she would go for him, and she went out, taking the child with her. In a minute I heard my friend's voice as if something was wrong. He came in, shook my hand, and asked me to take refreshment. I took some tea and meat, and gave him an account of my pleasant journey. Whilst we were talking, the same lady with another child entered the room, and almost immediately went out again. He gave me to understand that the children were his, and that Mrs. Finnerty, himself, and the children, would return to London together. He asked how I should go, and I told him that I should walk it. He asked when I should start, and I said I had no connections in Oxford, nor any business to transact, and I saw no reason why I should not set out that night, and had best be making my way. Of course, he said, if I preferred going, there could be no reason why I should not ; he then gave me his address in London, and said I must be sure and call upon him, and he would immediately on his arrival have some conversation with Mr. Perry about me, and he doubted not that Mr. Perry would put something in my way. I then got up, and taking me by the hand he bade me good-bye, and said I must be sure to see him in London. I said I would, and repeating his salutation, I came downstairs, and went into the street.

The shades of evening were closing over the city when I thus adventured to begin my journey. I had no luggage, save a small bundle and an umbrella, which I threw over my shoulder, and a stout ashen plant in my hand. I knew not which way to set forth, but went along the street towards the left, until I saw some respectable looking people, of whom I inquired the way to London ; and they gave me such directions as enabled me soon to quit the town and strike into the open country. I continued to walk and it soon became dark, and when night had completely set in, I could scarcely trace the road before me. I walked, however, briskly, and went a long way without meeting any person, or hearing anything, save now and then the tinkle of a sheep bell. At length, when I must have left Oxford four or five miles behind, I began to hear noises at a distance on my right, and soon after I saw gleams like those of lights in the windows of a town. In a short time there were lights before me, and I found they proceeded from a publichouse, into which I went and asked for some ale, which was brought to me, and was of most excellent quality. On looking around, I liked the appearance of the house also; the rooms were neatly furnished and clean, the company was apparently respectable, and the people of the house obliging. I inquired how far it was to the next village, and how the road lay, and they all gave such an account as made me begin to think I had best remain where I was ; the people of the house were of the same opinion, and so I took up my quarters there for the night.

Whilst we were chattering and enjoying ourselves comfortably with our pipes, some young fellows came into the next room, and called for ale. They were in high glee, and from their conversation, which we could not but hear, we learned that there had been a kind of battle-royal in the village betwixt some of the lads of the place and a party of collegians, and that the latter, after fighting bravely, which they allowed them the merit of generally doing, had been soundly thrashed, and compelled to retreat. I concluded that it must have been the noise of this row which had saluted my ears on the road. Some inquiries on my part, elicited an opinion from the company as to the general conduct of the young gentlemen at college, and it certainly, like all other human emanations, had its dark side, as well as its bright one, only rather more of the former, than should be expected, considering they were to become examples to and directors of others.

They were represented as courageous fighters, generous remunerators, and profuse spenders ; all of which most of the company allowed were good English gentlemanly qualities ; but then, in their intercourse with those not of their class, they were represented as being arrogant, wilful, and capricious ; and too prone to lay on hard when they got the upper hand.

It was not to be wondered at, said an elderly person who sat on the other side of the room ; it was not the young gentlemen's fault, but the fault of their "pa's" and "ma's" at home, and of the institutions of the country. If Will was schooled to be an officer in the army, would he not begin by trying to domineer over and command all who would submit to him ? If Dick was to have his father's broad acres, how could he better prepare for the enjoyment of them, as things went, than by learning to drink, gamble, and box ; by picking up stable slang ; and becoming a connoisseur in "dogs, horse-flesh, and women"—as they had it—and by an early imitation of that reckless self-willedness which he had seen practised by his class at home ? If James is for the Church, should he not learn to be combative when a boy ; inasmuch as he would have to contend against "the world, the flesh," and —another antagonist—and in favour of tithes, preferments, and fat livings ? and if Jack was preparing for the navy, what so natural as that he should practise with a bamboo, instead of a rope's-end, on the heads and shoulders of the King's subjects ? Great folks, he said, sent their sons to college, and they came there tainted with the vices of their order, and the follies of their parents : they were here planted thick together like young trees ; the rank and worthless dragged the others up ; the vicious overshadowed the virtuous, and when they had become noxious or morally withered, they went back into the world, as their fathers had done, to prepare a new race to succeed them. All allowed that the elderly gentleman's remarks were about the fact ; I begged leave to drink his health, the company followed my example, and the conversa-

tion then becoming general, and chiefly on rural affairs, I went
to bed.

I rose early; the morning again was as fine as could be
desired, and I felt happy at travelling beside broad pastures,
with the free wind blowing around me. I first traversed a
level plain, and then went up a rather steep eminence, after
which followed a road through woods a long way; all were
new and interesting scenes to me. I walked some twelve
or fourteen miles, and then made a hearty breakfast of bread,
cheese, and ale, at a neat-looking, road-side publichouse.
From thence I went on, through High Wycombe and Beacons-
field, where again I stopped a short time. I could not but
admire the cleanness and airiness of the town. Towards
evening I arrived at Uxbridge, and rested, after which I went
towards London, and had gone some miles in the dark and
rain, when a stage coach overtook me, and I mounted, and was
set down at the "Bolt-in-Tun," Fleet Street, where, perhaps,
it is unnecessary to say that I received very civil treatment,
and stopped for the night.

CHAPTER XXX.

MR. HUNT—SIR RICHARD PHILLIPS—AUTHOR'S PETITIONS TO PARLIAMENT—EARL GROSVENOR, AND HIS HOUSE AT GROS-VENOR PLACE.

THE morning after my arrival I went to the warehouse of a friendly tradesman in Cheapside to look after some clothes, and other requisites, which I had directed to be sent after me, and I found all safe. I next went and took private lodgings, and then sought out Mr. Hunt, whom I found at the house of one Giles, a bread-baker, in Wyche Street, Strand. He introduced me to Sir Richard Phillips, and I had, during my stay, many opportunities of conversing with that worthy gentleman and scholar. He was friendly towards Hunt, but did not like his overbearing manner. Once, I recollect, when Hunt came, he ordered the footman to say he was not at home, and on observing probably a degree of surprise in my look, he said Mr. Hunt was neither happy himself, nor would he let his friends be so. They must not only serve him, but they must do it at his own time, in his own manner, and to the extent he wished, or he would quarrel with them. His earnestness and vehemence he carried with him everywhere, and exhibited on the most trifling occasions; in consequence, he became annoying and oppressive, and his best friends were sometimes compelled to defend themselves by not being at home. I knew there was too much truth in Sir Richard's representations to blame him greatly for his conclusions, though I must own I did not like my friend Hunt, with all his faults, to be thus dealt with; but Sir Richard said there was no other mode, and he must either shut his door occasionally, or quarrel with him at once, and have done with him.

I gave Sir Richard my account of the Manchester affair, and at his suggestion, and under his care, petitions to the Houses of Lords and Commons were drawn up on my behalf, praying an investigation into the whole of the transaction, and offering to prove the allegations of the petitions at the bar of each House. Both petitions were duly presented, and with the usual result : namely, both were " laid upon the table."

But, connected with my petition to the Lords, an incident occurred, which, as it affords a glimpse of the great in London, I will narrate.

Earl Grosvenor was the nobleman selected to present my petition to the House of Lords, and Sir Richard went with me to his mansion, in Grosvenor Place I think it was. His lordship was not at home, and we were directed to call on a certain day. It happened that Sir Richard was then engaged, and I went to his lordship myself. The great burly porter, who wore a rich livery trimmed with gold lace, would scarcely admit me within the door, when he found I had not a letter of introduction. I explained to him my business with his lordship, but it was of no use, he could not send my message up. A fine table, with pens and paper, was near the window of the hall, and in my simplicity I made a move towards it, saying I could soon write a note to his lordship, but he said he could not allow me to write there ; it was contrary to orders, and would cost him his place if the other servants saw me. I accordingly bundled out, and went to a tavern and wrote a note, which I took back ; the porter then took the note, and told me to come again in about twenty minutes or half an hour. It was raining, and I had nowhere to go under cover, save the tavern, so I went there again—not much liking, however, this mode of noble housekeeping—and waited with impatience the time for the interview. I again went, and now the folding doors were thrown open long before I arrived at the steps ; the late surly porter received me with a respectful inclination and a smile, saying my note had been sent up, and his lordship would see me. He then rang a bell, and a servant appeared, to whom the porter announced my name. The servant asked me to follow him, and he led me into a very grand room, where he left me, saying his lordship would be with me in a few minutes. I had never seen anything like the richness of this place before, everything seemed almost too sumptuous, and too delicate for a human habitation, and to me it seemed a little museum of curious and costly things, arranged but to look at, and not to use. There were mirrors, and pictures, and cushions, and carpets glowing like silk; and delicate hangings; and curtains, as fine as gossamer in summer; then the tables shone like glass, and the chairs, with their high cushions trussed up, quite tempted one to sit. Well, I stood looking about me some time, and no one appeared, and at last I thought, "I'll sit down at any rate; if his lordship should come in, he cannot be so greatly offended at one taking a seat in his house." So I sat down, and was quite surprised; I almost sank to my elbows in the soft downy cushion, and immediately jumped up again, thinking those seats could never really be meant for human bones to rest upon, and I would not for the world have been taken by his lordship sitting there, with the cushion up to my elbows like a puff of soap suds. I began to make the thing right again, and was so busied, when I heard a slight creaking noise; immediately I resumed my posture of attention, and a tall, gentlemanly-looking person, forty or forty-five years of age, dressed in a blue coat with yellow buttons, undoubtedly of gold, entered and accosted me in a very courteous and affable manner, and immediately entered upon the business of my petition. I addressed him as "my lord," which indeed he was, and told him somewhat about the subject of my petition, which I now showed him, and requested he would be so kind as to present for me to the House of Lords. He looked at it a few minutes, and said he would present it. He then questioned me about the state of the country, and particularly of my own neighbourhood, to each of which I gave him brief and true answers, according to the best of my ability. He then questioned me about our new rector at Middleton, the Rev. John Haughton, and as I was bound in truth, though not at the time over partial to him, I gave his lordship a fair and honourable account of the worthy clergyman, whereat he seemed much pleased. Soon after I made my final bow, and was myself bowed out by the porter, and so I took my leave of that grand mansion and its immensely rich owner.

I frequently called to see Sir Richard Phillips, who always advised me to cultivate literature and poetry, as two friends who would be ready to console me at all times, and under all circumstances. He wished me to write something, in the metrical way, about the Manchester affair, but I never did; it never presented itself, as it were, to me in the form of poetry; it was too overpowering, too brimful of affliction, to be measured in verse. I made several attempts that way, but it would not do, and I never sought to describe it in any other form until this present publication. I felt grateful to Sir Richard, he gave me much useful caution and advice as to other matters in London. He acted the part of a real friend, and was the only professed scholar and literary character to whose acquaintance I can refer with entire satisfaction.

I called several times at the office of the *Morning Chronicle* to inquire if Mr. Finnerty was in town, and at last learned that he was so. I accordingly made my way to a suburb, somewhere west of the town, and following my directions, I knocked at the door of one of a lot of recently constructed edifices at the angle of a square. The same lady with the patten came to the door, and invited me to walk in, and showed me into a small, neatly furnished room on my right. Finnerty soon made his appearance, and, after mutual compliments, he asked when I arrived in town, what I had been doing, and such like, all of which I answered. He seemed, I thought, very mysterious and embarrassed in his manner, did not ask me to sit down or take anything, but at last said, " Would you like a walk round the square, Bamford ? " I, thinking he wished for more private conversation, said I would, and we went out. We paced once round this place, chatting about indifferent matters, I expecting him to introduce my business with the *Morning Chronicle*, and at last, on my mentioning it, he did say he had not been able to see Mr.

Perry yet. We had then arrived at the angle from whence we set out, and were opposite his own door, when, giving me his hand, he said, "Good morning, Bamford; I shall be seeing you in town some of these days," and with that he went into the house and shut the door. I was mute with astonishment; my first impulse was to send the panel in with my foot, but then I thought neither the door nor its owner had done me harm, and at last, consoling myself with the reflection that it was no place for a worthy, honest man, and that I was better out of it than within it, I went away.

I should not have been much troubled at the sudden termination of this friendship, which I had for some time suspected to be all on my side, had I not, on returning into the city, weary, disappointed, and hungry, found that I must change my last shilling for my dinner. I had paid several sums on the road for ostlers, baiting, and so forth, before Finnerty left me at Shipton, and I had also paid all the expenses of the journey from Shipton to Oxford, which Finnerty had undertaken to pay, and said he would reimburse on my arrival at the latter place. I had quite forgotten to mention these matters at Oxford, but now, forced by necessity, I probably should have done so in a delicate way, had Finnerty, as I expected he would, asked me to take breakfast with him. But, as I said, they had quite slipped my memory, and friend Finnerty's, too, as it seemed, and now I had the uncomfortable prospect before me of starvation, or a beggarly dependence on the hospitality of friends, neither of which conditions had I anticipated on leaving home.

Next morning I went to the house of Mr. Pearson, in Aldersgate Street, and stated to him my willingness to try my hand at writing in his office, at terms previously mentioned by him, namely, a guinea a week. He immediately set me to work at copying, and thus by a word I was metamorphosed from a rude Lancashire rustic into "a limb of the law." I worked hard until two o'clock, and then went out, not to dine, for I had not wherewith to purchase a dinner. At four I returned and wrote again until six, and then shut up, and went to my humble lodgings at London Wall. I did thus for three or four days, getting my breakfast and supper at my lodgings, and going without dinner. I began to feel unwell; I was cold, shivery, and nervous; I had never been quite well since the night I came drenched into London, and now, feverish as I was, the employment became intolerably irksome. At length I went to bed, and was so ill next morning I could not rise, I was in a fever, and the agitation of my mind added to the indisposition of my body.

The next day I went to Mr. Pearson, and told him that I had been ill, and hoped he would excuse me, but I could not bear to sit at the desk. He readily accepted my apology, and gave me a pound note for what I had done; he also invited me to come to his house that evening and take tea. I went and met him, his lady, a mild and beautiful young being, and a gentleman who was about to come out " as a phenomenon " at the bar. The day after I again went to Mr. Pearson's by appointment, when he took me to Peel's coffee-house, and set me to take memoranda from the newspapers, of passages from the addresses made by judges to grand juries on several State prosecutions. I gave him my notes, and believe I did the work to his satisfaction.

In a day or two after this I was informed that the London committee for the relief of the sufferers at the Manchester meeting had determined on presenting each of the persons who had been apprehended and held to bail with a sum of money—ten pounds, I believe—as some compensation for their loss of time and the inconvenience they had experienced. I accordingly went to the counting-house and manufactory of Mr. Alexander Galloway, the treasurer, whose place was then near Holborn, and presented myself for what belonged to me. He was at his desk writing, and I found him a cool, cautious, methodical man of business. He was very affable and mild, and I must say reasonable and convincing in his manner. On my stating who I was and the nature of my visit, he said he was sorry he could not pay me then, as, never having to his knowledge seen me before, he could not be certain that I was the person I represented myself to be, and he wished me to bring some gentleman, or produce a note from some one whom he knew, that I was the same Samuel Bamford who had been arrested and committed to Lancaster Castle. I mentioned Mr. Hunt, Mr. Harmer, Mr. Wooller, and Mr. Pearson, who I said would instantly verify, could I get to see them, but the afternoon was far worn, and I might not be able to meet with them that night; I, however, had a letter or two of Mr. Hunt's, and one of Major Cartwright's, which I offered to produce. Those, he said, would not do; they would not show that I was the person to whom they were addressed. I must confess I was now a little piqued and disappointed, for I was in want of some money for immediate necessaries. He saw, I thought, that I was hurt, for he begged I would not deem him needlessly cautious, as I must perceive, on reflection, how necessary it was, in a great place like London, to be quite certain as to the persons with whom they contracted business. He showed me, and he entirely conciliated me by the earnestness with which he did it, that he could not possibly have any wish to withhold the money from the person for whom it was ordered, and all he sought to ascertain was that I really was the person. I saw and appreciated his motive and his method of exactitude, and left him with the intention of obtaining a note from Mr. Harmer, whose office in Hatton Garden was the nearest place where I could expect to meet the requisite identification. Mr. Harmer was not within, nor would he be that night, and I gave the matter up until next day, submitting to the rather familiar inconvenience of going to bed dinnerless and supperless. On the forenoon of the following day I procured the necessary verification, and Mr. Galloway paid me the money, which proved a great present relief, as it enabled me to procure necessaries, and to pay off my lodging and other small accounts. I afterwards called on Mr. Galloway frequently, in a friendly manner, and at one of these visits I saw Robert Owen, who was then exciting attention by his plans for the amelioration of the condition of mankind; at another visit Major Cochrane was there, an officer who was with the 15th Hussars on the field at the great meeting at Manchester. Mr. Galloway's counting-house appeared to be frequently resorted to by literary and scientific men of all parties and of all professions.

My petitions to Parliament had been duly presented, and had appeaied, thanks to my friend Sir Richard, in several of the London journals. They excited some attention, and the committee of the relief fund deemed it proper that similar petitions should be presented by others of the sufferers. I accordingly, having now no further prospects or business in London, returned to Lancashire, and besides being of some use to Messrs. Hall and Service, who were sent down to select proper objects for relief, I promoted the getting up of petitions praying for inquiry, and when that had been done to a sufficient extent, I found the time at hand when it was necessary that I should begin to look about for evidence to produce at the approaching trial at York.

On application to my attorney, Mr. Pearson, I received a set of instructions for the collection of evidence.

Acting under these instructions, I wrote down with my own hand the examinations of about twenty-two witnesses, chiefly resident at Middleton, which examinations were copied literally by Mr. Pearson's clerk, and formed the basis of the defence relative to our proceedings. I next subpœned my witnesses, and they were requested to meet at the Dog and Partridge publichouse, at Middleton, at six o'clock in the morning of Monday, the 13th of March, in order that we might all go in a body on foot to York. On the evening preceding we took supper together, and we were joined by a number of witnesses from Manchester, who preferred to walk with us rather than go by coach. On mustering, I think we amounted to about three score, of whom probably a dozen were women, who, in high glee, chose to take the road with their relatives and friends. I should state that Mr. Pearson had placed in my hands a sum of money to pay the expenses, in which I was limited by my own discretion alone ; all my plans had been laid before him at Manchester, and he entirely approved of them. We set forward, therefore, with light hearts ; and amid this crowd of faces beaming with hope and the excitement of novelty, I could discover two only which wore a cast of thought and sadness. My wife and child were, as they always wished to be, with me ; they were going with us as far as Rochdale, whence they were to return; my faithful dog, Mora, also went gambolling on before us. I tried to be cheerful, with a view to promote the same feeling amongst all around me, and I could have succeeded, had I only been concerned; but when I caught my wife turning her head aside to conceal her emotion, and, looking down, met the tearful eye and inquiring look of my child, who held my hand, I could not but experience a pang that brought darkness and uncertainty to my heart, and which I endeavoured to conceal by smiles and consoling words.

At Rochdale we breakfasted at the Angel Inn, in Blackwater Street, and were there joined by witnesses from Bury and other places, who augmented our numbers to about four score. After an affectionate parting, full of hope on my side and of sadness on theirs, I left my wife and child to retrace their steps sorrowfully towards home, whilst I went forward, though somewhat thoughtful, amongst my joking, light-hearted companions. The ascent of Blackstone Edge, " the back-bone of the English Alps," as it has been termed, tried the marching qualities of the women, and by the time we arrived at the top, two of them were fatigued, and went on with a mail coach, which overtook us there. Their journey by this conveyance was a most unpleasant one; some " gentlemen " from Manchester were also passengers and they used coarse and abusive language towards the females. The coachman and guard were appealed to for protection, but they only laughed, and, to please the " gemmen," contributed their share of insult. The women " gave it them," however, told them what they were, and when the coach arrived at Halifax, they got down, and refused to go any further with the unmanly beings. This conduct we only learned on our arrival at Halifax, and I mention it to show the strong and unworthy feeling which our opponents, even of the class commonly deemed respectable, were wont to indulge in those days.

Mr. Hunt, with Johnson and Chapman, followed us in a post-chaise, and they were detained a considerable time at Rochdale, in consequence of the landlord at the "Roebuck" Inn, one Marriott, refusing to supply them with fresh horses, on learning who they were. ·He was even uncivil to the travellers, but soon found that he was not likely to get anything by that mode of behaviour, and horses having been procured from another house, the journey was proceeded with.

At Bradford many of the tender-footed men were lame, and I gave them money to go on with as best they could. Most of the women also had by this time enough of walking for that day, and they availed themselves of such modes of conveyance as were readily attainable; some, however, held out, and walked with us every step of the road to Leeds, where we were hospitably received by the body of reformers, and lodged for the night. The next morning we made a strong muster, being joined by numbers from Stockport, Hyde, Ashton, Stalybridge, Saddleworth, and other places, and now I believe we mustered about one hundred persons; some of the women, and an equal proportion of the men, were too lame to walk, and were sent forward by carriage; the main body, however, on foot, passed through Tadcaster, and arrived at York in a compact body at night-fall, on Tuesday, the 14th of March. We were lodged and boarded at a large inn, the " Elephant," I think, on this side the river Ouse.

CHAPTER XXXI.

OUR long expected trial, which had excited a strong interest in
the public mind, commenced on the morning of Thursday, the
16th day of March, 1820, before Mr. Justice Bayley and a
special jury. At an early hour the court was beset by
persons waiting for admission. At a little before seven
o'clock the reporters for the London and provincial press
were admitted, and soon after several individuals, principally
solicitors, and others connected with provincial newspapers, were admitted into the gallery. A number of ladies
also took possession of a box at the corner of the court, on
the right hand of the Bench. At eight o'clock a more general
admission of the public took place, and the front seats in the
two galleries were instantly occupied. A vast number of
persons immediately followed, till not one inch of either
gallery was left unoccupied. The box which the day before
was reserved for the attorneys was, on this occasion, appropriated for the reception of magistrates, except the front seats,
which had become occupied by some London reporters. In
the rush and confusion, however, many had invaded the
place who had no claim to seats there. These were forthwith
informed by the officers of the court that they must retire.
The mandate was reluctantly obeyed by some, but others
obstinately retained their seats, until they were finally removed
by order of the magistrates, when they arrived.

The number of witnesses put down for the prosecution exceeded eighty ; for the defence, one hundred and twenty.

At a quarter before nine, Hunt, Moorhouse, Saxton, Jones, Wilde, and Healey, went into the court ; soon afterwards I and Swift went up and applied for entrance at the common door of the court. We were informed by the keeper that no more could be admitted, the place being quite full. We smiled at this, and said we must be admitted, and desired him to open the door ; he stoutly refused, and we enjoyed the joke some time, and at last told him who we were, and that we should be wanted, and must take part in the trial. The man then admitted us, but almost as a favour, and we made our way up an avenue towards the witness box. Hunt saw us coming, and beckoned us to step over the backs of the seats, which we did, and I was presently by his side.

I may here remark, that at Manchester, both before and after the meeting, at Lancaster also, and at London, Hunt had uniformly worn a white hat, and it had in consequence become the Radical badge ; Johnson had also done the same, but here, before a judge and a jury of their country, they deemed it proper to display the common black hat. I, however, who never thought it wrong to be the same always and in all places, who saw not anything to be really ashamed of in the colour of my hat, and who would not, just then, have discarded it to please judge, jury, or king, threw it down innocently enough amongst the lawyers' bags and papers, and other hats of a different colour, some of which were the sombre ones of my co-defendants. There were some looking and smiling at the presumptuous appearance of a Radical hat on that table. Others of our party, like myself, stuck to their white colours, declaring they would not change them under any circumstances. I only mention this incident to show a trait of what the world deems prudence, and its judicious exercise, by some of our leaders.

At nine o'clock Justice Bayley took his seat on the Bench, and immediately the cause of the King against Henry Hunt, Joseph Johnson, John Knight, James Moorhouse, Joseph Healey, John Thacker Saxton, Robert Jones, Samuel Bamford,

George Swift, and Robert Wilde was called on. The names of the persons summoned to act as special jurors were then read.

At this time the court was most excessively crowded; all the bottom seats and avenues, as well as every inch of standing ground, a passage for the witnesses excepted, were closely occupied. In each of the galleries the people were packed like bees in a hive, and there was ground for apprehension that the fronts might be forced out. It was some time before order could be obtained, so eager were persons of all ranks to witness the commencement of this trial. The jury box had been partly filled by strangers and had to be cleared, and several common jurymen who happened to be in it made a remonstrance to the judge on the hardship of being turned, not only out of that box, but also out of the one which had always been assigned to the waiting juryman. This circumstance was occasioned by the arrangements which the High Sheriff, Henry Vansittart, Esq., and his subordinate officers had made for the accommodation of the public. The box usually assigned to the magistrates of the county was this day opened for the reception of the Manchester and Cheshire magistrates; the one usually reserved for attorneys was given up to reporters for the public Press, and the attorneys, being deprived of their usual place in court, went into the jury box, and filled it so entirely as to occasion the remonstrance just mentioned. Justice Bayley said he did not understand the arrangements of the court; the place was now full: if, however, there was any situation to which the waiting juryman had a right he would order it to be cleared and kept for their accommodation; the box was accordingly cleared.

The jury having been sworn, Mr. Littledale opened the proceedings, and the indictment was read, the substance of which, having been already given, I shall not now repeat. We, of course, all pleaded " Not Guilty," except John Knight, who, since being bailed out of Lancaster Castle, had again been committed on a subsequent charge for attending a meeting near Burnley.

Mr. Scarlett, Mr. Serjeant Hullock, Mr. Serjeant Cross,

and Mr. Littledale, conducted the prosecution : Mr. Holt was retained for Saxton, and Mr. Barrow for Moorhouse and Jones. Hunt, Johnson, Wilde, Swift, Healey and myself conducted our several defences and for that purpose we took our places at the barristers' table. Some conversation ensued respecting this arrangement, and Mr. Hunt expressed his willingness to agree to any other, but the judge decided that every individual conducting his own defence should sit there; the others must take seats behind their counsel.

Mr. Hunt said he had not been previously aware of the arrangements for the court, and he had therefore invited his co-defendants to the situations they occupied; room, how-ever, would easily be found for them behind the bar, as he intended to move that all the witnesses on both sides (and he knew many were in court) should be ordered out of it.

Justice Bayley accordingly ordered all the witnesses to withdraw from the court. Mr. Barrow added, " And out of hearing also."

The order was immediately complied with; and amongst those who retired were the Rev. W. R. Hay, the Rev. C. W. Ethelstone, Mr. Hulton, Mr. Sylvester, Mr. R. Wright, and several other of the Manchester magistrates, together with a number of gentlemen and tradesmen who had been subpœned as witnesses. The defendants who had retained counsel also took their places behind them on the seats usually allotted to attorneys, and the very inconvenient pressure in the court was considerably mitigated.

Immediately under the judge at the straight edge of the table, which was a half-round, sat the counsel for the prosecu-tion already named with their attorneys. On the judge's left, and occupying the curved edge of the table, were George Swift, Mr. Harmer, of London (who kindly suggested various matters to us), next myself, then Mr. Hunt, Mr. Pearson, Mr. Wilde, Mr. Barrow, Mr. Holt, Mr. Healey and Mr. Johnson —the two latter sitting near the witness box and almost directly in front of the judge. The further side of the table was occupied by attorneys and others; a number of elegantly dressed females were upon the right and left of the judge and occupying seats below and standing on the floor; the large box behind us, at first assigned to magistrates, and which had been almost filled by those of Lancashire and Cheshire, who vacated it on the order being given for witnesses to retire, was now filled with a crowd of ladies and gentlemen, chiefly, as we understood, residents in the county; many ladies had obtained seats in the body of the hall, and one was observed taking the likeness of the venerable judge as he sat in his robes.

Mr. Scarlett, after the opening by Mr. Littledale, proceeded to address the jury; but as it would be entirely beyond the scope of this work to give the proceedings of the trial, which have, no doubt, long since been placed amongst the public records, I shall only touch on such passages as concern myself and throw light on my conduct both previous to and during this important investigation. I shall intersperse such observations with brief remarks upon and descriptions of some things which occurred both in public court and were privately known to ourselves, and shall be content to be judged, so far as my name may be concerned, by the facts which I truthfully narrate. Mr. Scarlett's description of us should not, however, be omitted. It was as follows :—

Of Mr. Hunt it was unnecessary that he should say anything, because his name had been so much of late connected with these transactions as to leave no doubt on the mind of any man as to his character and avocations. The others were obscure; they were very little known, and he should therefore state who they were, premising that they were charged with assembling and inciting others to assemble to disturb the public peace. John Knight had formerly been in business; his occupation had been latterly that of an itinerant orator. Joseph Johnson was a brushmaker residing near Manchester, and he believed he also was in the habit of attending public meetings. Of John Thacker Saxton, all the description which he had was that he was some way or other connected with the office of a newspaper, called the *Manchester Observer*. Joseph Healey was represented as an apothecary. James Moorhouse was a coach-master residing at Stockport, George

Swift was a shoemaker at Manchester. Of Robert Wilde he knew nothing, save that he lived near Ashton-under-Lyne. Samuel Bamford and Robert Jones were individuals in humble circumstances. The jury, he said, would find by unquestionable evidence that these persons were connected in some secret design. He would be able to show the course which the parties took when he called his evidence, and therefore it was not necessary for him at that moment to state the specific acts of each; it would be sufficient to give a general view of their proceedings.

The learned counsel then indicated the line of accusation he should take against Mr. Hunt especially. He commenced with the Spitalfields' meeting at London in the June previous, setting forth the resolutions and describing .them as illegal. Mr. Hunt was next traced to Bullock Smithy;* thence to Manchester, connecting him with the proposed meeting on the 9th of August. Then he described the drillings at White Moss and the beating of Murray and his companions. He showed Mr. Hunt to have been stopping at the house of Johnson, at Smedley, where he said he received the visits of Knight and others of the defendants. Next he represented the people as marching from all parts on the morning of the 16th of August. They were, he said, provided with banners and inscriptions, and they marched upon Manchester with all the regularity of an army. From Rochdale, from Middleton, from Oldham, from Lees, from Stockport, and many other places, parties might be seen marching towards Manchester. "At Middleton Mr. Bamford was seen placing in marching order a body of two thousand men; they were without uniforms, but he displayed sufficient talent to put them through their evolutions. He addressed them and gave to each of them a laurel leaf, that they might distinguish one another. The town of Manchester was, in fact, surrounded by an immense force, who seemed as if they were going to invade it. Every road which approached the town was covered with parties marching in military manner, and amongst those who were marching to the town some of the individuals who

* The name of the place has been changed to Hazel Grove.

were seen training at White Moss were recognised. At eleven
o'clock Mr. Hunt and his party were preparing to enter the
town from the residence of Johnson. Mr. Hunt was attended
by a triumphant band; the Middleton and Rochdale force
had united, they became his guards, and thus surrounded he
entered the town of Manchester."

Next he commented on our banners, and some of his
strictures may show the difference betwixt the interpretation
of the laws in those days and the present. I will give a short
extract of that part of his address.

On some of the flags they would find the words, "Equal
Representation or Death." What could be the object of a
sentiment such as this? He would ask the jury to lay their
hands on their hearts and say, What good object could those
have in view who exhibited a flag bearing such a motto?
They were not met there to discuss whether the present state
of the House of Commons was the best that could be
imagined. Good and wise men differed on that point, but,
whatever difference of opinion might be entertained on the
subject, of this he was sure, that there was no man who
considered the question rightly that would not stand by the
law and the constitution of the country as they were now
administered; and if threatened with violence, that would
not resist to the uttermost an attempt to make a forcible
alteration of the system.

Another banner bore the inscription, "No Corn Laws."
He came not before them to discuss whether the law on the
subject of corn was good or otherwise; he had his opinions on
the question, but it would not be decorous or proper to state
them there. He knew that wise men might sometimes frame
a mischievous law, but it was not to be removed by riot and
violence. Would it not be a most dangerous thing to say to
a mob of sixty thousand persons, for the purpose of getting rid
of such a measure—particularly when the minds of the people
were irritated and inflamed—would it not, he asked, be an
appeal of a most inflammatory nature, to say to them, "We
will have no Corn Laws; we will force the legislature to do as
we please."

Next came the inscription, "Annual Parliaments." There were no doubt respectable and honourable men in the kingdom, who thought annual parliaments would be very useful; but would any of those individuals say that such a proposition was to be carried by violence, as the *sine quâ non* of their existence? Let the people meet to petition for reform—let them submit to Parliament what they think expedient for the public good—and no man can complain. But was it the business of a public meeting to dictate to Parliament, and to declare that it would effect a certain object, or would have nothing? The next inscription was "Universal Suffrage and Election by Ballot." These two points were the pretexts for calling this assembly; he felt considerable surprise that Mr. Hunt did not perceive that those three terms, taken together, meant nothing but the subversion of the Constitution, but as long as these questions were *sub judice*, what right had any man to say, "we will, in spite of all opposition, have these three things." To do so was illegal; and it was most unfit that, on the subject of public grievances, the mob should be suffered to dictate to the legislature. Let them meet and petition; let the weavers and shoemakers and other artisans in this kingdom who are destined to earn their bread by the labour of their hands inform the legislature of the best course to be pursued with respect to public affairs, if they have more wisdom than those by whom such affairs were conducted. The law enabled them to do this; but let not demagogues state to them that these three points were the only things which could be of service to them. Another inscription was, "Let us die like men, and not be sold like slaves." Who, he should like to know, had been selling the people of Oldham, of Rochdale, of Middleton, and of the other places, the inhabitants of which went to Manchester on that day? He never heard of any such sale; but some persons, who did not, perhaps, choose to speak those words, thought fit to place them on a banner.

Such were some of the constructions which the learned counsel attached to some of our banners and their inscriptions; constructions which, if followed in these days, would place some of the Chartist exhibitors in a rather perilous position.

Witnesses were now called, who traced Mr. Hunt through Bullock Smithy, Stockport, Heaton Norris, and from Manchester, to Johnson's at Smedley. On the examination of a witness named John Chadwick, who swore that he saw Murray at the White Moss, on the morning of the fifteenth, Mr. Hunt objected to his evidence, because he had said he did not know any one who was there by name.

Mr. Scarlett said he wished to show that some of the White Moss drillers had attended Mr. Hunt.

Mr. Hunt said it mattered not, unless some of those persons were among the accused.

Mr. Scarlett hoped Mr. Hunt would not be allowed to disturb the proceedings of the court.

Mr. Justice Bayley: Mr. Hunt has a right to take the objection, and I am doubting whether this is evidence.

The witness was here sent out of court.

Mr. Scarlett said he was about to show that some of these persons who were training, and who assaulted Murray, had attended the meeting of the 16th, and had also cheered opposite Murray's house; he would show that Mr. Hunt and his party had done the same. This, he conceived, was perfectly regular.

Mr. Justice Bayley: When you have shown that any of the persons of the White Moss party were at the meeting on the 16th, then it will be evidence, but I think you had better prove that first.

The witness was again called in and examined, and said the first person he saw at the meeting on the 16th was a man whom he had seen at the White Moss, with a letter brought from Manchester. A person arrived at White Moss after witness had seen Murray; the parties then formed into a square like four walls, and the man who was to read the letter was in the centre. The letter was not read, as they said there was no name to it, and they would have nothing to do with it; the man then joined them. The man who was to have read the letter was the man who led up the Middleton and Rochdale parties on Monday. This man was drilling the men, and giving the word of command.

Such was the first link of the evidence which, by inference, connected me with the White Moss affair. Why that link was not broken will hereafter appear. For the present Mr. Pearson advised me to sit still, and not cross-examine the witness; he would be sure, he said, to swear I was the man he saw at the Moss, he would swear right a-head, no doubt. It was for the witness to point me out, and not for me to offer myself to his notice. I accordingly kept my seat. This was the only evidence tendered on the first day of the trial which applied to me.

On the morning of the second day the court was crowded soon after seven o'clock. The rush when the doors were open was excessive, and a number of ladies again encountered the pressure of the crowd; they were soon, however, accommodated with such places as could be spared near the Bench, and in the magistrates' large box on the left. The defendants were assisted by Mr. Harmer and Mr. Pearson as on the previous day. Mr. Justice Bayley took his seat at half-past nine. Many persons of rank in the county were present during the day.

William Morris, the first witness examined by Serjeant Cross, said: I am a weaver, residing five miles from Manchester. In the month of August last I saw many groups of people near Middleton; Samuel Bamford used to be amongst them. Early on the morning of the 16th of August, I saw many hundreds of people put into regular form at Middleton, with two flags, and twenty-five men were in each section. I know not who formed them into sections, but there certainly was a large number collected—two or three thousand at least. They marched off four abreast, after being first drawn into the form of a square, in the inside of which was placed a chair, on which Bamford stood and said:—" Friends and neighbours, I have a few words to relate; you will march off this place quietly, and not insult any one, but rather take an insult. I do not think there will be any disturbance, or anything to do, if there is, it will be after we come back—there is no fear, the day is our own." He got off the chair and distributed laurel amongst the men who were to command the sections. They put it, some in their breasts, and some in their hats. Before they went away a large number of people came arranged in form from Rochdale, with a band of music before them, and bearing two flags. Both bodies joined and went off together, each with a cap of liberty. The men had nothing in their hands but bits of switches, or small sticks. Before that day I saw the Middleton people forming and arranging, both in fields and highroads. Bamford was with them at different times. John Whitworth, who had been a private in the Sixth Regiment of Foot, was drilling the men, but not on the 16th of August. John Heywood, who had been a private in the Sixth Dragoons, had also done the same.

In his cross-examination by me the witness said: I heard you recommend them to be peaceable, and understood you wished them to continue so during the whole day. Many thousands went with the Middleton and Rochdale people who were not formed with them, as well as a good deal of women and children.

Such was the evidence of this witness: it was, I dare say, as near the truth as he could recollect, and was, on the whole, strongly in my favour. I knew some points in his character which would have enabled me to put him through a severe cross-examination, but I forebore, not wishing to injure the testimony he had given on my behalf. Hunt, however, who could not miss an opportunity for display, took him up, and handled him most unmercifully; on which Serjeant Hullock remarked aside to one of his brother counsel, what a fool Hunt must be to destroy the man's credibility, he being to all intents and purposes *our* witness. The life of this man had been one of adventure and intrigue. He had been long in the army, and deserted from it whilst a sergeant on a foreign station, taking with him his arms and accoutrements. Soon after this trial he was apprehended for passing forged Bank of England notes, and was convicted, but, strong interest having been used to save his life, he was transported, and died abroad.

John Heaton being examined by Mr. Littledale, said:—I

live at Middleton, and am a plumber and glazier. On the
morning of the 16th of August I saw many people assembled,
and Samuel Bamford among them, and in front. They had
music and two flags. The inscriptions were—" Liberty,
Strength, and Unity," and something with a cap on a pole.
Bamford had a bunch of laurel in his hand, and many others
had a little of it in their hats.

In my cross-examination, he said : I saw nothing but small
sticks. I don't know your wife, but there were many women
and children, three, four, and five abreast, who appeared to
partake of the conviviality of the procession. The people did
not appear sulky ; they had no angry looks, but were more, as
it were, in joy. I have some little property, and had then,
but I felt no occasion to go home and shut my doors when I
saw this procession.

On the third day James Platt swore to having seen me
on the hustings on St. Peter's Field, and this finished the
evidence against me ; but the criminatory proceedings were
not closed until the afternoon of the fourth day. The court
continued to be crowded each day from an early hour. The
ladies seemed still as curious as at first, and their eagerness
to witness the proceedings induced many of them to seek
an entrance into the court, through privileged avenues, so
early as seven o'clock. At eight the public gates were
generally thrown open, and the galleries and area became
speedily filled, in the usual hurried manner, by a mixed
throng, which rushed into every seat and corner of the court
that was not defended by constables, for the use of magistrates, attorneys, and jurors.

On the evening of the second day, Mr. Harmer left us
to attend the trial, if I mistake not, of Sir Francis Burdett,
at Leicester. A Mr. Bryant, who I understood to be a kind
of chamber counsel at London, remained with Hunt and
Pearson, and assisted the former in making his points and
objections, but from him I derived no benefit. The time was
now approaching when I should be called on for my defence,
yet I had never had one minute's private conversation with
our attorney ; he had never, according to my recollection,

been at my inn, nor asked me to his, nor had he ever spoken
to one of my witnesses, or given me any instructions, except
those already noticed, for the collection of evidence; I was,
in fact, entirely left to my own resources. Every night after
the court had risen, he, Hunt and Bryant, retired and spent
the evening together, and remained unapproachable by, and
invisible to, the other defendants. Indeed, excepting those
who had counsel, Hunt, so far as I was enabled to judge,
was the only one of the party who had the benefit of careful
legal advice. During my cross-examination of the witnesses
against me, Mr. Pearson would occasionally suggest a question,
or advise the suppression of one; but in other respects I was
left to seek counsel from my own judgment. I regret having
to say this, but truth requires it. Every night Hunt retired
with his friends, discussing the occurrences of the day and
preparing for the next; consequently, he came into court
ready at all points, and, like a loaded gun, he only required
a sudden impulse to make a grand discharge. Under these
circumstances it was no wonder that he performed so well,
that he appeared to be so greatly talented, whilst his co-
defendants had not credit for the little talent which some of
them really possessed. This was just the position which
Hunt wished himself and us to occupy. He would be all in
all, and he could not endure that the humblest of us should
come betwixt the public and himself, that the smallest shadow
should intercept one ray of his luminous presence. This
intense selfishness was constantly displayed in all his actions.
I saw it and was astonished; I could not account for it except
by condemning him, and that was not to be thought of;
though the facts came oozing out like water-drops, I could
not harbour an unkind thought of our leader; "it was his
way"; "it was the way of great folks"; "it was perhaps
necessary that he should do so and so"; anything, in fact,
rather than allow the unwelcome truth to whisper that in
his weak points Hunt was the weakest of men. I had
recently some misgivings as to the integrity of his character,
but they had speedily vanished; I could not endure an
unworthy opinion of any of my comrades, still less of him

who occupied the most prominent station before the public. This may be called simplicity; it was the simplicity of an uncorrupted mind. I deemed all reformers as good as myself, and I knew that I could answer for the sincerity and dis-interestedness of my own intentions. It was not until years had elapsed that observation and reflection enabled me to penetrate the mist which had so long enveloped me. Then it was that I became aware of the real nature of past transactions and of the character of some who had been my political friends and fellow-workers in the cause of reform.

But during this important trial circumstances arose which compelled us at times to forget all anxiety and seriousness. Healey, as before intimated, was one of the five defendants who had a seat at the barristers' table. On the second day, Mr. Scarlett had a smelling-bottle which he frequently used, and then laid on the table before him. Our friend the doctor was seated nearly opposite to the learned gentleman, and I observed him once or twice cast very desirous looks towards the phial whilst the barrister was using it. Mr. Scarlett, however, did not, or affected not to, notice our surgical friend, and at last the patience of the latter being tried beyond control, he leaned across the table and very respectfully solicited the loan of the bottle, which was readily granted. "Oh yes, doctor! by all means," said Mr. Scarlett, politely handing it to him, who immediately applied it to his nose and evinced its pungency by very zestful sneezing, which obliged him to apply his handkerchief to his eyes. Of course there was some tittering around the table and Mr. Scarlett was declared to have "taken the doctor fairly by the nose." Hunt laughed till his eyes were brim full, whilst Healey sat quite unconscious and serious. Soon after the bottle was returned with compliments and the trial claimed our attention. On the third day Mr. Scarlett did not bring the smelling-bottle, and the doctor seemed disappointed. On the fourth day the doctor lugged a long, square smelling-bottle out of his pocket and laid it down before him. Mr. Scarlett took no notice. The doctor smelled and laid it down. Mr. Scarlett took no notice. The doctor smelled again. Mr. Scarlett did not see him. At length, determined not to be outdone in generosity, the doctor thrust it towards Mr. Scarlett with a bow and a request that he would use it. Mr. Scarlett coloured, but he good-humouredly took the phial and, having smelled, he politely returned it with thanks, which the doctor as politely acknowledged. The same ceremony was repeated once, if not oftener afterwards, and the doctor, then perfectly satisfied, gave up the farce.

On the morning of Sunday, the 19th of March, I retired to my little back room at a cottage opposite the inn, for I boarded at the latter place and lodged with a worthy couple across the street. I now read and compared my notes and spent several hours in framing the heads of my speech for the day following. On the morning of Monday, Mr. Chapman was sent by a committee of our friends, who were carrying into effect arrangements for the subsistence of the witnesses; the latter had been boarded at our hotel at the rate, if I mistake not, of five shillings per head per day, and it was found necessary to reduce the expenditure, else there would not be funds to carry us through the trial. The witnesses were thenceforth to provide for themselves and would have an allowance of three shillings per day for that purpose; all the money was to go into a common fund for disbursements. I accordingly handed to him what money I had remaining, and that cause of anxiety was removed from my mind.

It became apparent towards the noon of Monday, the fourth day of the trial, that the prosecutors were about to close their case, and that the defence must be commenced on the afternoon of that day. Whilst we were talking of the matter, Hunt said, "Bamford, you will be called on to address the court the first of all the defendants." I said I thought that scarcely probable, as we should most likely be called in the order in which our names stood in the indictment. Hunt said he knew that was contemplated by the opposing counsel, and particularly by Mr. Scarlett, who wanted to bring him out in the evening when he was exhausted, the court wearied, and the public satiated and listless. But, with an oath, he said

he was not to be taken aback that way, he was too old a bird
to be caught by such a manœuvre. He then opened to me
his plans and said that Messrs. Barrow and Holt, the counsel
for Moorhouse, Jones, and Saxton, would first address the
court, then I should be called on, next Healey, then Swift, and
lastly Johnson. I asked him if he thought the opposing
parties would acquiesce in that arrangement, and he said
if Mr. Scarlett objected, as he durst say he would, he himself
would make a special application to the judge on the subject,
or to adjourn the trial until the following day. "Now,
Bamford, by ——" he said, " I'll tell you what you must do
if called this afternoon." "Well, what should I do?" I
inquired. "You must talk against time," he said. "Talk
against time?" I asked, "what's that?" "You must keep
possession of the court an hour and a half at least," he said ;
"you must talk to put on time in order to prevent them from
calling on me under any circumstances to-night. I know well
that is what Scarlett is aiming at, and we must play our game
so as to put it beyond his power." "But I am not prepared
with matter for an hour and a half's speech," I said; "I
should break down if I attempted it." "Don't mind that,"
he replied, "don't mind anything, only keep on." "I should
make myself look like a fool, and they would be laughing at
me and stopping me," I replied. "Pshaw! and suppose they
did, you could listen and, when they had done, begin again."
"But I should not know what to say." "Say! say anything,
the d——est nonsense in the world, never mind what you
say, only keep on until they cannot call me to-day." Something like a glimmer of the naked truth flashed across my
reluctant mind and I replied: "No, Mr. Hunt, I will not do
as you desire, I will not exhibit myself before this court as
a fool ; I will speak as long as I can speak, to the purpose and
with common sense. I would speak until dark if that would
serve you, and I was prepared for the task ; but I am not, and
I won't make myself ridiculous." "Very well," said Hunt,
and looked another way, quite cool and distant.

I then showed the manuscript of my address to Mr.
Pearson, and he advised the striking out of a passage wherein

I alluded to the circumstance of my having slept at the house of my wife's uncle on the night previous to Murray being at White Moss, and to the fact of the servant girl having removed my shoes whilst cleaning the house after I went to bed, and my not being able to find them on the following morning and her having to find them for me. He said that passage should be erased; it had not been proved that I was at White Moss, and the attempt to explain away what had not been proved would rather strengthen the opinion, if such existed, that there was really some truth in the supposition of my having been on the Moss. I reminded him of what Chadwick had sworn, and of what Morris and Heaton had sworn, as to my leading up the people, but he said that was not sufficient to call on me for a replication; I had not been pointed out, not personally identified by Chadwick, and I had best not take any notice of that part of the evidence. I must confess I did not see this distinction clearly, but I yielded to his advice and the passage was struck out; the servant girl alluded to also was not examined as to that point by me.

I think it was about three o'clock in the afternoon when Michael Fitzpatrick, a reporter for the *New Times*, and the last witness for the prosecution, made his exit from the witness-box. Mr. Barrow and Mr. Holt then addressed the court on behalf of their several clients, and Mr. Hunt made application to the judge that I should next be heard, and the other defendants after me, in order that, as an indulgence, his address might be deferred until the following morning. Mr. Scarlett, I think, observed that such a course would be irregular, but did not strongly object to it, and the favour was granted. I accordingly addressed the court in the following terms :—

"My lord, and gentlemen of the jury,—Before I enter into a detail of the evidence which I intend to produce in my defence, I think it necessary to notice some expressions made use of by the learned counsel for the prosecution in the speech which he addressed to the court on the opening of these proceedings. I allude to that part of his address where he said that 'Bamford was seen training a body of ten thousand

men on the morning of the 16th.' If the brief which the
learned gentleman had before him instructed him to make
such an assertion, so much the better, and I sincerely wish,
for his own honour, that it may be so. [Mr. Scarlett intimated across the table that such were his instructions.]
But your lordship and the jury cannot have failed to observe
that the testimony of Morris contains no such proof, and he
alone has appeared against me with respect to the transactions that took place at Middleton, previous to our movement
towards Manchester. Indeed, Morris states that he knew
not who formed the people into section, division, and square;
that they were so formed, but by whom he does not undertake
to say. The learned gentleman also, in commenting upon
some of the banners and their inscriptions, described one as
bearing the words 'Annual Parliaments' and 'Universal
Suffrage,' and insinuated that such were put forth as a
demand, whence he inferred a design to subvert the constitution and government. Now, the mottoes on the banner
so erroneously described, were nothing more than an avowal
of what we considered, and do still consider, as our political
right. There was no such thing as a demand about it; why
should we demand that which we were going to Manchester
to petition for?

"With respect to drilling, I have, in common with my neighbours, heard much, seen some, and could have seen more; for
it was, to use a common, though very memorable, phrase, 'as
notorious as the sun at noonday.' If it will not be trespassing
too much on the time of the court, I will endeavour to give a
brief account of its origin and intention. In the course of the
last six years Manchester has witnessed many public meetings,
to all of which, with the exception of the last, great numbers
of people from the surrounding towns and villages proceeded
in groups; and on these occasions they were uniformly
styled by the Liberal and venal press of the place, mobs—
riotous, tumultuous, and disorderly mobs; they were ridiculed
as illiterate, dirty, and mean, having chapped hands and greasy
nightcaps. They were scandalised as being drunken and disorderly, as being libellous and seditious, dividers of property,

and destroyers of social order; and was it not then very natural that these poor, insulted, and vilified people should wish to rescue themselves from the unmerited imputations which were wantonly cast on their character? It certainly was natural that they should wish to give the lie to their enemies, and thereby show to the nation and to the world that they were not what they had been represented to be. They determined to give one example of peace and good order, such as should defy the most bitter of their enemies to criminate, and for this purpose, and this alone, was the drilling, so styled, instituted. Only one witness for the prosecution has sworn to having heard amongst the drillers the word 'fire'; all the others swear only to their facing, and to their marching in file and in line, which evolutions were certainly most suited to familiarise them with that uniformity of motion which would be necessary for the preservation of due order and decorum in their progress to the place of meeting. But as to these facts I do not tender to your lordship and the jury my own assertion only. I refer you to the papers laid before the House of Commons, relative to the internal state of the country. The particular document to which I refer in those papers is dated the 5th of August, only four days previous to the first proposed meeting at Manchester, which should have been on the 9th; so that if we suppose the drilling parties to have been in existence a week or a fortnight before the day on which the letter referred to is dated, the ground of my argument is strengthened. That military gentleman who did us the honour to stand so long before us on Saturday evening, and whose services, I trow, consisted in marching with Colonel Fletcher from Bolton to Manchester, and from Manchester to Bolton, talks of ' midnight drillings,' and of parties coming to the meeting in ' beautiful order.' The former representation is not, I presume, legal evidence, and, of course, will not appear on your lordship's notes. The latter confirms what I have said respecting the wish of the people to preserve the strictest decorum.

" Your lordship and the jury will find by the evidence which I shall produce that by nine o'clock on the morning of the

over memorable 16th of August, numbers of persons assembled
at Middleton; that they were formed into a hollow square;
and that whilst so formed I addressed them, earnestly
cautioning them to be on their guard against enemies, and
representing the advantage which might be taken of their
numbers to create a riot by persons who might be employed
for that sole purpose; that I advised them not to insult any
person, but rather suffer an insult on that day, as their
opponents would be glad of a pretext to accuse them of riot
and disorder; that I entreated them to bear towards every
one a spirit of good-will, in token of which I distributed
amongst them branches of laurel, emblems of purity and peace,
as described by Morris and Heaton; and having heard that
if I went to the meeting the police of Manchester would, on
its own responsibility, arrest me, I cautioned the people
against offering any resistance, if such an attempt should be
made, as I preferred an appeal to the laws of my country
rather than to force, that I insisted no sticks should be taken,
and that in consequence several were left by the way; that we
went in the greatest hilarity and good-humour, preceded by a
band of music, which played loyal and national airs; and that
our fathers, our mothers, our wives, our children, and our
sweethearts were with us. And this was the dreadful military
array which the learned counsel described as 'one vast army,
bearing from all parts to the invasion of Manchester'—poor,
forlorn, defenceless Manchester. These were 'the soldiers ready
to fight for Mr. Hunt'; with bare heads and with arms locked
—a fighting posture, forsooth—who terrified that immortal
author of green books, Mr. Francis Phillips; and of such
persons, oh, dreadful to relate! was formed that 'cordon,' im-
penetrable to everything, save the newly ground sabres of the
Manchester Yeomanry Cavalry."

At this time the judge arose hastily and motioned me to
cease speaking; the blood had gushed from his nose on the
cushion before him, and he retired, with the High Sheriff, and
one or two gentlemen that were near him. In a short time his
lordship returned, and I merely added some conversations on
the conduct of a magistrate who had detained papers of mine,

which, being a manuscript of one of Hoyle's games at draughts, the zealous functionary suspected it might possibly be the plan of a plot in cypher. I also said I should leave my share of the general defence to Mr. Hunt, whose superior knowledge and eloquence would, no doubt, obtain for us full justice, which was all we wanted.

In confirmation of this speech, I adduced evidence which showed that I inculcated peace and good order to the Middleton party before we left Barrowfields ; that there was not to be any opposition to the police, should they come to arrest me or any other person ; that the people were to keep themselves select, and return with their banners, and not to stop in the town drinking, nor loitering in the streets; that no sticks were allowed in the procession except to aged persons, and that several were resigned on the ground, or left by the way ; that the wives of several of the party accompanied their husbands, and that there were many young females and children with the procession; that we seemed quite cheerful on the road; that there were no symptoms of alarm in Middleton or on the road ; and that the drillings were public and in open day. In short, all that I advanced in my speech was fully confirmed by my evidence.

After me, Swift, Healey, and Johnson got up in succession. Healey had for a day or two appeared to be labouring under a cold with hoarseness. He sat opposite the judge, with a handkerchief thrown over his head, the corners drooping on his shoulders, exactly as the flaps of his lordship's wig drooped on his. He frequently looked up towards the glass dome above him, as if a stream of air came from thence and he was affected by it ; but he did not attempt to move to another seat, which he probably would have done, had he experienced illness from that cause. Whether this was the case or not, it is a fact that he had a speech to read which had been written by a friend at Lees, and he could not read it. He then had a cold, became hoarse, and the clerk of the court read the speech for him. This official was a well-fed, red-faced, snub-nosed personage, with spectacles on his nose, and a wig of legal cut on his head. He held the document at a considerable altitude, as if he were looking over his spectacles instead of through them, and he read the speech in a monotonous, half-speaking, half-singing tone, much as a school-boy, some twenty years ago would have droned out his lesson. The doctor stood at his elbow, his looks evincing surprise and disappointment, that his document should have fallen into such incapable hands ; next he became impatient, as was manifest by his varying attitudes and sharp gesticulations, by which he meant to supply the want of modulation and emphasis in the reader. An artist was in court sketching at the time, and if he took this pair of originals, his portfolio may some day turn out one singular illustration of nature.

Hunt had thus obtained what he so ardently desired, a night for consultation, reflection, and repose, and a crowded morning audience for his grand exhibition. I shall not dwell upon his defence, except to notice one passage relative to Richard Carlile. In the commencement of his address he said, " I am not only charged in the opening speech of the learned counsel with having attempted to overthrow the constituted authorities of my country, but also to extinguish in the flame of infidelity the altar of our holy religion. It has been industriously promulgated that I was connected with Mr. Carlile ; it has been promulgated that I am a man of his principles. Where is the proof ? Without it why should the imputation have been cast ? I shall not advert to the conduct of that man, because the law has imposed its punishment upon him, and he is now enduring the reward of his temerity. It would, therefore, be improper, and imprudent and unjust for me in open court to touch upon such a subject, but why was the topic introduced ? I will tell you, gentlemen—to connect our cause with that of irreligion, and to identify the cause of the reformers with that of Mr. Carlile. I profess to be a reformer, but not a leveller ; I profess to be a lover of liberty, but not of licentiousness ; sweet, lovely liberty, gentlemen, is pure and amiable as sacred truth ; licentiousness is a disgraceful as darkness and falsehood." And then in a subsequent passage, he said, " You have heard the miserable attempt to fix upon me an irreligious connection with Carlile. I have known the man, and if I do not say what I think of him, it is because he is now suffering the sentence of the law, and therefore is not a fit subject for anybody's animadversion. Of him I shall say nothing now, but I shall say that none of the principles, professions, or doctrines he is said to have espoused were ever, at any moment of my life, imbibed by or believed in by me. In the face of God and my country I most solemnly declare that I never read one line of the theological works of Carlile until Dr. Stoddart's libel upon me first put them into my hands in the following manner. Mr. Scarlett was then employed, as he is now, against me in the court of King's Bench. Carlile's trial was going on, mine was the very next, and I was bound to watch it, or else expose myself to the consequences of being absent when called on—a verdict for the defendant. Such was my unfortunate case, or else I should not have been in London, much less in court, when Carlile's trial was pending. I here further declare, in the face of heaven, that among the reformers, rich or poor, I never recollect to have seen one line of the theological works of Thomas Paine. Why, then, identify the reformers with such doctrines? Good God! was it not enough to charge us with crimes against our fellow-men, but that also we must be designated as infidels against our religion and our God."

Whilst Hunt uttered those last sentences the tears trickled down his face. "Good God!" I also mentally exclaimed, "Is it possible? are not my ears deceiving me?" Carlile, the reader will recollect, was one of those who went with Hunt in the carriage from Johnson's to the meeting on the morning of the 16th. He was so fortunate as to escape from the field, and had since been tried, found guilty, and sentenced to imprisonment for a theological work, if I mistake not; and was at the moment Hunt thus denounced and renounced him in prison. No human power, nor dread of human power, should have been able to compel Hunt to make use of such language at that time, and under those circumstances. Whatever Carlile was, good or bad, religious or the contrary, the law had for the present done its work with him, and that is seldom part done; and, above all other moments, that was not the one to aim a clumsy and treacherous blow at a late comrade, now bound and fettered. "Can this," thought I, " be also one of the fashionable levities of great folks? If it be, it is requisite that I should be more guarded and more self-governed in future." And so I was; I continued to respect Hunt for his good points, but I was no longer entirely blinded to his faults. I never could forget this scene.

It was about the second or third day of the trial that, in cross-examination, I put what was considered a leading question. One of the counsel immediately called it back, and said that was not the proper way to put it. I apologised on account of my ignorance of the forms of examinations, when Serjeant Hullock, nodding his head, said, "a pretty apt scholar, however, I think."

One morning I observed that Mr. Scarlett was reading some verses of mine (the Lancashire Hymn) in a Manchester newspaper. In the evening, when I was passing along the corridor from the court, I accidently joined Mr. Scarlett and Mr. Maule, the solicitor for the Government. They both recognised me respectfully, and I returned the salute. Mr. Scarlett said he had seen some verses of mine which were certainly open to comment by the prosecution, but he should not make any use of them to my prejudice. He also said he understood I had published a small poetical work, called "The Weaver Boy." I said I had. He then said, if it should so happen that I should have to come to London in consequence of the trial, he could wish me to bring him a copy. I said I would do so with pleasure, and if I did not come up, I would forward one to him. Mr. Maule said, "And let me have a copy also." I said I would take care he had one, and so with mutual civilities we parted.

After the defence was closed, and when Mr. Scarlett was making his speech in reply, I certainly felt more surprised than flattered by the distinction which he thought proper to make in my favour. "Bamford," he said, "and when he mentioned the name of that defendant, he could not but express his regret at the situation in which he saw him now placed; he (Mr. Scarlett) admired his talents and the respectful manner in which he had conducted his defence, and probably others as well as himself (Mr. Scarlett) were sorry that he was not found in better company."

One day I had done something which pleased Hunt mightily, and when the court broke up and we were in the yard, Hunt said, "Come, Bamford, take my arm, you are my right-hand man." I took his arm, and we walked down the street with a great crowd at our heels, shouting "Hunt for ever! Hunt for ever!" and huzzaing. Looking back, I saw the judge's carriage with his lordship in, and the horses restive in consequence of the noise, and I put out my hand and desired the crowd to be silent. Hunt heard what I said, and, giving me a sudden jerk, began cursing in his usual wont when in a passion, and asked who ordered me to stop the people from shouting? I pointed to the carriage then in the midst of us, the horses still prancing; but that did not pacify my shout-loving friend, and he continued his maledictions until I turned to go to my lodgings. A similar cause of displeasure was given by Moorhouse on another night when the mail-coach was passing, and was in danger of being upset. Moorhouse received his reprimand at Hunt's apartments, and was then invited to walk out of the room. He wept with mortification! I laughed, as I have often done since, when thinking of the circumstance.

A female witness from Middleton, a married woman, gave very important evidence in a most impressive manner, and was to return home the following morning. Before going she wished to see Mr. Hunt, in order to have the honour of saying she had shaken hands with the great man. I offered to introduce her, and we went to Hunt's apartments, but he was not there, and we were referred to a tavern, the "Black Swan," I think, in Coney Street. We found there that Hunt, Bryant, and several others were upstairs, and I sent in my name, and after standing in the bar a short time the waiter said, "Mr Hunt could not be seen, he was engaged." I thought there must be some mistake, and requested the man to give my compliments to Mr. Hunt, and say I should be glad to see him for a minute. The man did so, and came down again with the same result,

I was ashamed and offended at receiving such a slight; but, determined that he should not have any ground to plead a misunderstanding, I desired the waiter to go up once more, and say a lady who was going into Lancashire wished to bid him good-bye. The servant very obligingly went up again and returned as before, " Mr. Hunt could not be seen." The next morning I took my seat at a distance from him in the court, and it was not until repeated overtures on his part, and many fervent expressions of regret, that I resumed conversation with him. But I could scarcely have justified myself if I had suffererd any personal offence to alienate me from him during the trial. I considered the cause too great, too holy, to suffer injury in the least by any circumstance affecting one so humble as myself. I was, in fact, too simple-minded, too sincere, and too generous for the situation in which I was placed; and it was not until multiplied acts of deception and ingratitude had been practised upon me, that I learned (if I have yet done so) to value mankind according to their real worth. I narrate the above as a specimen of the intercourse and confidence which existed among us at York. The same really contemptible feeling of classism, the curse of England and Englishmen, and of Englishwomen also, existed in too great a degree amongst the witnesses. There were " the broad cloth " and " the narrow cloth" ones, the rich and the poor ; and the former seldom sought opportunities for inter-communication with the latter, but rather shunned them. This " pride that licks the dust "—for it is nothing else—has begot a counteraction as wrong as itself. It has filled the working classes with a fierce contempt and hatred of every one wearing a decent coat. This latter is being as mad as the other is being mean. The proper course for those who feel and contemn class distinction, is, first of all, to respect themselves; next, to invite a respectful equality by unoffending manners ; and thirdly, to assert their right position in society by withholding the smallest deference to mere assumption. This would be quite sufficient, without rudeness or noise, to restore the natural balance of society.

When the judge came to read over the evidence, the following passage occurred : " The next evidence, (for the prosecution) was that which related to Bamford, and it only showed that he recommended peace and order ; still he was identified with the placards if they thought them illegal. If a meeting for considering a reform in Parliament be illegal, he is an offender, but it was his (the judge's) duty to tell them that it was not. There was no illegality in carrying sticks unless they were for an unlawful purpose—nor banners, unless their tenor was such as to excite suspicion of the objects of those who carried them, or concurred in bringing them with an evil intention. As to numbers, they alone did not make a meeting illegal, unless attended with such circumstances as did actually excite terror, or were reasonably calculated to excite terror ; such circumstances were forbidden by the law. They had truly heard that where there was no law there was no transgression ; if the meeting was innocently intended, then the law was not violated. We next come," observed his lordship, " to Healey's admonitory remark to me, to take care, and not in anything I say to prejudice your minds against him. If I do, gentlemen, discard any expression of mine having such a tendency altogether from your minds. I mean to do my duty with integrity, to the best of my poor judgment. If I err, and err with intention, then, gentlemen, there is that power to which I am awfully responsible. Between the crown on one hand, and my country on the other, I shall do, I hope, equal justice. The defendants, I trust, shall suffer no undue prejudice at my hands—my conscience will uphold me in what I have to say to you ; and He who will sit in judgment on all our poor acts will have to determine what motive dictated them. I have now closed my observations upon the evidence for the prosecution, and before I sum up that for the defence, I wish to state that I have made a summary of it, which will bring its leading points with less fatigue to your minds. If, however, I omit anything material to any of the defendants, or, as I go on, shall miss one fact in their favour, then it will only be necessary to remind me of the omission, and I will read in detail the part to which my attention is called."

Mr. Hunt: Probably you will allow us, my lord, to avail ourselves of your kind permission, as you go on, without deeming our interruption obtrusive?

Justice Bayley: Yes, Mr. Hunt, I not only allow you, but I desire you promptly, as I go on, to call my attention as you please.

The learned judge resumed his charge, and said that, " with respect to Bamford, all that had been proved in his speech was a recommendation to peace and order. There were no sticks in his group, save a few common walking-sticks, carried by old men. There were women and children in the throng, and it was for the jury to consider whether Bamford and these people, carrying their wives and daughters with them to such a crowd, meant to create on that day riot, tumult, and disorder? With such an intention nothing was less likely than that they would carry to the scene those who were the dearest objects of their affection. According to the evidence for Bamford, the people in his party, so far from being tumultuous, were peaceable and joyful, and the drilling, as it was called, so far from being illegal and nocturnal, was open and innocent; the only object of it being merely to enable the people to attend the meeting as conveniently for each other and the public as it was possible." The learned judge then enumerated the names of the witnesses who swore that the Middleton party, on the 16th of August, went to the meeting in the utmost peace, and conducted themselves whilst there with equal tranquillity. "There was no act of violence," said his lordship, " according to these witnesses, committed by them, no violation of peace, which would bring them under the reprehension of the law; and so far in favour of Bamford." And again, whilst commenting on the various flags, his lordship said, "with respect to Bamford, who went with the Middleton flags, nothing could be more decent than his conduct throughout the day. If the account given by the witnesses he adduced be a correct description, he everywhere recommended peace and order."

At a quarter past twelve the learned judge closed his charge, and the jury retired. Shortly before five they returned into court, and the foreman read their verdict as follows :—

"Moorhouse, Jones, Wilde, Swift, and Saxton, not guilty. Henry Hunt, Joseph Johnson, John Knight, Joseph Healey, and (to the astonishment of the judge, the bar, and the audience) Samuel Bamford, guilty of assembling with unlawful banners, an unlawful assembly, for the purpose of moving and inciting the liege subjects of our sovereign lord the king to contempt and hatred of the government and constitution of the realm, as by law established, and attending at the same."

Mr. Justice Bayley : Do you mean that they themselves intended to incite ?

The Foreman : Yes.

Mr. Justice Bayley : Let the verdict be so recorded. You find, gentlemen, on such counts as the words of your verdict are applicable to. Do you find that they created terror, or incited it in the liege subjects of the king?

The Foreman : We mean, my lord, to find on the first count, omitting a few words.

The learned judge then requested they would retire and look over the counts of the indictment again, and say to which count they meant to apply their verdict.

The jury withdrew, and in a few minutes returned with a verdict of guilty generally on the fourth count, and not guilty on the remaining counts.

Mr. Justice Bayley : I take it for granted the defendants are still under recognizance ?

Mr. Hunt : We are, my lord.

Mr. Justice Bayley : Then let them now additionally, in court, enter into their own recognizances to keep the peace and be of good behaviour for six months, Mr. Hunt in the sum of two thousand pounds, Mr. Johnson in one thousand, and Bamford and Healey in five hundred each.

The parties immediately gave their several recognizances.

His lordship addressing the jury, said they had his best thanks for the patient attention they had bestowed on this arduous trial. He was very much obliged to them. Then, facing the body of the court, his lordship added, " I very much approve of the conduct of the court at the time the verdict was given in "—alluding, as was understood, to the universal silence which prevailed at the time.

The reader will perhaps not think that I speak too strongly when I say that the infamy of the verdict against myself has seldom been surpassed.

During the whole of the ten days' investigation I did not observe that any one of the jury took a single note of the evidence, or that they indicated by the action of a single muscle of countenance, that any impression was made on their minds. They sat motionless, and like men who were asleep with their eyes open ; and it was clear, from the bungling form in which they presented their first verdict, that they had agreed upon it from a vague recollection of some point in evidence, and a clumsy misapplication of the counts in the indictment.

In a short time after we had left the court I was somewhat surprised by the information that Hunt, Pearson, and Bryant were about to leave York that night. I therefore hastened to Mr. Pearson and represented to him that I had not any money whatever to pay my lodging and tavern bills, every farthing I had having been given up to Mr. Chapman. Mr. Pearson advanced me two pounds, and I went and discharged what I owed. The next morning the generous-hearted Moorhouse yoked up his coach and dragged a full load of witnesses and defendants to Huddersfield, where we stopped for the night. The following morning (Wednesday) Moorhouse found that, in consequence of the heavy load, he should want a pair of leaders to help him over the hills, and he applied at several places, but in vain ; no horse-keeper in Huddersfield would furnish us a pair for love or money ; and the Radicals of the place, indignant at the paltry annoyance, harnessed themselves to the vehicle, and drew it over the steep hills as far as Blackmoor Bottom. At Oldham our faithful and kind friends—alas, that so few of them remain !—met us, and conducted us to a good substantial dinner at the White Horse Inn. Here I was met by my dear wife and child, and our present joy was only saddened by the reflection that ere long there must be another parting. We were soon again in tender conversation by the hedgerows and green fields; and I arrived at Middleton " poor in gear," but rich in the satisfaction of having performed my duty well; in having, though condemned, largely contributed towards the vindication of the conduct of the reformers on the 16th of August; in having created a feeling of respect in my enemies, and a favourable impression in the upright judge who tried us; in having disclosed to a great assemblage of wealth and aristocracy, as well as to the nation at large, that somewhat of moral and intellectual respectability had been attained by the artisans of Lancashire, whom on this occasion I represented. From that time they advanced a step in the grade of society; they were contemplated with a mingled feeling of curiosity and deference, and they were no longer considered as " the swinish multitude," " the base unwashed helots," nor denounced as the " dividers of property, and destroyers of social order."

If I did this, or any part of it, for my working fellow countrymen, I was entitled to their gratitude. We shall see ere long how that just claim was discharged; how they remembered one who, whilst pleading his own cause, had never forgotten theirs.

CHAPTER XXXII.

THE terms of our recognizances were that we should appear
in the Court of King's Bench on the first day of the ensuing
Easter term, and not depart therefrom without the permission
of the court. On the approach of that time, I therefore
became anxious about the means whereby I should get to
London. I should have been miserable if from any circumstance I had incurred a risk of not being in court when called,
and had thereby forfeited the bail which my friends had given
with me. My Radical acquaintances, however, never asked
me when or how I was going, and I felt too much what was
due to myself and my situation to throw out the least hint
about the matter. One or two of the most sordid and ungrateful of my acquaintance, and God knows I had too many
such, even told me that I needed not expect any assistance
from them, even if I went to prison. I smiled in contempt,
and replied that it would be time to deny me their assistance
when I asked for it. Others there were who no doubt would
have acted with an honourable considerateness had I made
known to them my total want of funds for the journey, but I
deemed it their place to ask me, and not mine to ask them. I
could not but feel that I was about to be victimised on their
account; I knew what was my duty, and was prepared to do
it, but I would not condescend to remind them of theirs.

One day I was at Manchester, and in conversation about
these matters I asked Mr. Evans, the editor of *The Observer*,

if there were any funds in the town which would be available in assisting the convicted parties to London? He said he had some money in hand belonging to the relief fund, and asked me how much I should want? I said I should think three pounds would be sufficient. He said I should have it, and if I would call on him a day or two before I set off he would pay it me. I called on him the week following, and he gave me three pounds. I purchased a pair of strong shoes, a pair or two of hose, and some other necessary articles, and then I went home and prepared in other respects for the journey.

It would be of no use to dwell on the hours of care, thoughtfulness, and anxiety on my part, nor of the regrets and tears which I tried to soothe and to suppress on behalf of my wife and child. Every one with a heart susceptible of our common human emotions will understand and appreciate their feelings and mine. Suffice it to say that when the last moment had been spent on my hearth, I started to my feet, threw my stick and bundle over my shoulder, locked the door, gave my wife the key, and with her on my arm, and my little girl by the hand, I took my way down Middleton and towards Manchester. I could not but reflect that when I went that way on the 16th of August there were ten thousand with me ready to shout, sing, or do whatever I requested; now, as if they were afraid I should want something from them, not a soul came forth to say "God be with you." One or two whom I saw on the road did, as they passed, ask if I was "going off," to which I replied by a nod. The words stuck in my throat, I was ashamed both for myself and them; ashamed of my past folly and of their present faithlessness. At the bottom of the town we parted from our dear child, telling her to go to a certain neighbour's (as had been previously arranged), and be a good girl, and her mother would bring her something from Manchester. She looked at us alternately, in tears, and then said, "And when will you come, father?" I stooped, kissed her, and said I would come soon, and, dashing the drops from my eyes, I gave my arm to her mother, and we ascended the hill in silence.

We stopped at Harpurhey, and whilst there a Middleton

man, a weaver, came into the place, and said he understood I
was going to London; I told him I was, and he urged me to
accept a shilling, as he understood I had come away with but
little, if any, money. I thanked him, but refused to accept of
it, alleging that I was better able to struggle with my difficulties than he was to spare a shilling from the wants of his large
family. He then said that as he was coming through Middleton John Ogden, a shopkeeper, and a neighbour whom I well
knew, told him I was before him, and he would probably
overtake me, that I had gone away without asking for, or
receiving a farthing, and that if he overtook me he was to give
me the shilling (which he put into his hand) and request me to
accept it from him. I said that altered the case; John Ogden
was able to spare a shilling; I would therefore accept it, and
he must give my thanks to the donor for his good and kind
consideration. My neighbour then took a glass of ale and
smoked a whiff or two of his pipe, and hurried to the warehouse at Manchester; and, reader, that shilling was the only
Middleton coin which I had in my pocket when I started for
London to receive judgment.

So much for the shouting, huzzaing, and the empty applause
of multitudes. A young aspirant to public notoriety may be
excused if he feel a little tickled with the shouts of adulation,
but whenever I see a grey-headed orator courting such acclamations, I set him down as being either a very shallow or a
very designing person. I have no patience with such hollow
trumpery—with the fools who offer it, or the questionable ones
who accept it.

We stopped at the house of a relative that night, and the
next morning I left Manchester in company with my wife
and my friend and late co-defendant, Thacker Saxton. At
Stockport Saxton remained with some Radical friends whom
he found there. My wife still lingered with me, after having
often stopped and gone on again. At last we arrived at
Stockport Moor; the afternoon was advanced, and the sun
was descending.

> " I saw the tear from her young eyes
> Affectionately starting,"

as my friend Spencer Hall has so beautifully expressed it ; and here was a final pause and parting—that is, I left her standing with her looks bent towards me, and there she remained till distance closed the view.

I now walked on at a quick pace, and had not gone many miles before I overtook a young man and his wife, who I soon learned were going to Macclesfield that night. I said I was going to that place, and somewhat further ; and when I told them of my destination, and that I intended to walk the journey, they were quite glad of my company, and we agreed to travel together. I soon learned they were going from Preston to Loughborough, where they intended to settle amongst the woman's relations. They were a very good-looking couple—he a stout, florid young fellow, and she a tall, handsome-featured woman ; she was also a good walker, which he was not, being already foot-sore.

On our arrival at Macclesfield my companions rested at a publichouse, whilst I went in search of some honest Radicals, to whom Saxton had given me letters of introduction. They were chiefly working men ; some of them were in pretty good circumstances, being master weavers. I soon found them, and they took myself and fellow travellers to a decent inn, where we got refreshment, and spent a very agreeable evening. In the morning, when our bill was called for, there was no charge against me, the kind friends who were with us the night before having settled everything which stood to my account.

We set off from Macclesfield about six o'clock on a lovely morning, and soon were in a finely variegated and wooded country, as any one will allow who has travelled betwixt Macclesfield and Leek. After walking some four or five miles we began to talk about breakfast, and my male companion said he would have cheese and bread and ale, whilst I anticipated a good breakfast of tea, with a couple of eggs, if they were to be had. Soon after the man stopped, and his wife said as we went forward, she was glad I preferred tea for breakfast. I asked her why, and she said her husband was a very hard-working man, and a good husband on the whole, but

he was a little too greedy, and expected her to fare as he did
on the road, instead of letting her have a few indulgences, such
as tea and coffee.   It was not from want of money, she said,
for he had enough with him, nor was it want of kindness to
her—it was over-carefulness alone which made him so.   But
now, as I was for having tea, he would hardly for shame deny
her having some also.   I promised, if it was necessary, to put
a word in for her, and she thanked me.   Having travelled a
little further we came to a neat little tap-house, on the descent
of a valley, where the cool shadow of trees made the air
grateful and refreshing, and a tiny wimpling rill ran like
melted pearls over dark gravel, beneath young-leafed hazels,
and by green-swarded margins.   Here we agreed to stop and
take what the house afforded.   The smart-handed landlady
soon placed a nice repast of tea, bread-and-butter, and a couple
of eggs before me, whilst a jug of ale, with bread and cheese,
were presented to my fellow-travellers.   The woman said she
could not eat, and I asked her to come and join me at tea,
adding, very likely the cost would be little more for tea than
for the breakfast they had before them.   On hearing this
opinion, her husband told her to get some tea, and then with
great pleasure the woman came to my table and made a hearty
breakfast.

We rested awhile at this pleasant little hostel ; the man and
I (I might as well call him John at once) each smoked our
pipe, with the window thrown up, and the cool breeze wafting
around us.   It was delicious to breakfast as we had done, and
then to repose after a fine, health-creating morning's walk.
John, however, I soon found, had not many conversational
matters at his command.   He was a plain, honest bricksetter;
knew something of the value of work in his line, could make
out an estimate of the expense of buildings and such things, and
those were the most of what he understood.   Not so his wife,
she was a sensible, well-informed woman for her station, and
it was evident that on most subjects (except the purse-keeping)
she was his superior, and exercised much influence over him.
She had been, as she afterwards informed me, a servant at an
inn at Loughborough, where the young bricksetter, then

on tramp, fell in love with and married her. They went down to Preston to settle amongst his friends; he was very wild and reckless, and one day he fell from some scaffolding and was shockingly maimed, so that he could never be so stout again as he had been. Latterly he had been more steady, and had saved a trifle of money, and as they had no children she had prevailed on him to return with her and live amongst her relations, and that was the cause of their journey.

At Leek we rested again during an hour, took some refreshment, and then resumed our journey towards Ashborne. In passing through the streets of Leek we noticed a number of weavers at their looms, and obtained permission to go into the weaving places and see them. The rooms where they worked were on the upper floors of the houses; they were in general very clean; the work was all in the silk small-ware line, and many of the weavers were young girls—some of them good-looking, most of them very neatly attired, and many with costly combs, earrings, and other ornaments of value, showing that they earned a sufficiency of wages, and had imbibed a taste for the refinements of dress. The sight of these young females, sitting at their elegant employment, producing rich borderings and trimmings, in good, well-aired, and well-finished apartments—some of them approached by stairs with carpets and oil cloths on them—the girls also being dressed in a style which two hundred years before would have been deemed rich for a squire's daughter, was to me very gratifying; whilst to my travelling companions it was equally surprising, and they expressed their feelings by sundry exclamations of astonishment.

The afternoon was very hot, and we walked slowly—that is, I and the woman did—for poor John was sadly hobbled with his sore feet and we had to keep sitting down and waiting on the road for him to come up. At length we gave him an hour's respite by stopping at a publichouse about four miles from Ashborne. It was almost dark when we entered that very clean and pleasant little town. At the first inn we went into we found accommodation, and, after partaking a good

warm supper, with some hearty draughts of old ale and pipes
for a dessert, we sought that repose which had now become
necessary.

The next morning we were up again early and continued my
plan of travelling—namely, to walk a good stretch before
breakfast. We sat down after walking about six miles; our
meal was as good as we could wish—coffee and eggs for the
woman and myself, and ale, cheese, and bread for friend John.
We were now in a right farming country where large stacks,
barns, and cattle-sheds were quite common on the roadsides.
The roads were broad and in good condition, and there were
very often wide slips of good land on each side, apparently
much trodden by cattle. Occasionally we came to a neat,
homely-looking cottage, with perhaps a large garden and a
potato-ground attached, and with rose shrubs and honeybines
clustering around the door. These were specimens of our real
English homes; there was no mistaking them; in no other
country do such exist, and he or she who leaves this land
expecting to meet with like homes in foreign ones, will be
miserably disappointed. In England alone is the term "home,"
with all its domestic comforts and associations, properly
understood. May it long continue the home of the brave, and
eventually become the home of the really free!

We stopped but a short time at Derby; I visited, however,
the grave of Jeremiah Brandreth, in St. Cuthbert's churchyard, and paid to the remains of that deluded victim a tribute
of heartfelt emotion. I then joined my comrades and we
hastened on, as well as John's feet would allow him, towards
Shardlow. There he got into a cart, and the female and I
walked on, promising to wait at Kegworth till the cart arrived.
Some rain had fallen a few days before; the Trent had been
flooded, and of all the verdant pastures I had ever beheld,
none have surpassed the rich, vivid green of the meadows
between Shardlow and Kegworth. It was refreshing to look
upon them, and as the sweet air came across them, cooling
one's dewy brows, one almost felt tempted to stop and seek an
abiding-place in that delicious valley.

During our walk we had a very agreeable chat; I entered

into some particulars of my early life and into matters always interesting to females, namely, the histories of some tender attachments which I had formed, but which had lapsed, either through my own indifference, or, as I was pleased to suppose, the faithlessness of the objects I loved. This seemed to touch a tender chord in my companion, she was all attention, and when I paused, she put questions which compelled me to resume my narrative. I spoke of the noble and exalted pleasures of true affection, and pictured the sickening pangs of love betrayed, and the unhappiness which must eventually haunt the betrayer, whether man or woman. I repeated some verses of poetry, which heightened the picture, and at last, on looking aside, I found that her cheeks were glistening with tears. She now became more communicative, and informed me that she had somewhat to accuse herself of with respect to a young man, the first indeed whose addresses she had encouraged: that she now often thought she behaved coldly towards him without any just cause, and that, in consequence, the lad enlisted and joined his regiment before his friends knew what had become of him; that she soon afterwards was married, and he was killed in battle. Weeping freely, she added that at times she accused herself of having been the cause of his death. I consoled her as well as I could by the reflection that her conduct appeared to have risen more from youthful carelessness than want of feeling. She said he was an only child, and his mother was still living, and she thought if she could get settled down beside the old woman it would afford her some consolation to assist her and be a child to her in her old age. I approved of this with all my heart; and now, being at Kegworth, we stepped into a publichouse and awaited the arrival of the cart, which soon came up, and after a cup or two of ale betwixt John and myself, and a whiff of tobacco, we set forward, and a short journey through a pleasant neighbourhood brought us to Loughborough.

Nothing would satisfy my fellow travellers but my accompanying them to the house of the old folks, as they called them. I was not much averse to going with them, especially as I knew that I must stop somewhere in the town all night. I accordingly accompanied them along several streets and turnings, until we were in a humble but decent-looking thoroughfare, when, knocking at the door, the woman in a whisper told me her parents lived there. A tall, venerable looking dame opened the door, and in a moment our female traveller was locked in her arms. A cheerful, clear-complexioned old man at the same time got up from his chair and shook John heartily by the hand, and on John mentioning me as a fellow traveller, he gave me a like frank reception. He then embraced his daughter, and when the first emotions of tenderness were over, we sat down to a very comfortable but homely refection, and the family party became quite cheerful and communicative. Meantime the news had got abroad amongst the neighbours, several came in, and in a short time we were joined by a fine-looking girl, a younger daughter of the old folks, who had been at work in one of the manufactories. In short, we had a joyful family and neighbourly meeting; liquor was sent for, a young fellow tuned up his fiddle, and the old couple led off a dance, which was followed by others; liquor was brought in abundance, and the hours flew uncounted.

John and I and the old man were seated in a corner smoking and conversing, when I observed the younger sister come in somewhat fluttered. She took the old mother and her sister aside, and by the expression of their countenances and the motion of her hands, I perceived that something troublesome and mysterious had occurred. In fact, she was explaining to them, as I afterwards learned, that in going to the publichouse for more liquor she had to pass a stage-coach which was stopped, and that on looking up she saw a young soldier getting off the coach, with his knapsack slung on one shoulder and a foraging-cap pulled over his face, but she saw enough to convince her that he was Robert—the same who once courted her sister and who they had heard was killed in battle. This news, as may be imagined, was soon known in the house, and caused a great sensation, particularly amongst the women. We had just learned the cause of their whisperings, when the door opened and a young fellow, pale, slender, and well formed, wearing regimentals and an undress cap, and with a knapsack properly adjusted, stepped respectfully into the room and, seeing the old woman, he put out his hand and took hers and spoke to her affectionately, calling her mother. She gazed a moment on his face, as if incredulous of what she beheld. The company had drawn in a half circle at a distance around them; John, myself and the old man kept our seats, the younger sister stood beside her mother, and the married one was on a low seat behind her.

" I scarcely know what to say to you, Robert," said the old woman. " I am glad to see you have escaped death, for your mother's sake, but I almost wish you had not called here to-night."

" And why not, mother? my *other* mother," he said, trying to force a smile. " Why not call at a house where I left friends, and mayhap a little of something more than friendship ? "

" Nothing beyond friendship now, Robert," said the mother, endeavouring to appear cool.

" Why, where is Margaret ? " he said ; " I hope nothing has befallen her ? "

" Margaret is your friend," said the old woman, " but she is nothing more now. Yonder sits her husband," pointing to John.

John advanced towards the young man and took his hand, and, looking towards Margaret, said he believed she had been his wife about two years.

The soldier trembled, and staggered to a seat.

Margaret got up and gave her hand to the young soldier, saying she welcomed him home with all the regard of a sister. She was now married, as he had heard, and was about to settle in Loughborough, and if he had never returned, his old mother should not have wanted the tender offices of a child whilst she lived .

" Thank you, Margaret," he said ; " that is some consolation ; you wouldn't neglect my old mother, I know." He put his hand over his eyes and burst into tears.

" I would not, Robert," she said, " and if in former times I did not value you as perhaps you deserved, I was willing to make the only atonement I could by cheering the drooping years of your supposed childless parent."

"That is very good!" "very fair on both sides!" "very handsome!" said a number of voices. Neither of the interested parties spoke, they were both deeply affected.

The old woman and youngest daughter then conducted Margaret into another room. The old man shook hands with the soldier and endeavoured to cheer him. Meantime, information had been conveyed to Robert's mother, and she now entered the room, shaking and leaning on a stick. The meeting was most tender; it was such as could only take place betwixt a parent and child equally affectionate. The dancing had at first been given up; a warm, substantial supper was in a short time spread on the board; Robert and his mother took some of the refreshment and then went home. Margaret did not make her appearance. Shortly after supper I was conducted to lodgings at an inn, and spent most of the night in confused dreams of the strange scenes which, like those of a romance, had passed before me.

The following morning I breakfasted at the old folks, according to promise. I asked not any question, nor did I hear anything further. Margaret's eyes appeared as if she had been weeping. John was attentive to her, and she seemed as if she valued his attentions, but could not entirely cast the weight from her heart. I left the family, to pursue my way, and John accompanied me as far as Quorn, where we parted, and I never saw him afterwards.

I merely walked through Mountsorrel, and leaving Rothley on my right, where many Knights Templars lie interred, I pushed on to Leicester, where, having spent the remainder of the day in looking at various antiquities, particularly the chamber in which Richard III. slept on the night previous to the battle of Bosworth, and the bridge over which his dead body was thrown on its return, I took up my abode for the night at a respectable looking little pot-house. Here I met with excellent accommodation, and enjoyed the lively conversation of some stocking-weavers, who, when they learned from whence I came and the share I had borne in Lancashire politics, would almost have carried me in their arms.

The following morning I pursued my journey, and passing through a fine country, consisting of sheep pastures and arable land, I dined at Market Harborough, and in the afternoon went on to Northampton.

I scarcely knew where to apply for lodgings; there were so many snug-looking publichouses that I was spoiled with choice. At length I entered one of the said neat-looking places and asked a decent elderly woman if I could have lodgings there. She frankly said at once that I could not, they were full of soldiers; and, in fact, I had seen a large number on parade as I came through the town. I asked if she could direct me to a place, and she pointed to a respectable looking house a little higher in the street. I went there, but received the same reply; they were "full of soldiers," and I learned that the latter were but just come into the town and were on their march to Liverpool, for Ireland. I now was directed to a publichouse where coachmen and guards stopped, and where many travellers were in the habit of resting. It was getting late and almost dark, and I determined not to be shuffled out of this next place by any pretence. I entered a rather handsome bar parlour, where a numerous company was sitting, apparently farmers, who were taking their pipes and glass, after the fair or market. I asked the landlady, a smart but unassuming woman, if I could have a bed for the night. From the moment I entered she had been eying me over, and seeing, as I suppose, my shoes all dust, and myself a brown, and not a very polished-looking customer, she said she was very sorry, but there was not a bed to spare in the house, so many soldiers had brought billets that they were quite full. I drew my hand across my brows, looked at my feet, rather feelingly, and requesting she would serve me with a pint of ale, I sat down. The ale was brought, and I gave it a hearty pull, and then asked for a pipe and tobacco, which were placed before me. My next order was for something to eat, intimating that a chop or a steak, with a hot potato, would be preferred. Meantime, I drank up my ale and called for another pint, and sat smoking and chatting with the farmers quite in a comfortable way. When they heard I came from Lancashire they made many inquiries as to late events and present prospects, and I told them all they required so far as my information went, and as candidly and fairly as my judgment enabled me, and we became very agreeable company. When my supper was brought in I despatched it with a hearty relish, and then, having ordered some brandy and water, I called the landlady to receive my shot, observing that it was time I should look out for lodgings—for I wished to try what fair means would do first. " Oh ! " she said, " make yourself comfortable, young man ; you seem to be very good company, and we'll make you a bed somehow or other, you shall see." " Another glass, sir, did you say ? " asked the maid, who stood at her mistress's elbow. I nodded assent, and thus got installed for the night, and had a most excellent lodging.

I have been the more circumstantial in narrating this transaction, inasmuch as it contains a useful intimation to foot travellers. I have never since, save on two occasions, tried the experiment of getting lodgings at a publichouse in the way I put the question on this night, and on those occasions I took the plan more from curiosity than any other motive. A foot traveller, if he is really desirous to obtain lodgings, should never stand asking about them. He should walk into a good room—never into the common tap-room—put his dusty feet under a table, ring the bell pretty smartly, and order something to eat and drink, and not speak in the humblest of tones. He will be served quickly and respectfully —that is, if those two things happen to be understood at the house. After his repast he should take his pipe or cigar if he be a smoker, and whether he be or not, he should drink, chat, and make himself quite at ease until bed-time, when all he has to do will be to call the chambermaid and ask her to light him to bed. That will be done as a matter of course, and he will probably have saved himself a tramp round the town in search of lodgings, and probably, after all, the making of his own bed under a manger or in a hay-loft.

CHAPTER XXXIII.

STOKE GOLDINGTON—AN IMPORTANT FUNCTIONARY—A BETRAYED
ONE—A COUNTRY ALEHOUSE—AN ALARM—A SUDDEN DE-
PARTURE—A MAGISTRATE AND HIS CLERK—AN ACQUITTAL
—A WEDDING.

AT six o'clock the following morning, the weather still delight-
ful, I left Northampton. With feelings of veneration I
stopped to admire the fine old cross, as it is called, erected
on the spot where the body of Eleanor, Queen of Edward I.,
rested on its way to London. Near this place, as I was
informed by a finger-post, the road to Needwood Forest
diverged, and I longed for an opportunity to range through
these interesting haunts of our English yeomen of old, but my
imaginative wanderings were soon checked by the information
which a countryman gave me, that the forest lands were
nearly all enclosed.

At a little quiet, retired publichouse on the Northampton
side of Stoke Goldington I stopped for breakfast. I chose to halt
here for two reasons : the first, because I wished to pay my
respects to a worthy old couple, if they were still living, and
the second, because I had walked about eleven miles, and was
hungry. When, in my nineteenth year, I was absconding
from a ship at London, weary, exhausted, and anxious lest I
should be pressed, I called at nightfall at this publichouse,
then kept by a decent elderly man and his wife with several
children. I was in my sailor's dress, with but little money in
my pocket, and I told the good folks my situation. They could
not find me a bed in the house, but they took pity on me, and
shook me down some good clean straw in an out-building,

where, with the ducks for my companions in one corner, and the fowls in the other, I spent a night of sleep that might have blessed a king. The kind people also gave me a breakfast of milk and bread in the morning, and when very gratefully and willingly I offered payment, they refused to receive anything. I could not therefore pass their door without calling to thank them, but I found them not there; they were both, I believe, dead, and the people now at the house knew nothing about the circumstance which had made me a debtor to their predecessors.

Whilst I sat enjoying my repast, a portly country-looking personage, with an air of some authority, came into the kitchen where several others were. He was followed by a neatly and plainly attired young woman, who sat down at a respectful distance, and seemed to shun observation. I soon learned from the tenor of his conversation with the landlord that he was a kind of deputy-constable in some of the neighbouring townships, and that the young woman was going with him before a magistrate, on a charge which would send her to prison, for having become a mother without producing a legitimate father for her offspring. This was enough to interest me in behalf of the girl, even had not the coarse jokes of the constable and one or two others excited my disgust and strong aversion. I once or twice put in a word of a civil and rather exculpatory tendency, for which I almost got laughed at by the men, but was repaid by the modest and grateful looks of the poor girl. The son of the squire's coachman had, as I understood, been courting the damsel two or three years, but when she was in a way for bringing a charge upon him, he had nearly ceased visiting her, and had entirely given over talking about marriage. These circumstances, which to the young woman must be matters of deep affliction and shame, were to the country boors subjects for scornful and bitter joking, all of which she bore very meekly and, what made me think better of her, with a good sense and self-respectful manner which prevented her from making the least reply. She sat with her head not entirely downcast, but with an air of shame, indignation, and repentance, whilst blushes,

paleness,·and tears, were alternately visible on her cheeks.   I
ardently wished for an opportunity for getting her out of the
hands of these ruffians, and particularly of the one who had
charge of her, and as I had learned the constable and she were
going my way, I determined to avail myself of any chance for
that purpose.   I therefore fell to cultivating a good opinion
with the functionary; I gave him some tobacco, and my glass
to drink from, and in a short time he was telling about the
numerous perils he had gone through in his apprehension of
thieves, poachers, and trespassers; on the sound judgment his
office required, and the courage and activity he had on sundry
occasions displayed, whilst I wondered how so rare a constable
could have remained so long in a humble country situation.
At length he must go, and as he said he should be glad of my
company as far as we went, we all three left the publichouse.

We had not got far ere a young fellow, apparently a farm
labourer, climbed over a stile from the fields and joined us.
He was going to a doctor, he said, having had his face, some
weeks before, injured by a young colt kicking him.   His head
and features were bandaged so that none of them were visible
save his eyes and part of his nose.   He walked with us, saying
very little, but occasionally sighing, as it were from pain.   I
observed the young woman glancing rather doubtfully towards
him once or twice, but neither she nor the constable seemed
to know him.   After walking some distance the constable said
he had to turn off across the fields to a village.   He said I
might as well go that way, as the foot-road led into the highway again, and was as short, and there was an excellent tap at
the alehouse, where we could have a glass after his business
was done.·   I agreed, for I wanted to see something more of
this affair, and so I stepped with him, his prisoner, and the
young man into the meadow path—for the doctor also lived in
the same village.   We soon arrived at the little hamlet, and
the constable inquired of a servant in livery if " his worship
was at home ? "   He said he was, and would be downstairs in
half an hour, and if he called then he would see him.   We
stepped into a publichouse, where we ordered some ale, and

having found it very good, we began to smoke, having agreed, very philosophically, that it was the wisest course to " take things easy in this world." We had sat thus, blowing clouds for some time, and going on our second jug, when the young fellow came suddenly into the room, and, gazing wildly, said a person was killed just above, and the doctor had sent him for a constable, as they could not remove the body until one arrived. Our active officer then, potent with ale and authority, laid down his pipe, pulled out his staff, took a huge draught, and charging me with the custody of the young woman until he returned, he hurried out of the house. As soon as he had disappeared, " here," I said to the girl, " take that shilling, and run for thy life." The young fellow at the same time pulled his bandages from his face ; a scream burst from the girl, he laid hold of her arm, I turned to light my pipe, and the next instant they had disappeared.

I then hastened up the lane in search of my active coadjutor, and met him coming down swearing and brandishing his truncheon. " Where are they ? " I said, for I thought I would be first to speak. " Where are who ? " he asked. " Why the young Jezebel and that fellow with the broken face ? " " Where are they ? " he repeated, glaring on me with his two eyes as if they would have started from his head. " Where are they indeed ? " " You should know where one is at least." I then told him in a somewhat deprecatory tone that I only turned to the fire to light my pipe, and when I looked again both the prisoner and the young fellow were gone. " But you are not gone at any rate," he replied, " nor shall you go until you have been before the justice to answer for this. Come along," he said, " come this way," and laying hold of my arm he reconducted me to the publichouse. " Heigh ho ! " I said, " there's nothing like taking things easy in this world." " D—— you and your easiness," he retorted, quite in a rage. " John," he said to the ostler, " go and see if his worship is astir yet." John went and soon returned with the tidings that his worship was ready. My conductor and I then went into the house of the worthy magistrate, and were met at the yard door by a set of very cross

pointers and cock-dogs, who made a general assault as if they
would have worried us, and myself in particular, for they
seemed to have barked at my companion before. We were
conducted into a neat carpeted room, where his worship and
his clerk sat at a table covered with a green cloth, and with a
number of papers and writing materials before them. "Well,
Andrew!" said the clerk, a thin, sallow, suspicious-eyed
person, "where is the girl you were to bring?" "Lord bless
his honour's worship," said Andrew, "I left her in the custody
of this here man and he's let her run away." "How's
that?" asked his worship, lifting his eyes from a Game Act
which he had been perusing. "How did you come to leave her
in this man's charge? I thought you had been an older officer
and had known better than that," said his worship. "May it
please your honour's worship," said the constable, "I and the
girl and this said prisoner, that now is, were awaiting your
honour's pleasure in the publichouse, when in comes a scurvy
knave as was awaiting o' the doctor, and said there was a
person killed, and I must go and take charge of the corpse;
so I 'livered my prisoner into this man's charge, and away I
went arter the corpse, and when I had run up and down o'
the village, I couldn't hear o' no corpse, and the people all, sir,
a-laughing at me."

The clerk gave a dark and bitter frown, the magistrate
burst out a-laughing heartily. I laughed too; in fact, I had
been doing so in my mind during the last half hour. When
the clerk saw the magistrate laugh he was suddenly taken
with a like cheerful sensation, and we all three laughed at
Andrew, the constable.

"Well," said the magistrate, composing himself, "but what
has this to do with the loss of your prisoner?"

"Please your honour," said the constable, "before I went
a-seeking the corpse I left the girl in charge of this man, who
I believe is no better than he should be, and when I came back
he tells me the girl had run away whilst he was a-lighting of
his pipe."

"How was it?" asked the magistrate, addressing me. I
gave him the same account I had given the constable, on

which he first, and then the clerk, burst into a hearty fit of laughter, to the apparently sore puzzlement of the constable, who seemed to think it a subject of too grave a nature for such light entertainment.

" What do you wish his worship to do in this case, Andrew? " asked the clerk.

" I wish his honour would send this here man to jail instead of the girl," was the reply.

" Can we do that? " asked the magistrate, half serious, half joking.

" We can hold him in sureties if Andrew undertakes to prefer a bill against him at the assizes," was the reply in the same strain.

" Let it be done then," said his worship. " Andrew, you will be bound in a bond of fifty pounds to prosecute this charge at the next assizes."

" Please your honour's worship, I'd rather be excused," said Andrew, looking alarmed. " Who's to pay expenses ? "

" I rather think the prisoner won't pay, at any rate," said his worship; " those who prosecute will have the first chance of that."

" Then I couldn't do it," said the constable; " I'd rather not have any hand in the affair."

" Is the man to be discharged then ? " asked the magistrate.

" Yes, if your honour pleases," said the constable; " I don't like them ere bonds."

The magistrate then asked me what I was and where I came from, and I told him I was a weaver and came from Lancashire.

He asked me where I was going to and for what purpose, and I told him I was on my way to London in expectation of getting a place.

Had I relatives in London, and what sort of a place did I expect to obtain ? I said I had not any relatives in London, but I had some good friends, and I had little doubt of getting a situation under Government.

" Under Government," said he, with surprise; the clerk also elevated his eyebrows.

" Yes, sir," said I, half laughing ; " I'm going up in expectation of a Government place."

" The man is *non compos*," said the magistrate in an undertone.

" Very likely, sir," replied the clerk.

" You are discharged, then," said the magistrate. " We can't do anything with you unless there be an undertaking to prosecute."

I bowed respectfully to his worship, gave the clerk a questionable smile, and quitting the room, I made the best of my way to the publichouse, where I had left my bundle and stick.

Another person had come in whilst we were away, and the landlady had told him about the girl running off and my being taken prisoner. This person was an attorney's clerk, and he took up my cause earnestly, and advised me to prosecute the constable for a false imprisonment. He was giving me that advice when the constable returned. I pretended to entertain the project, and when the official became aware of the subject on which we were deliberating, he became very uneasy, and seemed almost willing to make any compromise rather than be under the clutches of the other " limb of the law." At length, after I had sufficiently tormented him, I agreed to a settlement, the terms of which were that he should pay for a quantity of ale, I and the attorney's clerk, whom I found to be a queer, ironical fellow, agreeing to pay for as much to come in after his was drank.

We had sat here rather a considerable time, and had got into high good humour with each other and the liquor, when the sounds of voices and a fiddle were heard approaching the house, and in a minute after in walked the girl we had prisoner in the morning, arm in arm with a young fellow, who, by his speech and dress, we recognised as the one with the patched face ; in short, they were the two runaways, followed by some half a dozen young men, two young women, and an elderly person fiddling. They had been at church and had got wed, the banns having been published there some months before. They were now all ready for dancing, singing, and

mirth; I scarcely ever saw a set of happier-looking countenances; the lad was in raptures; the bride seemed to have
more self-command than any in the place. She thanked me
most gratefully for the kindly feelings I had evinced; her
husband joined her, and I found it of no use offering to break
up from the wedding party. The constable was quite reconciled, as the charge, he said, would be taken off the township, and the ratepayers would deem it no bad day's work of
his. The attorney offered his friendly services in reconciling
the squire's coachman to the match, and the landlady brought
in a posset of spiced ale for the wedding feast. The fiddler
rosined his bow afresh, and played up a jig that set all the
lads a-capering. In short, we ate and drank and danced the
afternoon away. Evening followed, night came, and then the
noon of night; and the last scenes I committed to memory
were the fiddler falling from his chair and smashing his viol,
and the attorney painting the constable's face delicately with
a blacking-brush whilst the latter person was fast asleep.

The next morning I was at Newport Pagnel at an early
hour. The place had a most romantic appearance as I approached it. There must have been heavy rains upwards, for
the Ouse had overflowed its banks, and numerous cattle were
grazing on small green islets surrounded by the flood. The
weather continued all that a foot traveller could wish, and I
walked on leisurely, enjoying the cooling breeze, the odour of
flowers, and the music of birds some six or eight miles until I
arrived at the celebrated village of Woburn, where I stepped
into the first publichouse I came to on the left-hand side—I
think it was the sign of the " Bedford Arms." The place seemed
very fine, and the people I saw moving about looked, I thought,
in a strange supercilious way at me; none of them stopped to
ask what I wanted. At length I desired a woman to bring
me a glass of ale, intending it as a preliminary to breakfast.
She did not pause a moment to receive my order, but looking,
down, swept past me. "Bless us," I thought, "what sort of
a publichouse have I got into now?" No one attended to me,
and soon after I asked again for a glass of ale; this servant
also went away without speaking, but in a short time

a female of a superior appearance came and said they did not entertain foot travellers. I expressed my surprise at that, and assured her I was both able and willing to pay for whatever I called for. She said she did not doubt it, but it was an invariable rule of the house not to serve persons travelling on foot, and the rule could not be departed from. Could I not have a draught of ale? I asked. No, foot travellers could not have anything there. I accordingly rose, and replacing my bundle on my shoulder, I begged her to inform her employer that the rule of the house might bring trouble and humiliation sometime, inasmuch as, if other engagements did not press me, I would go before the nearest magistrate, or the Duke of Bedford himself, and prefer a complaint against the occupier for refusing to entertain a traveller without sufficient cause. She smiled at my law (as well she might, having scanned my appearance, and thence formed an opinion of my purse), and said there were other places in the village where I might have whatever refreshment I wanted; and then, probably thinking she had wasted time enough on me, she turned and walked off, and I came out of that inhospitable and pride-infected place. At another inn I met with a reception the very reverse of the first; the people, both landlord and servants, were very obliging and attentive. I made a good breakfast, rested, chatted, and received an invitation to call there again if I came that way.

I wonder whether the people of the Duke's Arms are yet in business? and if they are, whether, like scores of their arrogant brotherhood, they have not been so far humbled by those great levellers, the railways, that if a wayfaring man now enters their house he can have a cup of ale for money?

I walked to Redburn to dinner, which consisted of a plain but delicious repast at a very humble pothouse. Here I remarked a horseshoe nailed inside the weather board of the door, and on my pretending ignorance of its purpose, and asking what it was for, an old wrinkled dame, seemingly the mother of the household, told me with perfect seriousness that it was to keep all witches and bewitched persons and things out of the place, and that so long as it remained there nothing under the influence of witchcraft could enter.

At St. Albans I walked amid the ruins of the old Abbey, having previously passed a fragment of a wall in the meadows below, undoubtedly a part of the remains of the British city of Verulam. I lingered rather long with these scenes, and it was getting dark when I passed the Obelisk at Barnet, where the famous battle was fought in the Wars of the Roses. Every step I advanced to-day, the people, their houses, and their manners, became more Londonish ; and it will not then appear surprising that at the first publichouse I went into I was made welcome to comfortable quarters, and so remained there during the night. The next morning I walked into London, and took my breakfast at a coffee-house.

CHAPTER XXXIV.

A CRUISE AMONGST THE BOOKSELLERS—VISIT TO MR. HUNT—
LONDON POLITICIANS AND JURY REFORM—A PAINFUL DIS-
COVERY.

My next business now was to examine the state of my purse,
which was speedily done, and found scarcely able to make a
jink, however shaken. My next consideration was how to set
about replenishing it. I had, in contemplation of some such
dilemma as the present, brought with me from Lancashire
some manuscript poems, which I felt pretty confident of being
able to sell for a decent sum, should I be in want of money
during my stay in London. I was already in want of it, or
about to be, and I was thus driven to my last resource the
first day of my arrival. I wished to raise some money immediately, in order that I might be enabled to redeem some
things which I had directed to be sent by the carrier, and be
thereby enabled to appear before my friends in a respectable
garb.

I therefore inquired my way to Ave Maria Lane, and went
into a great publishing establishment there; but, without
waiting to see my productions, they told me they could not do
anything with poetry. At another place, in Paternoster Row,
I could not see the great man because I had not a letter of
introduction. I went down Ludgate, and into the shop of
William Hone, but he was out of town. At a shop in the
Strand the brown paper enclosure of my effusions was first
opened, a glance given at the contents, myself scanned over,
and the writings returned, with an assurance that "It wouldn't
take." At a grand place in Oxford Street the shopmen stood

laughing at me, as I verily believed, under pretence of being diverted by my Lancashire rhymes ; and at a similar establishment in one of the wide streets beyond Charing Cross I received the comfortable advice to return home and remain at my loom.　Alas ! I thought, I wish I could return home.

I had now enough of the poet's trade, at least for one day, of—

"The oppressor's wrong, the proud man's contumely,"

and, wearied and disappointed, I turned my footsteps towards the lodgings of my friend Hunt, at Mr. Giles's, in Wych Street.　To be sure the booksellers were not entirely blamable ; my appearance was, no doubt, somewhat against me. My clothes and shoes were covered with dust, my linen soiled, and my features brown and weathered like leather ; which circumstances, in consideration with my stature, and gaunt appearance, made me an object not of the most agreeable or poetical cast.　Still, I thought these booksellers must be very owls at mid-day not to conceive the possibility of finding good ore under a rude exterior like mine.　And then I bethought me —and comforted myself therewith, inasmuch as others had trodden the same weary road before me—of Otway, and Savage, and Chatterton, and of the great son of learning, as ungainly as myself—Samuel, the lexicographer—and, I might have added, of Crabbe, and others of later date, but their names had not then caught my ear.　And thus, musing as I went, and chewing bitters until they almost became sweets, I once more found myself in the shop of Mr. Giles, the bread baker, in Wych Street.

I asked for the good old man, and a plump, short-statured lady in mourning advanced from an inner room.　I saw in a moment that she was Mrs. Giles, and, smitten with a saddening thought, I ventured to ask for her husband.　She informed me civilly, but not in that friendly tone I had been accustomed to there, that Mr. Giles was dead, that she was keeping the business on, and that Mr. Hunt had removed to an address which she gave me, in Charlotte Street, Oxford Street.

The afternoon was far advanced, when, after traversing a

part of the town I had never seen before, I knocked at the
door of a very respectable looking house, and asked for Mr.
Hunt, and on sending up my name was instantly admitted.
I had not long been in the house before a very respectable repast of bread, butter, and a beverage made from roasted corn
was set before me, and I partook of it with a relish, though I
was never very fond of "corn coffee"; but as we all know,
"hunger is the best sauce." Many questions of course were
asked on both sides, and matters were discussed; and after
conversing about an hour, as night was setting in, I took up
my bundle and stick, received a hearty shake of the hand,
with an invitation to "come to-morrow"—"come any
time." And so, bidding my friend and his family good
evening, I left the house and turned into the street, to go
I knew not whither.

"This is not the way," thought I, "in which I treat my
friends from a distance when they call upon me in Lancashire.
I should not have let Mr. Hunt leave my dwelling, humble as
it is, without knowing whither he was going, and how he was to
be entertained." But then came the old excuse, "It is the way
of great folks," "one of the peculiarities of London," and
so forth; and cogitating on this and various other matters,
I retraced my steps, as well as I could find my way, to Mrs.
Giles's, in Wych Street.

I thought the widow seemed more friendly after I had expressed disappointment at my visit to Mr. Hunt. I asked her
if there was a decent tavern in her neighbourhood which she
could recommend as a comfortable place for lodging. She expressed entire ignorance of any of them, but said one of the
journeymen could possibly inform me; and she called one,
who recommended a house in Newcastle Street, close by, as
a suitable and likely place for stopping at. She sent him to
inquire if they could lodge a person from the country, and in
a short time he returned, saying I could have a very good bed
there if I chose. I accordingly went with the man, who
showed me the house, and I entered the public room, and,
taking my seat at a table opposite the boxes, I ordered a pint
of beer, as they call it, and bread and cheese for my supper.

I had finished my repast, and sat smoking, when three or four persons entered the room, and commenced a conversation which became animated. They were, as I soon learned, some of the London politicians of the working class, and the subject was the English jury system. It was, if I mistake not, the approaching trial of Thistlewood and his companions which led to this discussion. One party would have it that the English jury was one of the most complete inventions which human wisdom could have accomplished, and they lauded it as fervently, and with about as much sense, as a certain class of politicians are in the habit of lauding our "glorious constitution," a thing which exists in imagination only. Another party thought that the system was faulty, and instanced the packing of juries, and a third party thought the verdict should go according to the majority. I sat listening attentively, but did not interfere, until at last one of the speakers asked my opinion of the subject in dispute.

I frankly confessed that I differed from the whole of them, and thought the English jury one of the most bungling pieces of judicial machinery which could have been put together, and I noticed several instances of its clumsy and imperfect operation within my own knowledge, not, however, mentioning the late trial at York. I asked how it could be otherwise, seeing the manner in which jurymen were selected. In the country I came from I said they were generally men who had just the brute instinct of beavers, to scrape a little substance together and to keep it, but who for all other purposes were far behind their neighbours ; and infinitely so in qualifications necessary for deciding betwixt right and wrong, guilt and innocence. A time would come, as I ventured to suppose, when that piece of old trumpery would be done away with altogether ; meanwhile I would, had I the power, endeavour to render it more useful by ordering, in a legal way, that all jurymen should be elected by ballot in each township, that their appointment should be annulled at the will of those who appointed them, that property should not qualify, that five, seven, or nine should be the number, and a majority should carry a verdict, that all juries, whether grand juries, coroner's juries, or leet juries, should be taken from this body, and that they should be paid from county or other rates, independent of the crown. This plan was generally approved of, and I should have been honoured with a speech or two in compliment, but happily the girl came with the chamber candle, and so bidding my London patriots good night, I retired from their company.

After ascending several heights of stairs, I demurred, and asked the girl how much further upwards we must go? She begged pardon, and said the bed intended for me was on the second floor, and had been occupied by a lodger during a fortnight; he had gone away and they did not expect him that week, but he had suddenly returned and claimed his old bed. Against this I could not adduce any argument, especially as it was too late to go out that night, and so, following my guide, I climbed to the uppermost floor of the house. I looked at the apartment, which did not please me very well; it was of no use, however, beginning then to be very nice, and so I threw down my bundle and stick, whilst the girl, with the candle in her hand, reminded me that it was customary for strangers to pay before going to bed. "Oh! very well," I said; "how much is it?"—not thinking the charge would be more than sixpence at most. "Eighteenpence, if you please, sir," said the girl. I put my hand hastily into my pocket, and pulling out all the money I had, I counted it, and found it to be just a penny short of the demand, namely, one shilling and fivepence. "Well, lass," I said, "this is all the money I have in the world, and it is a penny too little," and I looked, as much as to say, "Will it do?" "Never mind, sir," she replied; "you will be calling some day in going past, and you can give the penny to master or mistress." I said I would do so, and the girl then bidding me good night, left the room.

I had never slept on so mean a bed as was presented on my turning down the clothes. I had slept for weeks on old sails in the half-deck of a ship, or in the cable tier, and slept comfortably, but I had never lain on anything that looked and smelled so filthy as the narrow, hard couch now before me. I, however, threw myself upon it and wooed forgetfulness, in order to escape from disgust, but there was such a racket on

the other side of the partition as for a long time forbade all
repose, and convinced me that I had got into a not very respectable house. When at last all was still and I was beginning to
sleep, the peaceful charm was broken by the entrance of a
drunken soldier, who rolled into another bed, and kept me
awake by narrating various sprees, as he called them, in which
he had been engaged during the day. At length he also became
oblivious, and his very welcome snore informed me that I was
at liberty to sleep if I could. The "sweet restorer" soon came,
and when I awoke in the morning my noisy companion was
gone, probably to attend an early parade."

I was not long in dressing, as may be supposed. I merely
coaxed the holes in my stockings a little lower, and turned my
neck-kerchief the cleaner side out, and my embellishments
were finished. There was no water or towel in the room, and
I would not make free with soldier Jack's blacking, as I had
nothing to satisfy his demand should he return and make one.
I therefore slipped on my shoes and clothes, dusty and soiled
as they were the night before, and grasping my trusty cudgel
and my bundle, I sallied from the room, wishful to get a breath
of sweet air, if there were any such in London. As I passed
along a kind of landing, a door opened just before me, and out
stepped, as quietly as an old hen off her perch in a morning,
as demure a looking piece of purity as the world ever exhibited.
As she turned to go down the stairs I caught a glance of her
face. She was almost forty years of age, with rather agreeable
features, modest and humble looks, as if she had been at
prayers, and was dressed in second mourning of the most
devout cut. "A mother in Israel," indeed, would that frail
dame have passed for. As I followed her towards the door I
really felt in a degree ashamed at being seen coming out with
her. I involuntarily turned towards the lady as she went
away, and at that moment she gave me a look which spoke as
plainly as a look could speak what was her unfortunate voca-
tion.

I sauntered down into the Strand, and turned towards
Charing Cross, not that I had any business in that direction,
but I thought a man without money might as well go one way

as another in London. I was half inclined to believe also
that the people I met seemed as if they knew I was penniless.
After wandering an hour or so, looking in at the shop windows,
and gazing at whatever was new, I retraced my steps on the
other side of the street, with the view of calling at the office of
The Black Dwarf, and a faint hope of receiving an invitation
to breakfast. Mr. S. was very glad to see me, and was very
civil, but he did not seem to have any thought about break-
fasting, and so, after a short conversation standing, I went
once more into the street. At Mr. West's, the wire-worker, I
was not more fortunate, and my friend, Sir Richard Phillips,
at whose shop I had called the day before, would not be at
home for several days. I consequently had no abiding place
save the street, and I " maundered about," as we say in Lancashire, devising new expedients, and conjuring up hope almost
against despair. I had become quite wolfish, and the sight of
good substantial meats and delicate viands in the windows of
the eating-houses, all of that which in my road I stopped before
and contemplated, tended to increase the pangs of hunger,
which were no ways allayed by the savoury fumes arising from
the cooking cellars. At last I wandered round Fleet Market,
and, coming to the prison, I found a poor debtor begging at
the gate.

" Please to bestow a trifle on a poor prisoner," he said.

" God help thee, lad," I replied, " I am more poor than
thyself."

" How is that ? " he asked.

" Why," I said, " thou has a room to retire to, and a bed to
repose upon, but I have neither home, nor lodging, nor food,
nor a farthing of money towards procuring them ! "

" Why, then, God help *thee !* " he said, " thou art indeed
worse off than myself, except as to liberty."

" And that I may not have long," I said.

He asked me what I meant, and I told him that I was come
up from the country to receive judgment for attending the
Manchester meeting.

" If that be the case," he said, " come back in an hour, and
if I get as much as threepence or sixpence, thou shall have it."

I thanked him sincerely and gratefully, and promised I would come back if no better fortune befel me, and so pleased that I had found one friend in the course of the morning, though a poor one, I bade him good-bye, and went on towards Bridge Street.

At sight of the bridge I recollected a gentleman on the other side of the river who had behaved very kindly to me the last time I was in London, and I thought I might as well call upon him, for at all events I could not be more disappointed than I had been. I therefore passed over the bridge, and soon found the shop of my friend in the main thoroughfare, called Surrey Road, I think. Several young men were busy in the shop, and I asked one of them if Mr. Gibb was within?

"Oh, yes," he said. "Is that you, Mr. Bamford? Walk forward; he's in the sitting-room at breakfast; he'll be glad to see you; step in."

I thought that was like a lucky beginning, at any rate, and, without a second invitation, I entered the room.

A glance of one moment brought the gentleman to his feet. He took my hand and made me sit down, and rang the bell, and ordered another cup, and more butter and toast, and eggs and ham. "You have not breakfasted, I suppose?" he said.

I replied that I had not—it was just what I had been wanting to do during the last hour and a half.

"Bamford," he said, as we went on with our repast, "what's the matter with you? You don't seem as you did the last time you were in London."

"How am I changed?" I inquired.

"Why, the last time you were up," he said, "you were all life and cheerfulness when I saw you, and now you seem quite thoughtful. Are you afraid of being sent to prison?"

"No," I said, "I was not."

"What's the reason you are so serious?" he asked.

I said "I could not help being so."

"What's the cause?" he said. "Tell me the reason of this great change?"

"Well, then, to tell you God's truth," I said, "I have not a farthing in the world, and I could not have had a breakfast if I had not come here."

"Oh! if that's all, man," he said, "make yourself easy again. Come! take some more, and make a good breakfast," and I took him at his word, I did make a good breakfast.

When we had finished he took me to his dressing-room, where were water and towels to wash. He also ordered the servant to clean my shoes, and found me a clean neck-kerchief and a pair of stockings. When I returned to the sitting-room I was quite smart, comparatively.

"Now, Bamford," he said, "this is my breakfast hour; at one we dine, at five take tea, and supper at eight; and so long as you are in London my table is yours if you will attend at meals. Take this one pound note (putting one into my hand), and if there is not a change in your circumstances for the better when that is done come for another."

I thanked him most sincerely. I never was more affected by an act of kindness in my life. He was in truth, "a friend in need, a friend indeed."

CHAPTER XXXV.

A CHANGE IN MY SITUATION—PROCEEDINGS IN THE COURT OF KING'S BENCH.

I NOW went to the warehouse in Cheapside, where my luggage had been directed to be left, and found it had arrived. I took it to a tavern, and put on a change of linen and articles of outer apparel, and then I went and engaged lodgings, to which I removed my things. I was now decent in appearance, and more comfortable in mind. I visited my friend Mr. Gibb, and did not forget the poor fellow in the prison. In the afternoon I again called upon Hunt, who received me very cordially, and I took some more of the "roasted" with him. The day following Healey and Johnson arrived in London, and on the 27th of April we all made our appearance in the Court of King's Bench, when Mr. Hunt moved for a rule to show cause why the verdict returned at York should not be set aside, and a verdict of not guilty entered on the record, or why a new trial should not be granted.

The Lord Chief Justice Abbott asked if the application was for Mr. Hunt and the other defendants.

Mr. Hunt said it was so made.

The Lord Chief Justice: Now state on what ground it is that you make this motion.

Mr. Hunt: The first ground, my lord, is a misapprehension of the learned judge who tried the case, in rejecting evidence which ought to have been received. It was evidence as to the acts of aggression, of cutting, maiming, and killing by the yeomanry cavalry, and other military, upon the persons of those who attended at the Manchester meeting. The next point is

the learned judge's admittance of evidence as to certain resolutions of a meeting held in Smithfield, and the admission of
evidence as to certain trainings and drillings at a place called
White Moss. The third point is the misdirection of the judge,
in consequence of such rejections and admissions; and the
fourth ground is, that the jury gave a verdict contrary to the
evidence.

The Lord Chief Justice : Have you any other ground ?

Mr. Hunt: Yes, I have a fifth and last ground, which is,
that the jury gave a verdict contrary to the direction of the
learned judge.

The judges not having before them the notes of the trial, the
determination as to the points urged by Mr. Hunt was post-
poned until Monday, the 1st of May, when we were ordered
again to be in attendance. We were accordingly in court at
the time appointed, with our solicitor, Mr. Pearson, but the
judges did not pronounce their determination, and we were
directed to appear on the 8th of the same month. The court
was each day crowded to excess.

On the 8th of May the judges delivered their opinion,
unanimously refusing the rule applied for by us. The Attorney-General then urged that judgment should be immediately
pronounced; but Mr. Hunt requested that time should be
allowed us to prepare. I was as fully prepared on the first
day as I was on the last, but coincided, through courtesy, in
Mr. Hunt's various expedients to put off the evil day to the
uttermost. The request now made by him was granted by the
court, and we were ordered to come up again on Saturday, the
13th of May, for judgment.

On that day Hunt, Healey, and myself, appeared before the
judges, and Johnson came shortly after. Mr. Hunt stated
that certain affidavits which he had sent for from Manchester
had not arrived, and he craved the indulgence of the court
until he was enabled to procure them, which he expected every
hour. This was accordingly granted, and we retired once
more. Soon after two o'clock we again went into court, and
Hunt tendered an affidavit, setting forth that the person who
had been despatched to Manchester for the affidavits had not

arrived, nor had any letter been received from him. Mr. Hunt next stated that since the above affidavit was sworn a letter had been received by Mr. Pearson, wherein it was alleged that the writer had been unable to procure the affidavits by the time appointed, but there was no doubt they would arrive in the course of Sunday.

The Lord Chief Justice then ordered the case to stand over until Monday morning.

This being the day appointed for pronouncing judgment, the court and the hall were crowded at an early hour by spectators, and hardly on any former occasion did public curiosity appear to be more excited. Several persons of distinction were present in court during the greater part of the day. Among others, we observed Lord Binning, Lord Apsley, and Mr. Tierney.

About half-past eleven o'clock, the Attorney-General having prayed the judgment, we all came into court. We were accompanied by Mr. Pearson, the solicitor, Mr. Wooler, and other friends. The whole of the proceedings occupied the attention of the court from the hour above mentioned until past six o'clock in the evening.

Several affidavits were put in by Hunt, Johnson, and Healey. I did not tender any affidavit; indeed I had not been a willing party to these fruitless procrastinations.

The Chief Justice asked the Attorney-General whether he meant to put in affidavits on the part of the crown?

The Attorney-General: Not at present; it will depend, my lord, on the contents of the affidavits now put in.

The first affidavit read was that of Mr. Hunt, which entered into a history of the transactions that took place at Manchester on the 16th of August.

The joint affidavit of William Brundret, Dwarris Hart, Joseph Holland, Richard Sheridan, Samuel M'Cabe, George Burney, William Hunt, William Gregory, John Riley, Henry Barrett, William Mackelroy, and Alexander Anderson, all of them persons who had signed the requisition for calling the meeting, was next put in and read. These persons described themselves as housekeepers at Manchester and its neighbourhood, and weavers, &c., by trade. They described the dreadful state of depression and poverty to which they had been subjected as the motive for calling the meeting, in order thereby to obtain, by legal means, a redress of their grievances. They stated that with the utmost industry, working fourteen hours a day, they could not earn more than eight shillings per week.

The affidavit of Ann Jones, a married woman, occupying a house which commanded a view of all that took place at the meeting, was next put in. She deposed that the meeting was quiet and perfectly harmonious until the yeomanry cavalry broke in upon the unresisting crowd, who were cut down and trampled upon with merciless fury. Her house afterwards became the refuge of the wounded and dying, to whom she administered such relief as her means would afford. She likened her house to an hospital after a military slaughter.

The affidavit of Nicholas Whitworth stated that after the sanguinary transactions of the 16th of August he had made it his business to inquire into the extent of the mischief, and he had seen and spoken with near four hundred persons who had been wounded by the military. Some of these persons were injured from sabre cuts, and others by gun-shot wounds.

Part of the affidavit, which merely spoke to the deponent's information and belief as to other circumstances connected with the transactions of that day, were rejected as not admissible.

The affidavit of Robert Willis Hall stated, that the deponent had seen and spoken with three hundred persons, men, women, and children, who had been injured by gun-shot and sabre wounds, received from the military on the 16th of August.

The affidavit of Joseph Rayner stated, that the deponent had seen and conversed with three hundred and eight persons injured from the like causes.

Mr. Hunt said that before the other defendants and himself proceeded to offer any observations in mitigation of punishment, he must entreat their lordships to confine their attention solely to the fourth count of the indictment, upon which the conviction was founded. In order to this, it was necessary that their lordships should distinguish the evidence which supported that count from that which was adduced to sustain the others, of which the defendants were acquitted, but which embraced much more heinous charges. This caution was the more necessary, not only because it would be the height of injustice that, by blending all the evidence together, they should be punished for offences of which they had been acquitted, but because one of their lordships (Mr. Justice Best) had misconceived many parts of the evidence, and had made comments upon them with that warmth which was natural to him, and which could not but have a prejudicial effect upon the minds of the other judges in meting out the punishment they were called upon to award. He therefore prayed that the learned judge who tried the case would read such parts of the evidence as applied to the fourth count only, so that the court might see upon what foundation their sentence was to proceed. He, however, would leave this matter entirely to the discretion of their lordships.

The court assured us that in awarding the punishment they should confine their attention solely to that part of the evidence which was applicable to the count on which the jury found their verdict.

Mr. Hunt then prayed, as a matter of indulgence, that the other defendants might have the priority of him in addressing the court in mitigation of punishment.

The court said they saw no reason for departing from the ordinary course of their proceedings. Mr. Hunt's name stood first on the record, and therefore he would begin.

Mr. Hunt then addressed the court in a long speech, during which he was several times stopped by the judges for irrelevant matter, and once by Justice Bayley, who, as at York, requested that he would forbear to use complimentary language. Mr. Johnson followed in a speech more condensed and to the point, whilst, when Healey's turn came, he produced a speech ready written by his friend at Lees. It was all to no use, however—the doctor could not make out the polysyllabic words without spelling, and I, who stood behind him, had to

look over his shoulder and read for him, whilst my cheeks
burned, and my ears tingled with mortification, amid the
suppressed titters of the gentlemen of the long robe and the
spectators. When he was fast, and I was not attentive, he
would look over his shoulder supplicatingly, and say in an
undertone, "Prompt, Bamford! prompt," and then I set him
going again. At last this was beyond endurance, and I said,
"Throw that confounded paper down, man, and speak off-
hand." He accordingly wrapped the paper up, and went on
very fluently, arguing that the inscription, "Universal Suffrage
or Death," which was on the black banner from Lees, was
only meant as the expression of an opinion, and was not a
demand, with death as the alternative. "Suppose," he said,
"that one of your lordships had a bad leg." The gentlemen
of the long robe looked aghast, wondering what would come
next; for it was well known that Justice Best, who was on
the bench, had two of the worst legs in England.

"Suppose," said our imperturbable friend, "that one of
your lordships had a bad leg, and I, amongst other medical
and surgical gentlemen, was called in. Well, we hold a consultation, and we pronounce it to be a bad case—a case of
gangrene, my lords; and my opinion as to the mode of treatment is asked, my lords. I say, amputation or death! my
lords, amputation or death!" And so he went on to argue
that bribery and corruption having produced a political gangrene in the State, there must be amputation of the corrupting
influence, or political death would ensue.

Hunt sat on a low seat behind Healey, and when this scene
was passing I, half-diverted, half-ashamed, looked down at
him, and saw him nearly suffocated with his efforts to refrain
from laughing outright.

I spoke somewhat as follows :—

My lords,—I understand that the evidence upon which I
was convicted relates to the motto, "Unity and Strength."
I must, however, confess myself at a loss to understand how
guilt can be implied thereon. If we examine that part of the
evidence for the crown which applied more immediately to my
case, we shall find that the unity and strength which I incul-

cated, and which was also expressed upon the banner from
Middleton, was of a quite contrary description to that imputed
to me by the verdict.   Morris, in repeating, or attempting to
do so, my address to the people upon the Barrowfields, says
that I made use of the following expressions :—" Friends and
neighbours, I have a few words to relate ; you will march off
this ground quietly, not to insult any one, but rather take an
insult."   Heaton declares that " the people did not seem
sullen and sulky.   They had no angry look, but were more, as
it were, in joy."   Now, my lords, herein you will perceive a
full comment upon this short text.   Here is the " Unity and
Strength " of which our banner spoke.   But if we go further
on to read the evidence of Dyson, who was one of my witnesses,
we shall see the utility of this motto still further exemplified.
Dyson says that I made use of the following words in my
speech to the people, previous to their departure from Middleton : " Friends and neighbours, those of you who wish to join
in the procession will endeavour to conduct yourselves orderly
and peaceably, so that you may go as comfortably as possible.
If any person insult you or give you offence, take no notice of
them.   I make no doubt but there will be persons who will
make it their business to go about in order to disturb the peace
of the meeting.   If you meet with any such, endeavour to keep
them as quiet as possible, and if they strike you, don't strike
again, for it would serve as a pretext for dispersing the
meeting."   Before proceeding further, I solemnly and firmly
assure your lordships that I never again will advise my
countrymen to exercise that degree of patience which I here
did, until every drop of blood shed on that day has been amply
and deeply atoned for.   Never again will I recommend forbearance until the perpetrators of all the horrid murders
which I then witnessed, and from which I miraculously
escaped, have been brought to condign punishment.   My
lords, I speak this not from a spirit of vindictiveness, or from
a wish for indiscriminate vengeance, but from a high sense of
the wrongs and injuries inflicted on my country, and from an
indignant feeling that justice has been denied.   Dyson proceeds—" If the peace officers come to arrest me, or any other

person, offer them no resistance, but suffer them to do their
duty. When you get to the meeting, endeavour to keep yourselves as select as possible, with your banners in your centre,
so that if any of you should straggle away, you will know
where to find each other by your banners: and when the
meeting is over, keep close to your banners, and leave the
town as soon as possible, for if you should stay drinking or
loitering in the streets, your enemies might take advantage of
it, and if they could raise a disturbance, you would be taken
to the New Bailey." Now, my lords, this is the kind of
" Unity and Strength " which I recommended to the people,
accompanied by a degree of patience, which, as I before said,
I will never again recommend until justice be obtained. This
is surely not a criminal Unity—this is surely not a Strength
calculated to overawe the authorities, and to fill " his
Majesty's liege subjects with terror and alarm." This is
only that " Unity and Strength " which is the foundation of
liberty and the security of property. How often since my
arrival in London, for the purpose of waiting upon this honourable court, have I heard boastings about the liberties of
Englishmen—but if such a thing does really exist, how can it
be secured without a moral " Strength " on the part of the
people for its maintenance ; and where shall we find strength
without " Unity ? " This unity and strength, therefore, is
nothing more or less than the foundation of all the glory and
happiness which we enjoy ; and shall it be said, then, that in
this enlightened age an Englishman shall be persecuted and
punished for inculcating those maxims upon which the glory
of his country depends. If such must be the case, the era is
every way worthy of the deed. Another instance of this unity
and strength may be adduced in the situation of Middleton,
which is a considerable manufacturing town, and situated in
a populous district, and yet to secure its peace and tranquillity
there are only two constables annually sworn in, and not a
soldier quartered upon us ; yet we have had no breaches of the
peace, either on the part of the people or the authorities. It
was, indeed, at one time, deemed expedient by some individuals to raise a posse of special constables. This measure,

however, I most strenuously opposed, and happy am I to inform your lordships that the good sense of the people prevailed, and the affair was dropped. Now, here again is that "Unity and Strength" exhibited, to which our motto so aptly alluded. Surely if any persons had a right to such a motto, it was the inhabitants of that place, whose conduct had beautifully illustrated it. I concluded my speech, of which the foregoing is only an extract, by assuring their lordships that I appealed not to their humanity, not to their commiseration, but to their justice. Humble as was my situation in society, I would not condescend to beg the boon of mercy from any man or set of men, however exalted their situation. I would disdain to receive that from their pity to which justice entitled me.

The Attorney-General spoke at considerable length in aggravation of punishment, and contended that the conduct pursued by the defendants in this last stage of the proceedings was an aggravation of their guilt. The only topic fairly addressed to the court in mitigation of punishment was the hardships which the defendants had suffered after they had been apprehended; but those sufferings were the natural consequences of their own crimes, which he still thought approached as near as possible to the offence of high treason. There could be no doubt of the illegality of the defendants' conduct in every part, and for the sake of the public welfare he called upon the court to pronounce such a sentence on the defendants as would, through their example, teach others to abstain from pursuing conduct equally criminal and dangerous to the peace of society, and the security of government.

The Solicitor-General declined offering anything on the same side, but left his learned friend, Mr. Scarlett, who was present at the trial, to say what occurred to him on the subject.

Mr. Scarlett rose principally to correct a mistake under which Mr. Hunt seemed to labour, namely, that he (Mr. Scarlett) was selected to conduct the prosecution. There could not be a greater misapprehension. It was purely matter of accident, from the circumstance of his situation at the bar, and the absence of his senior, that he was employed in the case. As to any resentment he might be supposed to entertain towards Mr. Hunt, nothing could be more erroneous. He never entertained any towards that individual, of whom he knew nothing but what he happened to read of him in the public papers, and to suppose that he was selected to conduct the prosecution on account of this resentment, was really absurd. If such a selection could have taken place on such an account, he could only have treated it as a personal insult towards him on the part of the Attorney-General. Adverting to the case under consideration, he entertained no doubt of the illegality of the defendants' conduct, who, he said, endeavoured to divert the attention of the court and the public by introducing matters which had nothing whatever to do with the offence for which they were called upon to answer. He insisted, that whatever might have been the conduct of the magistracy and yeomanry of Manchester, it was wholly irrelevant to the question of the defendants' guilt or innocence of the crime imputed by the indictment.

Mr. Serjeant Cross followed on the same side.

The court having deliberated upon their judgment for nearly half an hour,

Mr. Justice Bayley proceeded to pass sentence, and in doing so he entered into a long commentary upon the case. The case had been fully submitted to the jury, and the court, having no reason to be dissatisfied with their verdict, were pronouncing such a judgment as would satisfy the justice of the case between the public and the defendants. Taking all the circumstances of the case into consideration, and giving the defendants the benefit of such mitigatory suggestions as had been urged, the sentence was—That Henry Hunt be imprisoned in his Majesty's gaol at Ilchester, in and for the county of Somerset, for the term of two years and six months, and at the end of that time to enter into security for his good behaviour for five years, himself in £1,000, and two sureties in £500 each; and that the other defendants, Healey, Johnson, and Bamford, be severally imprisoned in His Majesty's gaol of Lincoln for one year, and that they do severally enter into securities for their good behaviour for five years, themselves in £200, and two sureties in £100 each.

Mr. Hunt : I hope, my lord, the confinement is not to be solitary ?

Mr. Justice Bayley: We make no order on the subject. 1 make no doubt that the persons to whose custody the defendants will be committed will show them every indulgence consistent with their safety. Their duty will be performed under the inspection of the magistracy, and we take it for granted that everything will be done to avoid aggravating the inconvenience of imprisonment.

We were then taken into custody, and when we reached the hall we were greeted with the acclamations of the assembled multitude.

CHAPTER XXXVI.

IT is now requisite that my narrative should return, as it were,
and trace some events and occurrences parallel in time to those
already recounted, from my entrance into London until the
last scene in the High Court at Westminster. The narrative
will then merge into one channel, and will so continue.

It is perhaps almost unnecessary to say that I made no
more attempts for the present in the publishing line. My
friend Sir Richard Phillips, whom I frequently called upon,
advised me to drop the idea, as a volume of poetry, unless of
an astonishing kind, would be quite unsaleable.

I received a letter from my wife, informing me that a
number of friends came from Oldham, expecting to see me the
Sunday after I set off for London ; that they were quite grieved
when they learned I had gone away unprovided for, they having
very promptly and liberally got up a subscription, whereby
they put a handsome sum into Healey's pocket to come up
with.

In a day or two I saw Healey, and he told me how he had
managed matters. He had heard about my poor departure,
but he determined to try another plan. He got a number of
small circulars printed, informing his friends that " Joseph
Healey would be under the necessity of taking his departure
for London on such a day, to receive judgment in the court of

King's Bench; and as he was entirely without funds to carry
him up, he would thankfully receive whatever sums the friends
of reform contributed for that purpose," or words to such
effect. The consequence was that a number of the Oldham
and Lees Radicals took the matter in hand, and went round
collecting, and the following morning he had fifteen pounds
given him at Oldham, besides which he collected money at
Hollinwood, Failsworth, and Newton, where he made calls,
and was surrounded by friends who contributed handsomely.
From his account it appeared probable that at the time he
arrived at New-cross, he would have twenty pounds in his
pocket.

Such was the difference betwixt his departure for London
and mine. But then the means were different. Had I begged
it must have been from the generosity of strangers, and not
from those who were indebted to me.

Mr. Johnson was in respectable lodgings, in the Strand, I
think. Healey lodged with Mr. Chapman, of Manchester,
who had come up, at a cousin of the latter, in some street on
the other side of Smithfield, whilst I got a cheap and cleanly
but humble domicile at the "One Bell" tavern in Fleet Street.

When Healey had been a few days in London he wrote to
his friends in Lancashire, giving an account of the heavy
expenses he had necessarily incurred, and stating that he had
only tenpence left. I had not quite expended the pound my
friend Gibb had presented to me.

One morning I recollect, when the pound was done, and I
was daring to entertain the question whether or not I should
take my friend at his word, and ask for another, I stumbled
upon Healey in the street, who pulled some money out of his
pocket, and wanted to know if I had got mine. I did not
understand the question, and told him so, on which he informed
me that the relief fund committee had awarded to each of us
defendants ten pounds; that he had drawn his the day before
and I should get mine on applying to Mr. Galloway. I
accordingly lost no time in seeking the counting-house of
that gentleman, Healey went with me, and I received the
money. Thus, by the very kind and considerate attention of

the committee, all further anxiety as to the ways and means of existence for the present was done away with.

We now indulged ourselves with a trip by water to Richmond—that is, Healey, I, and Chapman—but there was either nothing very extraordinary in the landscape, or I was in no humour for appreciating it: I thought nothing of it. A walk through the Tower was more attractive, and I paused long beside the helmets and cuirasses and weapons from the field of Waterloo, all hacked and crushed, and still rusted in gore. At the Waterloo Museum in Pall Mall I doffed my hat before that of Napoleon, and I reverently touched the sword of Ney and the truncheon of Murat. At the British Museum I wondered and admired, but nothing interested my feelings as did the mementos of the brave and unfortunate of our own days.

The detection of Arthur Thistlewood and his companions took place, if I mistake not, during our trial at York; it caused a great sensation at the time, and the conviction of the same misguided men occurred soon after our arrival in London. It was the subject of general conversation, and particularly the intrepid bearing of the prisoners during their trial. Mrs. Thistlewood had an asylum with the family of our friend West, the wire-worker in the Strand, and I frequently saw the unfortunate woman there. She was rather low in stature; with handsome regular features, of the Grecian cast; very pale, and with hair, eyes, and eyebrows as black as night. Still she was not what may be called interesting: she had a coldness of manner which was almost repulsive. She seemed as if she had no natural sensibilities, or as if affliction had benumbed them. She wore her hair very long, and when she went to visit her husband, which she did with devoted attention, she was strictly examined, and, among other precautions, her long hair was unbound and combed out. Hunt frequently indulged in imprecations against Thistlewood and his party. He aspersed their courage, the fame of which seemed to have hurt him. But the worst thing I ever knew him do was his slandering of Mrs. Thistlewood, whom he represented as carrying on a criminal intimacy with West during her husband's incarceration. A baser, more unfounded, or more improbable slander was never uttered. Its atrocity was its antidote. In fact, he would have said anything of any one against whom he entertained a pique. My blind adherence to Hunt could not but be much shaken by such oft-repeated instances of an ignoble mind.

On the morning of the execution of the conspirators I remained in my room, earnestly praying God to sustain them in their last hour; for though they professed not to believe in a future existence, I did, and could therefore sincerely say, "Father, forgive them! they knew not what they did." At noon, when all was over, I came downstairs. The execution was the subject of conversation in every place, and I soon heard, as perforce I must, the particulars of the disgusting transaction. When I met Healey he told me that he and Johnson had been to see it, and had paid a rather heavy price for places at a window nearly opposite the scaffold. I said he was welcome to the gratification such a scene could afford; for my part, I would not have gone on any account; and such places were the very last at which persons of our description should be seen. He put it off by saying he merely went from curiosity, to see how such things were done. The executioner, he said, bungled in severing one of the heads: he could not hit the joint of the vertebræ, and when at last the knife touched it, the head went off in an instant.

The day before we received sentence I called on my friend Gibb, and he not being at home, I enclosed in a letter of thanks a bank note for the one I had received from him. A day or two after my arrival at Lincoln Castle a letter came to hand from my kind friend, enclosing the same note, and making me welcome to it. Such traits of generosity ought not to be forgotten.

We were conducted from the court to a small and darkish room at Bellamy's coffee-house, where Hunt expressed himself in strong terms respecting the sentence on himself. We endeavoured to console him, as did also Mr. Pearson, but he continued giving fitful vent to his feelings until our conductors again invited us to take their arms. They ushered us into a couple of stand coaches, and we were driven to the King's Bench prison, where Hunt engaged two rooms at the tavern which is within the prison. Johnson, Healey, and myself got lodgings in the wards of the building; and thus, reader, was I domiciled in the fifth place of my confinement.

If the verdict of the jury at York may be termed infamous, how shall the sentence upon me of twelve months' imprisonment be described? As infamous also, no doubt. The former circumstance can be attributed to political fanaticism only; it was contrary to the evidence and the oath which the jury had taken. The latter circumstance may, I think, be fairly imputed to that quite uncalled-for passage in my address to the court, where I said I would never again recommend so great a degree of forbearance as I had done, until the blood shed at Manchester had been atoned for. That sentence I should have acted quite wisely and patriotically enough in withholding · it was a declaration which my situation did not require, and which my fellow Radicals had no right to expect. I should have been advised against any extravagance of the sort; but as at York, I had no counsel save my own discretion, and here it failed me. But then, where was the justice of imprisoning me, not for a crime committed, but for a speech delivered? Yet so it was I am sincerely of opinion. I believe, and not without reason, that Judge Bayley did all he could to prevent that sentence being passed on me; but there were four judges on the bench, and the majority govern, and three being probably against me, he would be necessitated to deliver the sentence in which the three concurred.

The same evening, Sir Charles Wolseley entered the prison, he having been sentenced to eighteen months' imprisonment in Abingdon jail, with heavy recognizances at the expiration of his confinement, for attending a reform meeting at Stockport. I met Sir Charles on the flags, and with him a gentleman whom he introduced to me as Colonel ——, of the Guards. Both the colonel and Sir Charles complimented me on my address to the judges.

It was a curious place which I had got into this time. It seemed to be an epitome of the great world we had left, only there was not any spinning or weaving going on here, nor rushing of horses, nor rattling of chariots, but all the degrees of luxury and want, of careless pleasure and thoughtful woe, were presented; all the extremes and contrarieties of our English condition might here be observed.

No sooner had we stepped inside the gate than we were accosted by several men, who offered to let us apartments entire, or lodgings, or shares of apartments, but we declined making any immediate engagements, preferring to look round and get some information from those who knew the place.

A crowd was collected near the gate, some waiting the arrival of prisoners like ourselves; some taking leave of friends, or creditors, or attorneys, or members of their families, returning into the great city; and others, whose acquaintance was perhaps now but slight with the world, would be standing there smoking, and sharing, mayhap, by sympathy, in the painful or pleasurable emotions of their fellows. A number of young and athletic men were stripped and playing at racket against the high walls of the prison, whilst numerous lookers-on sat smoking and drinking, blaming or applauding the players, and betting on the games. Some were hanging out dingy, half-washed linen to dry near their windows; the cobbler's hammer was at work; the barber had stuck out his pole and displayed his pomatum, tooth-powders, and perukes, as if people there had nothing to care about save cosmetics and curls. The broken-down, starved dandy stalked gaunt as a winter's wolf; the ruined gamester; the over-speculative stock-jobber; the player in his last act; the honourable tradesman ruined; the spendthrift with nothing to spend; the fox-hunter, hunted at last to his earth—all were here. The warrior found bars of vulgar iron too strong for his polished steel; the miser, in his living rags, hutched beside the priest in his lawn; the banker was here bankrupt; the statesman without estate. The senator in vain called "order, order," each man was thinking, acting, reading, resting, singing, praying, eating, drinking, weeping, or smiling for himself and his own concerns, just as in the wide world outside. But here all of human reason and passion, of pleasure and pain, of hope and despair, was pent up like the rolling, tossing, boiling wave of a volcano that comes not up to the brim.

The day after our committal to this prison a son of Mr. Cobbett came to visit Johnson, but, if I recollect aright, he was not introduced to any of the other political prisoners. His father, since his return to England, had been at variance with Hunt, and he had suffered his personal feeling so far to estrange him from the common cause as to neutralise his powerful pen on the subject of the Manchester meeting, and the extraordinary proceedings at York. In fact, Cobbett was jealous of Hunt's popularity, just as Hunt was jealous of Thistlewood's fame; the same unworthy and unseemly spirit had now possession of both our great leaders, and the result was that they hated each other with a most sincere hatred. Not so the worthy Major Cartwright; he was always the same. The day after our sentence I found him in the coffee-room, promising Healey to write to some of the magistrates of Lincolnshire on our behalf, should our condition when there require it. He questioned me as to the mode in which I purposed spending my time in prison, and on my expressing a desire to learn something of the Spanish language, he promised to send me some books on the subject; and he kept his promise, but I never made any advance in the study. My wishes were greater than my endeavours.

We were visited by Dolby, the publisher, by Wooller, of the *Black Dwarf*, by Mr. Pearson, our, or rather Hunt's, attorney, and by one or two others, but, somehow or other, most of our London friends seemed to have forgotten that we were yet in the land of the living. They never came to ask for us any more than if the prison had been our tomb. Alas! how many unfortunates in that place have made the same reflection! How many, on coming forth, have found that not a friend was left to welcome them back to the world.

The day after my arrival, I announced my situation to my wife in a letter containing the following lines :—

" I never will forget thee, love !
Tho' in a prison far I be ;

I never will forget thee love!
   And thou wilt still remember me.

I never will forget thee, love!
   When wakes on me the morning light;
And thou shalt ever present be,
   When cometh down the cloud of night.

I never will forget thee, love,
   When summer sheds the sultry ray;
And thou shalt be my comforter,
   Amid the winter's cheerless day.

Oh! they may bind, but cannot break,
   This heart, so fondly full of thee;
That liveth only for thy sake,
   And the high cause of liberty."

On the morning of Wednesday, the 17th of May, Mr. Hunt was sent off in custody to the jail of Ilchester, pursuant to his sentence, and on the following morning, myself, Healey, and Johnson, were called into the lodge preparatory to our removal to Lincoln. Here was a number of turnkeys and other officers, and the first movement was the unclasping of some handcuffs for the purpose of fastening us before we set out. Healey and Johnson demurred strongly, and showed a disposition to resist, seeming to consider it a great affront and degradation. I said the degradation was with those who offered the insult, and not with those who were compelled to receive it. We were then hand-chained and ushered to the door of the prison, where we expected a coach would have been in waiting; but there was not any, and we were informed we should have to walk to the booking-office. Here was another demur, my fellow prisoners expressing a strong repugnance to walking the streets of London handcuffed. The person who seemed to have the superintendence of this transaction, said we should have had a coach, but there was not any on the stands at that early hour. So we set off, and I endeavoured to soothe the spirit of repining by observing that an iron manacle, worn in a just and righteous cause, was more honourable than golden links worn by a tyrant or his minion.

But few people were in the streets, and without encountering much observation we arrived at the "Saracen's Head," on Snow Hill, where we entered a four-horse stage coach and were soon, to my great satisfaction, dashing along a broad highway, past meadows, cornfields and trees, in all the verdure of spring.

I do not recollect having ever noticed two worse-looking fellows than the twain now our conductors. One was a middle-aged man with a villainous physiognomy, and features as immovable as if chiselled in stone. I looked, and looked, and looked again, but he appeared always the same trained and inscrutable being. He seemed to have just learned how to do a turn churlishly in open day, but would be more at home in lending a hand in a lonely place at midnight. I never, to the best of my recollection, so thoroughly disliked a man for his looks and manners. His comrade was younger and somewhat more urbane and better-looking, but there was a restlessness and a lurking distrust in his every glance and action which indicated an acquaintance with, if not the habitual practice of, wily and unrelenting scoundrelism. I never, before or since, set my heart so against two strangers—God forgive me if I was wrong in my estimate of their characters—and I thought I shouldn't at all wonder if something occurred that would lead me to defy them before we got to Lincoln. These fellows sat outside the coach, we were inside ; they seldom opened their lips to us nor, I believe, to any one else. I could perceive that they were armed with pistols. Our fellow traveller inside was a gentlemanly looking personage. He rode a considerable distance before any conversation ensued. When he understood who we were and what was the cause of our being chained, he became quite chatty and agreeable, but nothing occurred which claimed a place in my recollection. When we stopped for refreshment, our conductors, like two mutes, were always with us ; the hand-chains were removed, and replaced before we set out again. And thus we travelled through a rather wet day and all night, and at dawn on the following morning the coach stopped at Newark, and we had to take a fresh conveyance.

We were now only sixteen miles from the place of our
destination, and I proposed that we should wash ourselves
and adjust our dress before we made our appearance at the
jail.   This favour was, after some hesitation, granted, and
we were not long in finishing our toilette.   The elder fellow
then approached me with the clasps ready for my wrists, but
I said I would not have them on any more.   He looked
surprised, and moved as if he would compel me; but I bade
him keep back, for no force he could command should induce
me to submit.

Healey and Johnson expressed a similar determination, and
the two fellows asked the reason for so sudden a resolve?

I said it was not a sudden resolve on my part, for I never
intended to enter Lincoln with the chains on.   I cared but
little how I appeared in London or the country through which
we had passed, and where I was, as I should probably remain,
a perfect stranger; but I knew the consequence of a first
appearance in a seemingly degraded state before persons with
whom we must remain twelve months.   There was no
necessity for the handcuffs, I said; he might put them in
his pocket.   I would give him the word of an honest man
that I would go with him peaceably without the shackles, but
I would not go at all with them.

Healey and Johnson gave a similar pledge and expressed
a similar determination; and the fellows, seeing the point was
not to be carried by force, gave it up; and a post-chaise being
waiting at the door, we stepped into it with one of our
conductors, the other riding on the seat, and in this form
we passed through a fine level country and approached the
ancient city of Lincoln, the cathedral and castle looming in
the distance, long before we could distinctly see their outlines.

At length we were upon a pavement, and soon entered a
street which we passed along, and then began to ascend the
hill on which the upper town stands.   Our nags dragged
hardly and slowly for some time, until, having got on a level,
we went forward more rapidly, and in a minute we stopped
before a huge gate which, after the application of a heavy
knocker, was soon opened, and we drove into a fine broad

yard and alighted at a strong nailed door, which we passed, and were conducted into the governor's apartments, where the warrant for our detention was read, and we were received formally into his custody.

CHAPTER XXXVII.

OUR GOVERNOR—OUR APARTMENTS—INTERVIEW WITH THE
MAGISTRATES—SKETCH OF THE PRISON—A SINGULAR
MUSEUM.

OUR new governor came from his chamber in his morning
gown to receive us. I thought there seemed to be a little aim
at effect in this. His voice was clear, his utterance rapid, but
distinct, and accompanied by considerable action. His complexion was brown, his features rather attenuated, his eyes
quick, clear, and deep-seated, his forehead capacious, his hair
rather thin and a little grey, his age forty-five or fifty, his
stature about the middle size, and his motions very lively.
Such was John Merryweather, the governor of his Majesty's
castle of Lincoln, as the impression of his appearance on the
morning of Friday, the 19th of May, remains on my recollection.

After our disagreeable conductors had retired, our governor
showed us the apartments we were to occupy. We mounted
two heights of stone steps, and our rooms were the first two
on the right hand. Our day-room was a very good apartment, with fireplace, table, chairs, and every requisite; lofty
overhead, a smooth floor of hardened mortar or composition,
and a sash window, with a strong grating of iron before it.
Our bedroom was the next to it, and of the same dimensions.
In it were two good clean beds, a table, some chairs, and, I
I think, a cupboard or two, for clothes or other articles. The
rooms were remarkably clean, airy, and agreeable, and we
expressed more than satisfaction, thankfulness, for the in-
dulgent feeling which had assigned us such comfortable

quarters. Mr. Merryweather gave us some general directions as to the manner in which we were required to comport ourselves towards the other prisoners, and then retired; but was quickly followed by the turnkey, a stout, active man, named Tuxford, who after some further explanatory chat, went down and sent to us the woman who made the beds, and attended on the debtors by going errands for them into the town· With her assistance, we soon had materials for a good breakfast and dinner; a fire was burning in the place on our arrival, and whatever cooking utensils or eating vessels we required were quickly procured. And thus, friend reader, thou seest me located in the famous castle of Lincoln, the sixth place of my confinement for alleged, or suspected, political offences.

We had scarcely set our breakfast things aside, when, after a knock at the door, the governor again entered, accompanied by about half-a-dozen gentlemen, one or two of whom seemed to be clergymen. They were, he informed us, magistrates of the county, who had business to transact in the adjoining court, and had taken the opportunity to visit us on our arrival. They asked if we were satisfied with our accommodations, and we assured them we were perfectly so, and quite grateful for their attention to our comfort.

The Rev. Dr. Caley Illingworth, chairman of the bench of magistrates, expressed a desire for himself and the others to afford us every indulgence compatible with our situation, and their duty to the executive, provided our conduct was such as justified them in pursuing that course towards us. The only restraint they wished us at present to observe was the avoidance of the company of the debtors, the holding of conversations with them on religious or political subjects, and the circulation of publications containing opinions of which they (the magistrates) could not approve. They also required that we should not receive the visits of any persons without the knowledge of the governor.

We promised obedience to their injunctions, and after many assurances of good feeling on their part, and suitable acknowledgments on ours, the gentlemen withdrew, leaving us still

more pleased than before with the situation we had fallen
into.

The worthy guardians of the peace and morals of the
county were evidently apprehensive lest our presumed
opinions should contaminate those of the other prisoners;
but when they saw, after many weeks' trial, that we acted
with good faith, avoiding the debtors, and not seeking opportunities to speak on unpleasant topics, the injunction was no
longer held in force; and, when in time, the governor saw us
take part in the sports of the place, he expressed his satisfaction; and afterwards there was little distinction betwixt us
and the debtors.

The outer turnkey was a merry, loquacious, little fellow,
about seventy years of age. He proved to be very obliging,
fond of money, and somewhat singular in his way. He kept
a kind of curiosity shop, consisting of instruments of murder,
or murderous assault, such as hedge-stakes, splintered with
breaking skulls, poles broken and bloody, hatchets, bars, and
bludgeons. Then he had an arrangement of the skulls of
murderers, male and female, and highwaymen; and, next,
halters, each ticketed with the name of the man or woman
who had suffered in it. This impressive exhibition he displayed with apparent satisfaction, especially when the visitor
slipped a piece of silver into his hand.

All around the prison building I have thus sketched arose
high stone walls, some parts of them appearing to be of a
great age. They comprised, as I was informed, an area of
about eight acres, one part of which was a large green in front
of the jail, on which the prisoners for debt took exercise; in
the centre of this green was a shrubbery, and the green was
bordered on three sides by a long slip of garden ground, embracing the foot of the wall, appropriated to the use of the
governor, and cultivated by the more orderly of the felons.
On the wall opposite the governor's apartments was a round
tower, on which executions took place; and an ancient keep,
called Lucy's tower, in the rear of the jail—part of the original
fortification—was now kept locked, and was tenanted only by
owls, and an immense number of shell-snails, which completely

formed its floor. In a hollow at the foot of this tower were seen the green heaps above the graves of felons who had died within the prison, and of criminals who had been executed; and on a more level plot behind the Town Hall (which building fronted the gates at the extremity of the yard) was the place of interment for debtors, some with stones and inscriptions, and others with only the green mantle of their mother earth lapping over them.

> " And these had once been lov'd full well,
>   Though some might hate or fear them;
> But now they slept in narrow cell,
>   Nor wife, nor child lay near them."

High above the gates and prison walls, at a short distance outside, rose the towers of the venerable and magnificent cathedral. The Lady tower contained a peal of bells which were only rung twice a year: on Lady and Michaelmas days. They were the sweetest-toned bells I have ever heard. One of the towers was cracked, and men were employed in boring through it to brace it with iron. This was the tower of the great bell Old Tom, which boomed forth the hours to us, as they too slowly joined the eternity of the past.

As I was walking in the yard the day after my arrival, several gentlemen in clerical garb entered the gates, apparently on a visit of curiosity to the place. As they approached my line of walk, I noticed the Rev. Jabez Bunting, Wesleyan preacher, a native of Manchester, amongst them. Recognitions were given and received, and I mentioned to him the circumstance of having often sat under his ministry at Middleton, when he was but a young man and I a boy. I called to mind also the names of some of his old friends at that place, who were relatives of mine; and I thought I somewhat interested him, when stating a fact of which he seemed not to be apprised, namely, that my grandfather, Daniel Bamford, was the first who opened a door to the preachers of his sect at Middleton; and that John and Charles Wesley, George Whitefield, John Nelson, Samuel Taylor, and others of the old band, were frequent expounders under that humble roof.

The gentlemen soon departed, and I mention the circumstance only because it gave rise, after they were gone, to a series of very pleasant recollections of my young days, which served during half an hour to dispel gloomy thoughts, and lead me back to "that sweet morning time" when—

> " With hymns we went praising
> By rindles and bowers;
> Or, sheltered, sat gazing
> At rainbows, in showers."

One thing, however, struck me as a falling off from the good old apostolic customs of the preachers in my younger days. The reverend gentleman went away with his company without vouchsafing a blessing or a word of advice to me, not that I cared much about it, but I thought old John Gaulter, or little Jonathan Barker, would not have done so.

We had not been long here before we had reason to expect that we had either some very insidious foe, or some very indiscreet friend in the neighbourhood. One morning, Tuxford came and requested to be allowed to examine the paper we used in our letters. There seemed to be something mysterious in his manner, but we readily showed him all we had, and allowed him to take away a sheet of each sort. Soon after he returned with the governor, who explained the reason for the proceeding, when to our astonishment it appeared that Lord Sidmouth had received an annonymous threatening letter, bearing the Lincoln post-mark. The letter was sent to the governor, with a request that he would examine into the matter so far as he was able, and with the view of ascertaining whether the letter was written on the sort of paper we used.

We, of course, as in truth we must, entirely disclaimed all knowledge of the document or its writer, and strongly condemned the feeling which could lead to the writing of anonymous letters under any circumstances. The governor expressed himself as perfectly satisfied with the examination, so far as we were concerned. He then similarly examined the debtors, but no clue was obtained towards connecting any one in the castle with the infamous document, and the only result was, that henceforth we stood better in the governor's opinion, as well as that of the visiting magistrates.

Our governor was a genius in his way; he was not an educated man, but had the reputation of being an adept in astronomy. He had a handsome mounted telescope, and frequently spent whole nights in star-gazing—a very proper employment, I thought, for the governor of a prison. One or two desperate attempts at escape had been promptly foiled by his vigilance and that of his sub-officer.

The story of Elizabeth Barton, his housekeeper—for he was a bachelor—was rather a romantic one. She was now about fifty years of age, a clean and industrious woman, and withal, was very tender-hearted to the prisoners. She was now rather infirm, but had been an uncommonly handsome woman, and in the prime of her charms she was the wife of a man of desperate habits, who initiated her into the business of passing forged banknotes. She was taken in a transaction of that sort at Lincoln, and committed for trial, at that time almost equivalent to death; whilst her husband was equally unfortunate at York. Both were convicted, and the husband was executed, but the situation of the youthful widow, now resigned to her fate, excited a commiseration so lively, that strong means were used to have her life spared, and it was so, on condition of a long confinement. This she spent in a manner which obtained for her the good opinion of her superiors and the good wishes of her fellow prisoners; and she had ever since been the manager of the governor's household.

When we went our doctor became her medical adviser. He gave her physic, and a lotion, or something of that sort, for her legs. But there must have been a mistake this time, for she soon dispensed with his attendance, complaining that his medicine made her very ill and his lotion burned the stockings off her feet.

Every morning the servant from a publichouse near attended at the gate, and served the debtors with ale. Each debtor was allowed to purchase a quart per day, but many went without, and others took it in their stead and kept it for sale at the price of a shilling a bottle, thereby gaining fourpence.

Pipes and tobacco, and indeed ale, might be had to any
reasonable extent, provided the money was forthcoming.
Spirituous liquors were prohibited: I did hear that such
articles might be obtained secretly, but I never saw anything
of the kind during my twelvemonths' stay in the place.

After I was sentenced a number of my friends at Middleton
bestirred themselves, and besides making a present collection,
they put down their names for a regular monthly contribution
so long as I remained in prison, and thenceforward I received
from them one pound per month. Without this aid I should
have been sadly put to my wits as to the means of living, for I
never would have asked them for a farthing or made known
my situation. However, I accepted it as tendered, in goodwill,
and the most friendly relations continued betwixt us. Healey
complained that he had not the means for supporting himself
and paying for his room and bed, and on making a representation to that effect to the governor, a room above was assigned
him with a bed, free of any charge, together with the county
allowance to prisoners, consisting of three loaves a week, one
pound of butcher's meat, and a quantity of coals.

Soon afterwards it was understood that Mrs. Johnson was
in a critical state of health, and was about to come to Lincoln
to visit her husband. On that occasion I wished to give up
my share of the apartments Johnson and I held, in order that
he and his wife might be more comfortable during her stay. I
accordingly mentioned the circumstance to Mr. Merryweather,
and intimated that I should for the present be willing to take
a part of Healey's room. Mr. Merryweather assented in a
moment, as he always did to whatever was reasonable, and I
had a bed put up for me in the room above; which room was
the identical one previously occupied by my late friend
Finnerty, when he was confined here on a charge of libel. It
was a very pleasant room, with a fire-grate, cupboards for
victuals, and places to put coals, potatoes, or other matters in.
We both had iron bedsteads, and very comfortably I slept,
considering circumstances, and very grateful I was for the
accommodation I experienced.

I was in the habit of receiving a considerable number of

letters, newspapers, and pamphlets—perhaps four or five where Healey received one. Letters of a general nature I read to him, those of a private nature I of course did not. Letters containing money for myself I sometimes read to him, and sometimes did not, as I judged most proper; those with money for both of us were open to both, and when I divided the money I always took his receipt for it, giving him mine when he had to pay. The circumstance of so many letters coming to me I soon found excited envy and jealousy in his breast. He suspected that I did not disclose to him all the letters that contained money on our joint account. This was, perhaps, his most weak point, and it was not long ere I discovered that an influence was at work with him which at length entirely put a stop to all confidence and friendly feeling betwixt us, and rendered me during the remainder of my imprisonment a stranger to the society of my two fellow prisoners. This, to be sure, was no great loss, and as such I treated it; but my equanimity was assailed by the means taken to annoy me, and to lower me in the estimation of my friends.

I was soon, as may be supposed, in active correspondence with some of the most distinguished reformers. Hunt and Sir Charles Wolseley each wrote to me about once a fortnight, the latter also furnished me with a daily newspaper; his letters breathed, as in fact they always did, an exuberance of spirits.

Mr. Swan, Member for Grampound, who was in the King's Bench for bribery at the election, wrote to me, inquiring about the treatment we experienced on leaving the prison. The Honourable Robert Bligh, brother to the Earl of Darnley, did the same. The reader will thus perceive that, though condemned and in prison, we were not entirely disregarded by some who had influence in high places.

One day, as I was lounging in the yard, the Rev. Mr. Nelson, one of the prebendaries of the cathedral and a county magistrate, accompanied by a gentleman whom I did not know, came up to me. Mr. Nelson introduced the gentleman as Sir Montague Cholmley, a Member of Parliament for the county and a magistrate. Mr. Nelson said he wished to ask me a question in the presence of Sir Montague, and he hoped

I would answer him in all sincerity and truth. I promised him I would, if it appeared to me a proper question, and I did not suppose that he would require an answer to one that was not so. He said he certainly would not. The question was, whether or not I was satisfied with my treatment at that place? My instantaneous reply was, "Perfectly so." Was there nothing, then, in the conduct of the governor or the regulations I was subject to, of which I had to complain? My reply was, "Nothing whatever." Then I never had complained, either verbally or in writing? "Never! such a thing never entered my mind; on the contrary, I was most grateful for the indulgence I received." "Did I suppose," asked Mr. Nelson, "that I was as well treated there as I should have been if confined at Lancaster?" "Yes," I said, "and a great deal better, I was of opinion. In my own county I should probably have been put in the worst dungeon the magistrates could have found."

Was I aware of any grounds of complaint on the part of either of my fellow prisoners, I was next asked. I was not aware of any such cause, I answered. Sir Montague then informed me that a letter had been sent from Lincoln to a gentleman in London, whose name I have forgotten, containing allegations of great cruelty on the part of the governor towards us, and of most uncalled-for treatment generally, and he was come down purposely, he said, to ascertain the truth or falsehood of the charge. I said that, so far as I and my two fellow prisoners were concerned, the charge was most false, and I was certain they would bear me out in my statement. But, I added, "your worships can see them, and let them speak for themselves." They assented, and I led up to the room occupied by Healey and myself, and, opening the door, walked in, inviting the gentlemen to follow. I could not see the doctor at first, and thought he must have gone out, but a kind of splashing noise directed my looks to the door, and there he was behind it, as it stood open. "Here is Doctor Healey, gentlemen," I said, as they advanced into the room. I never saw a look of greater mortification and embarrassment than the doctor exhibited at that moment, as the gentlemen bowed to him and smiled at each other. The doctor was busy washing his shirt, and was actually up to his elbows in suds, which he vainly tried to conceal, first by holding his hands behind him, and when he saw that posture did not avail, by wiping the suds off, and rolling down his sleeves. After a moment or two spent in civil inquiries as to his health, and so forth, the same questions were put to him which had been to me, and nearly the same replies were elicited, whereupon the gentlemen expressed themselves quite satisfied, and left the castle.

We had a regular scene after they were gone. I dearly liked a harmless joke, and had many opportunities for seeing my comrade exhibit himself in his various moods. " Well," said I, " I never knew such a thing in my life." " Such a thing as what," asked the doctor, who, rather sulkily, was preparing to go back to his suds. " Why, such a thing as that a learned doctor should be caught up to his elbows in suds and washing his shirt," and I laughed until my sides almost cracked. The doctor looked fiercely, and giving me a hearty malediction, said I had no right to bring them up ; I brought them purposely, and he knew it ; I had done it to lower his respectability. I laughed louder than ever, pretending great sorrow that so celebrated a character should have been caught in the suds—laying emphasis on the latter words. The sense of humiliation I suppose now recurred with double force, and in his passion he caught up the mug and offered to throw the suds upon me, but I stepped out of the door that moment, and the doctor's foot slipping, in the wet, he came down on the floor, and, smashing the earthen vessel, all the suds were soon floating around the room. I then thought it time to retreat, and stepping downstairs I escaped into the yard, doubled up with laughter. The doctor ever afterwards took care not to be surprised washing his shirt.

I may here mention a trait in the natural instinct of the feathered tribe. The governor had a splendid peacock, with a hen, and a young one which had the run of the grounds. One fine clear day, the cock and hen were beside the shrubbery, and as it happened I and some other persons were at the time

near the place. The hen suddenly turned her head, side upwards, and uttered a kind of cry, in which the cock joined,
and the chick was instantly close to her wing. I looked up,
but could not see anything, and the two birds keeping their
heads aside, turning them as if following a moving object with
their eyes, I was convinced there must be a bird of prey
within the ken of their vision. I again looked in the direction
they seemed to be doing, and at length descried a small black
spot at an immense height over head. It seemed to move in a
circle; and in some time I could perceive that it was gradually
descending. It came lower and lower, the fowls still keeping
a steady eye on it, and the young one being under wing, and at
last it came so near that we made it out to be a fine glede hawk.
He took a few circles around the castle, as if he intended to
make a stoop, but, probably seeing too many of the wrong
sort, he at length gave a wheel, and swept out of sight.

The worthy Major Cartwright, faithful to his promise, did
not forget to use his influence with some gentlemen of the
county in our favour. Happily, we had no need of that,
though he was not to be thanked the less, for the magistrates
evinced every disposition to be kind towards us, and the
governor and his subordinates, though naturally a little fond of
power, never gave us reason to suppose that they wished to increase the small portion of restraint we necessarily experienced.
The governor, I must say, like the magistrates who directed
him, never hesitated about doing us a good turn. I had
hitherto paid him a sum per month for the use of a bed and
bedding which he found me, but immediately on my application to be allowed to find my own bed, which a worthy old lady
offered to provide for me, the application was granted, and
the county allowance was also given me on a subsequent
application.

My best and firmest friend was the above venerable lady,
the wife of a blind and aged minister of the church, who
was living at Lincoln on a small allowance. This good old
woman was like a mother to me, reproving me when blamable, advising me in difficulty—for she was a sensible strong-
minded woman—consoling me amid vexation and ingratitude,

and defending and encouraging me in the right. I sometimes thought that if spirits of the departed were really permitted to return to the earth, it was not improbable that the spirit of my departed mother might be the animating principle of the good being whose benign influence watched over me. I shall ever love a good woman for the sake of Mrs. Stainton ; she was to me what my own mother would have been had she lived.

It was scarcely to be expected that two men so entirely dissimilar in person and mind as Healey and myself should long remain together, perforce, without having cavillings, differences, and ultimately dislikes. It is all very well to have a ramble through a countryside with a man, or to be in company once or twice a week, but to have to endure the company daily of one we cannot thoroughly esteem, is rather too much for human patience ; at all events, it was often too much for mine. Nothing sooner tried me than an exhibition of duplicity and false pretension, and of these, God knows, I had enough. I was surfeited to disgust. But I forbear.

The room which Healey and I occupied opened into a lobby where there was a back window looking down into the condemned ward, and over a great extent of country even to Belvoir Castle, the flagstaff of which we could see with a glass on a clear day. This lobby, in consequence of the view, was also visited by strangers, particularly on Sundays, and it was my wish and endeavour to keep it in a state of neatness and order. This very proper desire was, however, often thwarted by Healey, who would put his offal and the scrapings of his dishes on the window-sill, and his potatoes with their peelings on the floor, near the door, and in sight of every one who came up. One Sunday, on his doing this, I remonstrated with him in terms which led to warm words on both sides, in which I upbraided him with his mean jealousy on account of the letters received, and of being perfidious under the guise of friendship, and I concluded by likening him to the viper which stung the bosom of its benefactor. This enraged him beyond endurance, and he came at me with a two-handed blow with the poker. I caught the weapon in my hand, and in

trying to wrest it from him, he having a very tenacious grasp,
I lifted him off his feet, and laid him, with but little violence,
on the floor, and tore the thing out of his hands by main force.
I then held the heel of my shoe over him, and said if he was
not so utterly contemptible, I would stamp the breath out of
his body. I then flung the poker under the grate and went
out of the room, and on returning I found him on his feet,
pretending to spit blood from his lungs, which he said I had
injured by crushing him. The fact was that his lip was a
little swollen and cracked, having probably come in contact
with his own knuckle, or mine, during the scuffle, and that was
whence the pretended blood from the lungs came. I will not
repeat the terms of reproach which I flung away upon him.
He went downstairs and brought up the turnkey, and accused
me of having knocked him down, beaten him with the poker,
dragged him on the floor, and stamped on his breast, and concluded by spitting out streaks of blood as before. I then gave
a true version of the affair, showing the turnkey the state in
which the lobby and window were, and requested him to
examine Healey's lip and see if that was not bleeding inside.
He did so, and found it bruised, and blood oozing from it.
He then told the doctor he did not believe a word he said; that
he had found him in falsehoods before, and that if he were not
more circumspect in his conduct he would report his behaviour
to the governor, and have him removed to the other side of the
prison. Healey thus took nothing by his motion, whilst I
took only the resolution to get out of his company as soon as
possible.

But it was not at Lincoln alone that I was doomed to be
annoyed. The grossest slanders were propagated at Middleton and other parts of Lancashire, and in some cases they
were but too coldly combated by those who called themselves
my friends, but who alas! knew little of the " generous
friendship," which

> " No cold medium knows;
> Burns with one love, with one resentment glows."

One hoary-headed slanderer, who hated me because I had

prevented him from imposing on the relief fund and obtaining money to which he had no right, circulated a report that I was actually a Government spy, that I had sold the Middleton blue banner to the authorities at Manchester for twelve pounds, and that if the banner were sought for, it would be traced to the police-office at the said town. The fellow actually went about the town swearing most confidently that such was the case. A committee was appointed to investigate the charge, and a deputation waited upon my wife, who opened a chest, and pulling out the banner, displayed it; and yet the scoundrel afterwards went up and down persisting in what he had said.

It may be readily supposed that the fine yard the prisoners had access to would induce them to take much out-of-door exercise. This was the case, and I in particular of our party, frequently joined in the running, leaping, and football matches which took place. I generally entered with ardour into the game, and being a good footman, was not considered a mean auxiliary to any party. Often, however, when the game was over, and I was quite warm with the exercise, would I fling myself down on the grass, and perhaps take a nap until some fresh sport called me again into action. By such unthinking conduct I took many colds, and neglecting to diet myself, or take medicine, the colds struck to my weak part, the lungs, and in time I began to have my old tightness at the breast and my night cough, as at Lancaster, only much worse, attended by profuse perspirations and other weakening symptoms.

It was about the beginning of August that my dear wife, hearing of the state of my health, expressed her wish, in a letter, to come over and see me, and I gladly assented, provided the necessary means could be obtained. I had, at Hunt's request, written a piece called "the Song of the Slaughter," which first appeared, I think, in his memoirs, and was afterwards published at the *Observer* Office, Manchester; and with three pounds, accruing from the sale of it, and one pound which my wife borrowed, she was speedily in a condition to join me, and announced her intention of doing so.

About this time the Rev. Mr. Nelson, and other magistrates, came to the castle on business, and before they went I took an opportunity of stating to them my wife's intention of coming over, and requesting the use of a room to ourselves during her stay. They asked if there was one anywhere unoccupied, and I said that fortunately there was one, the very next to that I was now in. They directly went into the turnkey's lodge, taking me with them, and sending for Tuxford, they ordered him to get the room I had mentioned coloured and cleaned, and to put up a bedstead, and give me the key of the place, that being my apartment during my wife's visit. Then, turning to me, Mr. Nelson said, " We [meaning himself and the other magistrates] do not approve of all that the Manchester magistrates have done, any more than of some of your proceedings, but we consider you to be here as prisoners under peculiar circumstances, and we should be sorry to be the means of depriving you of any little indulgence compatible with your safe custody, especially, so long as you comport yourselves as you have hitherto done. There is one thing, however," Mr. Nelson added, after a pause, " which we must enjoin upon you, and that is, that you do not make any public statement as to this matter ; that you do not mention it to the newspapers, or make a noise about it. It is an indulgence, and at variance with the rules we ourselves laid down for the governance of the prison, but, as I said, under the peculiar circumstances of yourself and your fellow prisoners, we will do all we can to make you comfortable so long as, by your conduct, you enable us to be kind towards you."

I expressed my unfeigned gratitude to the worthy magistrates, and promised to obey their injunction. The place was immediately whitewashed and cleaned, and the day following, to my very great comfort, I removed to that welcome domicile, with thankfulness of heart to those who had been so kind, and with extreme satisfaction at being thus left alone, and to my own thoughts.

It was on the 18th of September that my wife was to arrive. Our meeting was both mournful and tender. The sight of my features, so much altered for the worse, and of my pale and wasted hands, renewed her tears, and it was not till after a fit of downright crying on her part, during which I let her feelings have uninterrupted vent, that she became more calm, and we unburdened our minds of whatever lay heaviest and most painful there. And of such matters, what with the falsehood or apathy of friends, and the open or insidious detraction of enemies, God knows, we had enough.

CHAPTER XXXVIII.

THE PATRIOTS OF OLDHAM—A COMFORTER IN PRISON—A MELANCHOLY SPECTACLE.

AMONGST the best and truest supporters of persecuted Radicals, and the Radical cause, were a small but firm band of patriots at Oldham. Their like never, to my recollection, existed previously in Lancashire, nor has it ever since. To them I owe an especial acknowledgment, and if a grateful remembrance of the men and their good deeds, and a public recognition of their good words, through a medium so humble as this, be any equivalent for their kindness, they have it. Some of the best have long since been called to the reward of "the good and faithful servant." Some still remain, but scattered and bowed by the storms of life. A few winter's gales, and we shall all be gone to, I hope, "where the wicked cease from troubling, and where the weary are at rest."

It may easily be conceived that the society of my wife was a great solacement. I had now always one true friend to converse with, and though the replenishment of my "basket and my store" was somewhat more frequently required, we did not regret on that account; since, if there were plenty we partook it, and if not, with Milton, we could sit down to our "herbs and other country messes," and be thankful for them. Our greatest cause of anxiety now was the absence of our child; but as she had been left with her uncle and aunt, in whom we had unlimited confidence, we were the more easily reconciled to her having stayed at home. My wife certainly saved something by going to market herself. She could go out and return without a single question at the gate, without any rude hand examining her basket; and then, when at night I was locked up, it was in company with the one most fitted to administer to my wounded mind; one who with me could retrace the hours and days from childhood, and leading me to bright recollections, could wile me from present ill to past happiness, until the present also at times became tinged with brightness.

In the beginning of October my wife returned into Lancashire. Our parting was fraught with saddening anticipations. I still kept up appearances as well as I could, and partook of active exercise, but my health was no better, and the means I took to restore it were just the opposite of what my case required.

In January, 1821,* my wife returned to Lincoln, in accordance with my earnest wish.

I was witness about this time to a very affecting incident which took place at the prison. A young, good-looking countryman had narrowly escaped being hung for an atrocious case of housebreaking. He was sentenced to transportation for life, and had sent for his mother to come and take leave of him before he went off. She was a little neat-looking woman, pale, and rather browned, and attired in a plain but very cleanly habit. She stood before the barred gate leading to the dungeons, and when she heard the clank of chains coming along the dim passage, she startled, clasped her hand convulsively, and listened. Her son soon made his appearance, dragging his chain. He extended his arms towards her, and she rushed into the gloomy passage, and to his bosom— uttered his name—and fainted. They rubbed her temples, and tried to give her water, but in vain. Her teeth were fast set, her colour deathly pale, and she continued thus long—he standing weeping over her and uttering words of endearment. " Mother ! Mother !—Dear Mother !—Oh ! that I should have brought you to this ! " Many eyes unwont to melt were also in tears, but no one, save the son, spoke. At length they motioned him to return, but he broke away, and kneeling, caught his mother in his arms, and pouring tears fast on her

* She stayed with him till his release, in May.

face, he reverently kissed her wan forehead and her cheeks, and resigning her to the attendants, he said, " Now let me go !—I've killed my poor mother !—I've broken her heart ! " and they led him away. Then they carried her out for air, and when, after some time, her senses returned, she cast a look around and peered down the passage. " He is gone," said one of the by-standers, on which she sighed, and departed slowly out at the castle gate, weeping.

I was indebted this spring to Mr. Berry, one of my late sureties, residing at Failsworth, and some other friends, for a suit of new clothes, which I had begun to be in need of. They sent me a sum of money, with a request that I would fit myself out decently to come home, and I obeyed their directions, by which I lost some friends.

Mrs. Johnson, the wife of my fellow prisoner, never recovered from her indisposition. She kept declining in health, and returned home to die. I mention this painful circumstance because I am desirous to render that testimony to the conduct of the magistrates and governor, which it so truly merited.

I believe it was the wish of Mrs. Johnson that her husband should, if possible, come to see her before she died; and an application was made to Lord Sidmouth by him for that purpose, but without effect The visiting magistrates, and the Rev. Mr. Nelson in particular, then took up the affair, and memorialised his lordship, but with no better result than before. The magistrates of the county next got up an urgent but respectful memorial, which was presented to his lordship by the county members, but without effect; Lord Sidmouth assigning as a reason for his refusal, that if he conceded the point in this case he did not know on what grounds he could refuse it in others which might occur, and that the practice would lead to endless confusion and evasions of the law. Mr. Johnson did not therefore see his wife, though it was not the fault of the magistrates that he did not; and when they could not do anything more, they gave him the entire range of the grounds within the walls—every indulgence, in fact, excepting walking out of the castle gates. Most of his time, when out of doors, was thereafter spent in the gardens, apart from the other prisoners. I was frequently asked why I did not claim the same privilege, and I replied by reminding the interrogators that my case was different. I had the society of one whose companionship was a greater blessing than the range of any length or breadth of land could bestow. His privilege was not necessary to my happiness. I was content with what I had, and, moreover, whilst a claim of that sort would not benefit me, it might injure him, by causing his confinement to our common bounds. I therefore never interfered; and I should have acted a very selfish part if I had.

The expiration of my imprisonment was now fast approaching, and I and my wife often amused ourselves by conjectures as to how we should get home. It was soon decided, however, that we must walk it, and she, laughing, boasted what a light step she would lead me when we were on the road. Some perplexities as to the means for travelling, whether on foot or otherwise, were happily dissipated by the same beneficent friends who had smoothed our path at London. Healey, entirely unknown to me, had written to Mr. Galloway on the subject with respect to himself, and the result, to my great surprise, was a letter from that gentleman, directed to me at Lincoln, which set all our apprehensions at rest on that score.

Two of my friends in Lancashire—namely, the aforementioned Mr. Berry, of Failsworth, and Mr. Mark Smith, of Heywood—became my sureties for five years, in one hundred pounds each, and it now only remained for me to give my recognizances in two hundred pounds, previous to my liberation.

It was a very fine morning, I recollect; there was a large meeting of magistrates in the county hall, and many of the debtors were in court, for it was held for their relief also.

My wife took my arm and we entered the court and were shown to a seat opposite the chairman, Dr. Caley Illingworth. The Rev. Mr. Nelson was also there, and several other magistrates whom I knew from their frequent visits to the castle.

"Joseph Johnson," was soon afterwards called, but he did

not answer. "Joseph Healey," was next called, but neither did he appear. I was then called, and, standing up, was invited to go across the table near the chairman. I did so, and entered into my own recognizances in the usual terms, after which I returned and sat by my wife. Healey and Johnson shortly afterwards came into the court, and when some business had been disposed of, they were each directed to pass over the table as I had done, and then they severally went through the same form and took seats below the chairman.

Dr. Illingworth then called our names, and we stood up whilst he congratulated us on the near termination of our imprisonment, thanked us for our good behaviour, which had enabled the magistrates and the governor to afford us some indulgencies which we otherwise could not have had, and hoped that in future the reflections which must have presented themselves in prison would, during the remainder of our lives, produce a line of conduct which would render unnecessary any further visitations of the law—or words to that effect.

I looked at my two fellow prisoners, expecting that something would be said by them, and especially by Johnson, who had experienced so largely the best endeavours of the magistrates on his behalf; but neither of them spoke, they both sat down.

I, remaining on my feet, then thanked the magistrates and the governor for their kind behaviour towards me and towards my wife during my imprisonment. I could not, I said, suffer that opportunity to escape without expressing to them how unfeignedly grateful we were for all they had done on our behalf. Their kindness was such as I did not expect when I came to that place, and was certainly such as I should not have experienced in my own county. It had made a deep impression on both our hearts, and for myself I must say that if any course could wean a man from error by creating a grateful feeling in his mind, it was a course such as I had experienced at that prison. It would have an effect more powerful with me than the harshest measures that could have been adopted. I again thanked them most sincerely and gratefully. I should remember their kindness, I said, to the last day of my existence.

I then sat down, thinking that now, at any rate, my two fellow prisoners could not avoid following so proper an example. They, however, kept their seats, and spoke not one word. Then, in a few minutes, Johnson got up and walked over the table, out of the court, and the moment after Healey followed him.

I need not intimate what impression this scene created on the minds of all present, nor repeat the observations it gave rise to. I will only say that I the next day left the castle with the good opinion and good wishes of all who had known me, whether rich landowners, or reverend magistrates, or poor prisoners. The governor spoke well of me and ordered that I should be admitted to the castle on any day, so long as I stopped in Lincoln. But my most welcome applauder was my own conscience, which told me that, whilst I had in a becoming manner submitted to the authorities of the country, I had also deserved their esteem, had disarmed, perhaps, some animosities, had done some good to the cause of reform, and had, by my conduct, made one more appeal for those of the class in life to which I belonged.

When I came to settle with the "Old Daddy"—the turnkey at the gate—which prisoners generally did by making him a present before leaving, he begged I would give him my wooden shoes, for so he called my Lancashire clogs, which I wore in the winter. I gave them to him, and he expressed great delight, saying he would place them in his collection of curiosities, for it seemed that clogs had been but very rarely, if ever, seen previously in Lincoln.

CHAPTER XXXIX.

OBJECTS AT LINCOLN—TOM OTTER—BARTON FERRY—GREAT
MARKHAM—A SCRUPULOUS LANDLADY.

WE stopped a day or two in Lincoln, at our friend Stainton's, and having sent our luggage to the carriers, we examined many of the venerable ruins of the place, particularly the fine Roman arch called "The Stone Bow," one of the most perfect specimens of Roman architecture in England. The splendid and venerable cathedral also attracted our particular notice, and we could not but lament the ruthless and insensate havoc made amongst the images and statues by the soldiers of the stern Cromwell.

It was on the afternoon of Wednesday, a fine day, that we bade adieu to Lincoln, and passing over the race-ground, we stopped at the "Eel-pie House," where we partook of their celebrated dish, "collared eel," and had our parting glass with some friends who accompanied us. Proceeding thence, we passed Saxmundham on our right, and at Dringey Nook we came in sight of the gibbet of Tom Otter, who, in the dark shady lane in which he then hung, murdered his sweetheart by beating out her brains with a hedge stake. We stopped at a very decent inn, at a short distance from the gibbet, and from thence continued our journey through a level country, full of woods and plantations, till the broad waters of the Trent suddenly appeared before us. A shout and a signal brought the ferryman over, and after some persuasion, with fear and trembling, my wife at length went on board and we were ferried over and landed in the county of Nottingham. A short and very agreeable walk through a rural country, with pretty English cottages embowered in gardens and fruit-trees, brought us to the village of Great Markham, where we entered a snug little publichouse and took up our quarters.

We sat chatting over our tea until it was nearly bedtime, and when I requested that we should be shown to our room, the landlady gave an inquiring and dubious glance at us, and retired, evidently to take a second thought upon the subject. The servant woman next came into the room, pretending to fetch something, but once or twice I observed her taking side looks at us; and as I perceived there were misgivings of some sort, I ordered a glass of liquor and a pipe, resolved to amuse myself by watching the shifts and manœuvres of these simple country folks.

The mistress brought the glass, and the girl brought the pipe, and each gave a scrutinising glance, which we seemed not to notice. We were both ready to burst into laughter, only my wife was a little apprehensive lest we should be turned out of doors. I thee'd and thou'd her in their presence, as a man might do his wife, and talked to her in my ordinary careless way; and at last the landlady came and, begging we would not be offended, asked if the young woman was my wife? I now laughed outright, and my wife could not refrain, though she covered her face. I assured the good woman that my companion had been my wife many years. Nay, she had no ill opinion of her, she said, only she looked so young. But, young as she appears, she reckons to be my age within about three weeks, I said; and she was mother to a fine girl, now in the ninth year of her age. Oh! she was sorry to have mistaken us, she said, we should have a comfortable bed ready in a few minutes. And so saying, she left the room, satisfied, no doubt, with the explanation which had set at rest her troublesome qualms of conscience. We had most excellent lodgings; and in the morning we rose early and commenced our journey, by lanes and shady footpaths, sweet with the breath of flowers and echoing the music of birds.

Elksley. What associations in a name! The ley—the pasture land—the lair of the elk. Where was now the elk? Where the wide wold, with its " grc wolf " and the elk stalk-

ing, the dimly-seen monarch of a misty land? All had
disappeared—the elk, the wolf, were no more—and the dun
moor and black moss had become laden with pastures and
fields of grain, and garlanded with orchard blossoms and
dotted with cottages as white as lilies on a garden bed.

Here we breakfasted with the landlady, a tidy little body,
and a delicate-looking young girl, who had come from Nottingham to stop here for her health. We found this a most agreeable resting-place; everything was fastidiously clean; the tea,
the sugar, the bread, were of the best quality, whilst the
butter—if I may be allowed a new compound—was most
butter-fully rich. We, of course, much enjoyed our breakfast,
for—

> " We together far had come,
> Among the dews that morning."*

And I believe our hearty eating made the poor lass from
Nottingham quite hungry. She said she had not taken such
a breakfast for a long time.

From hence we travelled a long way, nine miles, I think,
chiefly through woods and plantations belonging to the Duke
of Newcastle. We seldom saw a house, and the solitude was
unbroken for long distances, except by the whirring of the
pheasant or partridge across the road, or the bounding of the
hare. At Shireoaks we passed a large mansion and some
substantial homesteads, and entering Worksop, with its ruined
abbey on the right, we again rested and partook some excellent
ale. At South Aston we entered Yorkshire, and near Aston
crossed the Rother river; and successively passing Hands-
worth, Darnal, and Attercliffe (Qy. why not Ottercliffe, or
Addercliffe?), we entered Sheffield when near nightfall, and
having been directed to The Axe publichouse, or "Hammer
and Axe," I forget which, we soon found the place, on our left
as we entered the town, and there took our quarters for the
night.

We intended to stop a day here, to look about us, and survey the curiosities of this great city of Vulcan, and well should

* Spencer T. Hall, the poet of Sherwood (*Bamford*).

we have been repaid for the delay, no doubt, but as important events not only frequently arise from small causes, but are baffled by them, our dreams of all the shining jewels of this wondrous cave, shrouded in smoke and sulphur, and glaring red fire, were quickly annihilated by a very significant object. As I sat up in bed, I was almost startled by a sudden exclamation of my wife, who discovered one of those noisome flat insects so common in the beds of towns and crowded places, crawling up my shirt. This determined her. " She would not stop in that place," she said, " for the world—she could not eat in it—and we must set off directly ; " and suiting the action to the word, she was dressed in quick time, and fidgeting to be gone—to get out " into the green lanes," and to " breathe the sweet country air." I rather thought, however, that the wish to see her child affected her ; perhaps she had been dreaming of her ; at all events, I am sure the anticipated pleasure of embracing my dear little girl once more had considerable influence in my acquiescence to quit the town thus suddenly.

Well, we soon paid the shot, and were on our way out of the town. We got, however, on the wrong route, and, before we were aware of that, we found ourselves climbing the foot of the great hills which divide Yorkshire from Derbyshire. For several miles we continued to ascend, and everywhere we came to a small flat, and hoped we had surmounted all, when a few paces discovered to us another eminence. I wondered how my little women stood it, but she this morning showed me her light foot indeed, and with all cheerfulness we breasted the hill, anon looking back, to see how far we had travelled towards home. At length we entered on a broad wild moor, where for miles and miles towards Yorkshire all was a scene of dun heath and shelterless plain ; whilst downwards, over Derbyshire and Cheshire, the eye commanded what seemed an almost illimitable expanse of mountain land.

> " But where the vision began to fail
> There seemed to be hills of a cloudy pale."

In the valley we had left—now as we could discover of a

beautifully undulating surface, and gaily green in the sun—lay the town of Sheffield, shrouded in its furnace clouds. On our right and left were the wild and boundless districts I have mentioned, and before us was the wrinkled front of Mam Tor, frowning like an eld, in witch-land.

We walked to the height of Hathersage Grange, and there stopped to survey the vast, solitary, yet pleasing scenes. My wife was seated on a grassy knoll, whilst I stood beside her with my stick and bundle over my shoulder, my back towards the sun, whose beams were somewhat mitigated by light clouds, and my looks directed over the wold towards the Yorkshire border.

" Well, I am convinced now," I said, breaking a long silence, " that Burke was not so far wide of the truth after all."

" What did Burke say ? " she asked ; " for my part, I never heard him say much of either truth or falsehood."

She thought I was alluding to one of the simplest of my Radical comrades, whom we had nicknamed " Burke."

" Pho ! its Edmund Burke, the great orator and political apostate, that I mean."

" And what did he say ? " she asked.

" Say ? He called the people ' the swinish multitude ' ; and I am convinced he was right, for I have discovered I am one of them."

" What do you mean ? " she again asked, now more interested.

" I can see the wind," I said, " and that's a sure sign I'm one of the swinish herd."

" See the wind ! And what's it like ? " asked she, looking up and laughing.

" It's the most beautiful thing I ever saw," I said, " and it thou'll come here, thou shall see it also."

I will suppose that the curiosity natural to the sex was excited, for she instantly was at my side.

" Now look over the top of the brown heath with a steady eye, and see if thou canst discern a remarkably bright substance, brighter than glass or pearly water, deeply clear and lucid, swimming, not like a stream, but like a quick spirit, up and down, and forward, as if hurrying to be gone."

" Nonsense ! " she said, " there is not anything."

" Look again, steady, for a moment," I said ; " I still behold it."

"There is," she said, "there is ; I see it ! Oh ! what a beautiful thing ! "

I gave her a kiss, and said I loved her better than ever. She was the first woman who, I believed, had ever seen the vital element, the life-fraught wind.

" Is that the wind ? " she asked.

" That is the wind of heaven," I said, " now sweeping over the earth, and visible. It is the great element of vitality, water quickened by fire, the spirit of life ! "

I know not whether I was quite right in my philosophy, but we bowed our hearts, and adored the Creator ; and in that we were both right, I hope.

We stood gazing in wonder and admiration ; for still, like a spirit-stream, it kept hurrying past—or as a messenger in haste ; and so we left it glittering and sweeping away. This was on the morning of the 19th day of May, 1821.

And, reader, I dare be bound with thee that, if having a good pair of eyes, thou wilt at the same season of the year, and on a day like ours—with a mild sun and a quick breeze out of Yorkshire—if thou, at such season, and on such day, climb to the top of Hathersage Grange and stand with thy back to the sun—Mam Tor visible on thy left hand—then also shalt thou see the beautiful apparition—the spirit of life— which we saw. It will repay thy trouble well, I assure thee. Neither I nor mine can ever forget it whilst memory is ours.

At Hathersage we heard the sound of a shuttle, and my wife remarked that we were getting near home. Fortunately we stepped into a little publichouse, never exceeded in neatness and comfort, except by the one at Elksley. Our breakfast was all that could be desired, and we did justice to it, having walked our ten or eleven miles, and over such a country.

At this place, in the churchyard, are shown two small

stones, marking, as people say, the grave of Little John, the faithful companion of the bold Robin Hood. A picturesque low cottage, situated in a garden, and overgrown with ivy and other creepers, is still shown as the one in which the broken-down outlaw took refuge after the dispersion of his band; and where he also died. Both objects are worthy the attention of the travelling antiquary. Such a place would be a likely shelter to a proscribed man; whilst the moors and the forest glades, then but little known, and seldom penetrated, would yield plenty of game to a good bow, and no one be the wiser of the trespass.

At Hope, where we called at the house of the village black-smith, to ask for a draught of water, it being a warm day, we were, with old English hospitality, presented with a jug of good brown ale, and also pressed to sit down and partake the family dinner of hot potato pie; but, with all gratitude, we declined the latter and went forward, not stopping at Castle-ton, for we had now fairly set our hearts on getting home.

In climbing up the Winnits (Wind Yates) we sat down to rest, and to view the rocky scenery around and above us. A spring of clear water was trickling near, and with that health-giving beverage we quenched our thirst. A fine hawk was circling over head, and a couple of ravens disturbed the death-like silence with their croak. The place was mysterious, and had an air of savage grandeur. The imagination might easily expand in such a vast and darksome gorge. Were it indeed the portal—the palace gates of the wind? of the wild, and beautiful, and powerful existence which we had seen that morning? And if so, whither did it lead? We mounted to the top, and found ourselves again entering on a wide dun moor. Mam Tor, with her bold, storm-channelled front, on our right; the sun in his mid-height above us, and a long and weary waste, with swampy bottoms, and grey grass waving in the wind, before us.

Not wearily, but cheerfully and lightsomely, along this desert track we went, and having gone a far way, we began to descend, and eventually rested again at a publichouse in the pleasant little town of Chapel-le-Frith.

Here I was certainly taken to be a fellow who was running away with some old woman's daughter. The landlady could not, at first, believe that my wife was my wife; and when I told her, as I did the good woman at Great Markham, that she had been a mother nine years, she called John, her husband, to partake in her amazement, and "wonderfully strange," to our great amusement, they both deemed the case to be.

We stopped not at Whaley Bridge, for the sun was getting low, but hastened to Disley, and after a brief rest there we again started, though neither I nor my fellow traveller were so alert as in the morning. In fact our feet began to be worse for our two days' travel, and when we got upon the paved causeway, betwixt Bullock Smithy and Stockport, it was like treading on red-hot stones. Thus, long after nightfall, we went limping arm-in-arm into Stockport. We found the dwelling of our friend Moorhouse at the lower end of the town, and knocking at the door, were received with every hospitality.

My friend and his wife bustled about, and did all they could to make us comfortable. We got a supper of good refreshing tea, and then essayed to go to rest, but my poor little companion had to mount the stairs on her knees—she would not be carried up—and when her stockings were removed, her feet were found covered with blood-red blisters. I got some hot water and soap—washed her feet well—wiped them carefully, till quite dry—wrapped them in her flannel petticoat, and put her to bed. I then washed my own feet, for they were not much better than hers, and committing ourselves to Divine care, we were soon oblivious of all weariness and anxiety, and on awaking the next morning, our feet were as sound, for anything we felt, as they were when we set out from Lincoln.

Our walk to Manchester the next morning was a mere pleasure trip. We scarcely stopped there, but, hastening onwards, we entered Middleton in the afternoon, and were met in the street by our dear child, who came running, wild with delight, to our arms. We soon made ourselves comfortable in our own humble dwelling ; the fire was lighted, the hearth was clean swept, friends came to welcome us, and we were once more at home.

> " Be it ever so humble
> There's no place like home.'

CHAPTER XL.

AND now, friend reader, thou hast seen me, at last, through all the places of my imprisonment and back to my home. Have I not led thee a somewhat strange and painful, yet not altogether unpleasing, pilgrimage ? whilst the consciousness that thou wast all this time treading the ground of reality, of this earthly world, must have rendered thy sojourn more strange. Even so it is ; reality is always romantic, though the romantic is not always real.

Having written of myself and others, it may not appear unseemly if I give a short history of the origin and progress of the present work, and conclude with some general, but I trust not unimportant, observations on the present condition of the country, the fallacious views of parties, and the means to be adopted for our safe transition to an approaching state of society.

I make no excuse about the " partiality of friends " having induced me to take the step of publication. I have not any friends who, in that respect, either could influence me, or would attempt it. They would know it was not necessary to do so ; they would have the confidence in me to feel assured that I should produce a book which, whilst it interested the reader, would form a tablet of facts, a group of characters which otherwise would have passed into oblivion ; and that it would, so far, be useful to the future historian of the days recorded. In the performance of this task, however, I have sought counsel only of myself. A long train of fruitless exertions, of disappointed hopes, of harassments of body and

mind, of young days and years wasted and flung away for
nothing, except to find selfishness, ingratitude, and detraction,
where I should have met every generous and manly virtue,
could not have weighed on any heart as they did on mine,
without producing a will of its own, a purpose beyond the
ordinary motives of human nature : therefore impervious to
them, and, in some respects, also above them.

I had friends, however, and I am proud to acknowledge them,
who, when my purpose became known, lent me every assistance in furtherance of my object ; but their friendship was not
of that cast which—though some of them were public men—
sought its reward in the public emblazonment of their names ;
therefore on that point I am silent. They expected something better from me, and they have had it—the sincere though
unpretending gratitude of my heart. Still I may say they
are not great men, in the ordinary sense of the word ; nor rich
men, in the golden hue of richness ; nor poor men, from a
penurious craving spirit ; nor high men on the stilts of gaudy
pride ; nor low men, degenerate through ignorance and vice.
Some of them are poets, and of imperishable name too ;
others are encouragers and admirers of literature, of the
genuine uneducated, as well as the educated stamp. Some
are men " well to do in the world " ; some are humble, but
trustworthy servants ; and others in more distinguished situations : but all are of that class which is privileged to—

> " Hear the muses in a ring,
> Aye, round about Jove's altar sing.

Such are they who enabled me to bring my memoir before
the public. Without their aid I might have written—as
indeed I should—for posterity : to the pecuniary benefit,
mayhap, of some thankless " next of kin," or to the emolu-
ment of that very respectable set of tradesmen who are said
to " drink wine out of authors' skulls."

But there were others, besides friends, whom I had to
encounter, to smile upon, when I was full of sadness, to look
up unto when my hopes were drooping; for in a case like mine,

where a purpose of novel execution had to be prosecuted like a piece of market business, we must try all, likely and unlikely, and spare none, shun none, on account of their looks, or creeds, or of our own suppositions. How many bitter disappointments then fell to the lot of him who travelled the great world, with nothing to exchange for its bread save the unperishing food of the mind—the etherial for the substantial, the spirit for the body ! But why do I expatiate ?

One of that class, about the education of which so much is now being said—a self-taught writer—produces a book which is certainly not to be despised on account of its morals, its politics, or its religion. He waits on some of the richest of those who profess to be friends to the working classes, and to them he respectfully presents his humble production, when, what is the reception he and his book experience ? One " never buys books, he has not time to look at them." Another has " hundreds of volumes, chestsful he has never read." One says, " the book won't suit him " ; another " never reads such things " ; and another superciliously walks away, he " is not in that line, that morning."

But I will not give way to the language which waits for utterance when I recur to these things. I will turn rather to the consolatory view, and recollect how indifference at the office of one rich man was more than atoned for by a courteous reception at that of another—how rudeness at one place was followed by encouraging attention at the next—how to the bustle and importance of the warehouse succeeded calm and respectful discussion—how ignorant superciliousness was rebuked by thanks for my attention—how, in short, many received me with civility, many with kindness, many heard me with patience, many wished me success, and gave me earnest of their wish, many recommended me to friends, many referred me to others, several led me to their hospitable boards, and some who declined my work laid me under an obligation by the manner in which they did so.

The booksellers were certainly the most amusing class I had dealings with. One wrote to me for the work whilst publishing in parts, and sold it well for me. Another, whose windows were crowded with old tomes and his counters with the numbers of " Master Humphrey's Clock," " Jack Sheppard," " Nicholas Nickleby," and such like serials (a house of long standing in the trade), looked at the volume—looked at the title—turned the book over, and gave it back, declining to sell it on any account ; another objected to a word in the title —it " wouldn't do for his customers " ; one wrote to me from London, offering to become my agent, at forty-five per cent. of course ; and another London house " begged leave to decline the publishing of it at all."

Amidst such variety of quickly succeeding incidents, some pleasing, others discouraging, some of them ups in the world, others decided downs, but with more of the latter than the former, how could a man struggling to rise comport himself ? It would be difficult ; but old John Bunyan has a verse which answer the question.

> " There's no discouragement,
>   Shall make him once repent,
> His first avowed intent,
>   To be a pilgrim.
>
> Whoso beset him around
>   With dismal stories ;
> Do but themselves confound,
>   His strength the more is.
>
> Nor lions can him flight,
>   He'll with the giants (tyrants) fight,
> And he shall have his right,
>   To be a pilgrim "

To the effect which this and other small works of mine have produced I think I may refer with some degree of certainty and satisfaction. The publication of my small poem—or rather versification of Berenger's " La Lyonnaise "—with its accompanying notes and postscript, was quickly followed by that most important assemblage of the trading and working classes, the operative Anti-corn-law banquet at Manchester ;

a decided step, and one, too, " in the right direction." That was the first time the two classes had come together to shake hands, and look manfully in each other's faces. A few more such meetings, and the occupation of the incendiary demagogue, the real " divider and destroyer," had ceased. Its moral influence was greater than that of a hundred bazaars or conferences.

Since the publication of the present work, the question of the education of the working classes has seemed to have received a fresh impulse, and the agitation on that subject still forms an engrossing topic of discussion. A minister of the Established Church at Manchester has thought the matter of sufficient importance to claim the advocacy of his pen, and he has given it in a most excellent spirit.

A gentleman of Salford, heretofore of Conservative principles, also put forth a tract on the necessity of uniting the middle and working classes ; and just latterly, Mr. Sturge, of Birmingham, who, if I mistake not, has had one of my books in hand, has come forth an advocate for " complete suffrage." The ruthless tone of Chartism has been softened, and I know that some of the leaders have had my books. The more rational and honest have become loosened from the violent and unprincipled; and as, ultimately, the latter must wither of their own madness, so the former may be expected to adhere to realities only, dropping the extremes of things, until all the practical good has been obtained, wisely applied, and permanently adopted. If I may not claim to have been the pioneer in some of these and other salutary movements, I may certainly, at any rate, take my place in the advanced guard; and it is some reward to find one's self so honourably stationed.

Still, much remains to be done, and I am ready to do my share, in my own way, and for—THE NATION ! That is the only party I will serve; though, if all things were finely balanced, even my country has only a step-mother's claim to my services. I have given more to her than I have received, and far more than many of her most favoured sons had either the heart, or the brains, to contribute. But enough of this, I am willing still to lend a hand to the old lady, unkind though she has been. Let us, then, inquire how she is situated.*

Behold the crown without influence, and the sport of faction; the factions themselves strong enough to enact evil, but too weak to effect much good. The aristocracy blindly clutching their rents, whilst their very acres are in jeopardy, as if they could not perceive, and would not be made to comprehend, until too late, that cheap bread for the people means also, all they seem to care about, cheap pride, cheap pomp, cheap distinction for themselves.

Next are the priesthood, scrambling for worldly gain, and squabbling as to which sect or party shall have most hand in moulding the young brains of the rising generation; as if they had something else in view besides making them into good men and women; as if there were a precept, known only to themselves, and superior to that, " Do unto others as ye would they should do unto you."

Then there are the land-tillers, blind and blundering serfs to the landowners, though the latter knock them about like the clods of their own fields, and for the same purpose too, to make them yield rent.

Next come the manufacturers, working at the wrong end, and trying to make a pitiable impression on the heads and hearts of a class that never, since the days of Cromwell, was pervious to anything at variance with its own will, save a battle-axe or a bullet. There they are, striving for cheap bread, as if it were present salvation, and forgetting what all history is constantly proclaiming, that nothing human is fixed: that crowns, sceptres, dominions, institutions, establishments, and monopolies are ever changing, ever departing from their old seats, springing up anew in other places, and leaving deserts where they formerly flourished. Tyre, Sidon, Carthage,

* It must be borne in mind that this was written in 1842, a time when, as Mr. Spencer Walpole observes, the social condition of the nation touched the lowest point in a long and continuous decline. It was just before the Free Trade epoch. Bamford's remarks convey a graphic and painful impression. He considered the state of things desperate. He lived to witness a great change.

Greece, Rome!—all the departed nations of the world warn us of this; and still we remain as if we were unconscious that our time must come, is coming,—nay, is almost at the threshold.

What, then, " shall we do to be saved?" We must look our difficulties in the face like men. The times which have been never will return; we cannot recall that which has departed, and is still going; we cannot, any more than we can still the ocean, prevent our manufactures from being set up in other nations. We have read them too profound a lesson for that. We have exhibited the spectacle of a small community combating the world, and buying or beating it all round. We have shown the secret of our strength, of all our warlike strength—and they will act upon it. We have shown them how our manufactures produced commerce, which produced wealth, which created credit, which supplied taxes and loans illimitable, and enabled us to wield, with tremendous effect, all the resources of our vast navy and our numerous armies; beating those we encountered, and subsidising the remainder until we either had time to beat them ourselves or could get others to beat them.

And will not the nations lay hold of this wonderful power, and try to render it available to their own interests? Most certainly they will. The novelty of the thing itself would be a great temptation; and though no one nation may manufacture to the extent that we have done, they may manufacture for themselves, and they will do so. America, with its cotton-fields and its teeming population, will spin its own yarn and weave its own cloth, whether we will or no; and the nations of the Continent will do, are doing, the same. They have nothing else to do in peace, nor can anything be more natural than that they should do so. We cannot, must not, always be spinners and weavers for the world; and if we could, I do not see that it is desirable we should. Let these truths be impressed on our minds, and let us, like a community of sensible men, calculate all our disadvantages, and prepare for the worst.

Whether or not we shall be prepared depends on the exertions of the wise and good of all classes. If preparations are made we may be a suffering family, but we shall be an united one, and half our evils will be obviated. Those we must endure will be borne in a noble spirit; whilst those we surmount, and they may be many, will be subjects for our common triumph.

Let all the sufferers, then, of whatever class or description, all who love their country, all who would promote the happiness of posterity and of mankind, unite to procure by peaceful means a suffrage co-extensive with direct taxation, an annual accountability of members to their constituents, cheap food for the hungry, cheap clothing for the naked, cheap labour for the industrious (we must cut a straightforward swathe—we cannot turn aside to leave nooks and corners for classes), cheap rents for the cottager, cheap rents for the farmer, cheap education for every one, cheap law in our courts, cheap justice on the bench, and real justice too, cheap religion, and freedom with it, a cheap, money-despising, vanity-shunning priesthood, a cheap, noble-minded, open-handed aristocracy, elder brothers and fathers of the people, and lastly, or firstly if you will, a cheap government, and a cheap but firm Executive.

I would not, like the O'Connorites, insist on having the whole of these things, or nothing; I would take any part, and think well of it, and get the others as soon as I could.

A bond of union like this, entered into and prosecuted without noise, without agitation or frothy declamation (with which the ears of the people are dinned nowadays, and which is but the pumping out of so much energy to the winds), would put down all demagoguism, all trading agitation, all jealousies, all dissensions, all recriminations. It would bring together good men and true of all grades, and would create a brotherhood which, whilst it directed the masses, would also prepare them for whatever vicissitude was at hand. Like the veterans of an army, it would show its comrades how to bear as well as to dare.

But the whole extent of the evil must be steadily scanned: there must not be any half-measures, any exemptions for this or that interest, for this or that portion of the community.

During fifty years the English nation has been engaged in a gluttonous scramble for wealth, and now the time is coming when there must be a disgorging from the highest to the lowest. We shall be never the worse for it, after all, but better, more long-lived, both as individuals and as a nation, provided we get the crisis over pretty smoothly, and that depends upon ourselves. Our weaver lads must put up, as their grandfathers did, with jannocks and barley bread, and barm dumplings, and brown ale; our farmers' "ladies," as the daughters of farmers are commonly called, must don their clogs, and milk their own cows, and make their butter, and darn their own stockings. "The Mrs." may ride behind Robin instead of taking out her gig; whilst the manufacturer's lady must not deem it beneath her to sit basting a good Yorkshire pudding, without a firescreen, instead of perching on a screw stool thrumming a piano. We must all take our share in the humiliation, and be thankful it is no worse. We must work like a willing crew, or the ship will be lost.

Yes, the change must be prepared for in our towns, our villages, our homes, our manufactories, and our seaports, as well as at the seat of government. The evil does not all lie there. Our present condition is the consequence of our folly as a nation, and of the natural course of events. Our grandfathers and fathers were all mad for war with the French, and the most wise and popular government that could have been established would have gone mad too, with a mad people under it. The wars which plunged us into irredeemable debt were the acts of the nation, and the nation must submit to its own infliction.

The very same cause which removed the silk manufacture from Spitalfields into Lancashire, namely, cheapness, is now taking our manufactures into other countries. So that even the repeal of the Bread Tax, desirable as it is, would not save our trade, unaccompanied by such other measures as would cut down all other taxes to the very core, and place our expenditure on a most rigid scale of economy. We must all be prepared to make sacrifices. We must determine to deserve redemption; the nation must act as one man, or at least the influential portion of it must, and the sooner it is set about the better.

If we honestly lay our shoulders to the wheel, and lift all together with a long pull and a strong pull, and a sober and noiseless one, we shall get over the slough upon firmer land, and into better ways. If not, and we stick fast and begin to sink, how inglorious it will be to be reminded by the gods that we are perishing because we did not perform our whole duty.

Reader, consider these things seriously—and FARE THEE WELL.

July 27, 1842.

THE END.

UNWIN BROTHERS, LIMITED, THE GRESHAM PRESS, WOKING AND LONDON.

THE LIBRARY OF LITERARY HISTORY

Each with Photogravure Frontispiece, demy 8vo, cloth, **16s.**

. The idea of the Series is to take the intellectual growth and artistic achievement of a country and to set out the story of these in an interesting way. Each volume will be entrusted to a recognised scholar, and, when advisable, the aid of foreign men of letters will be invited.

---

1. **A Literary History of India.** By R. W. FRAZER, LL.B.

   "A work which, for the first time, renders it possible for the English reader to understand the part which literature has played not only in ancient or in mediæval or in modern India, but in India from the earliest times to the present day."—*The Times.*

2. **A Literary History of Ireland.** By Dr. DOUGLAS HYDE.

   "If we are not greatly mistaken, this is a book of very exceptional value and importance. We are quite certain there exists no book in English which attempts what Dr Hyde has accomplished, namely, a clear account of the whole literature produced in Irish Gaelic, and a reasonable estimate of its value."—*Spectator.*

3. **A Literary History of America.** By BARRETT WENDELL.

   "Learning it has, and style, and thought ; the information is full, the order lucid . . . Professor Wendell has put forth an admirable, a suggestive study of his country's writers. To me every page is interesting."—*Bookman.*

4. **A Literary History of Persia.** Vol. I. From the Earliest Times until Firdawsi. By Professor E. G. BROWNE.

   "Professor Browne, beyond doubt the first living authority on Persia, is singularly qualified to present the history of Persian thought in a scientific, and at the same time, in a popular form."—*Athenæum.*

6. **A Literary History of Scotland.** By J. H. MILLAR.

   "This is a brilliant but satisfying work. The author . . . has keenness of vision, a cultivated taste, a vivid style, and independence of judgment."—*Speaker.*

T. FISHER UNWIN, Publisher, 11, Paternoster Buildings, London, E.C.

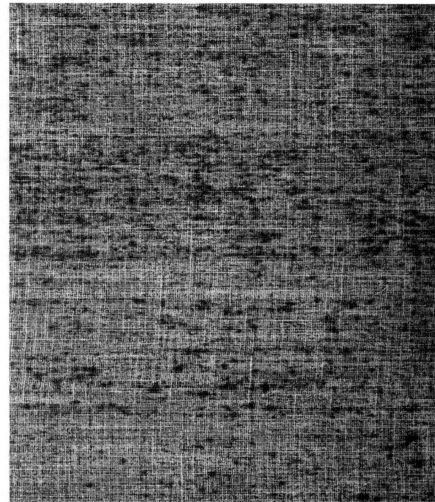

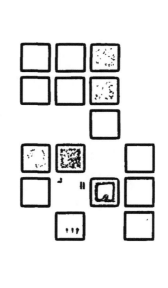

Lightning Source UK Ltd.
Milton Keynes UK
UKHW022233120122
397052UK00003B/149

9 781373 696465